Tracing the cultural legacy of Irish Catholicism

MANCHESTER
1824

Manchester University Press

Tracing the cultural legacy of Irish Catholicism

From Galway to Cloyne and beyond

Edited by Eamon Maher and Eugene O'Brien

Manchester University Press

Published by Manchester University Press
Altrincham Street, Manchester M1 7JA
www.manchesteruniversitypress.co.uk

British Library Cataloguing-in-Publication Data
A catalogue record for this book is available from the British Library

ISBN 978 1 5261 0106 8 hardback
ISBN 978 1 5261 2963 5 paperback

First published by Manchester University Press in hardback 2017

This edition first published 2018

Typeset by Out of House Publishing
Printed in Great Britain
by TJ International Ltd, Padstow

To our wives and families: Liz, Liam, Marcella and Kevin; Áine, Eoin, Dara and Sinéad; for their unstinting support and for putting up with us

Contents

Figures and table

Figures

Contributors

Justin Carville teaches Historical and Theoretical Studies in Photography and is Chair of the Photography Programme at the Institute of Art, Design and Technology, Dun Laoghaire. A former Government of Ireland Senior Research Scholar in the Humanities and Social Sciences, he has guest-edited a special Ireland-themed issue of the *Journal of Popular Visual Culture* and an issue of the journal *Photographies* on the photographic image and globalisation. His publications include *Photography and Ireland* (2011) and, as editor, *Visualizing Dublin: Visual Culture, Modernity and the Representation of Urban Space* (2013). He is currently researching the connections between photography, anthropology and the representation of Irish identity, for which he was awarded an Irish Research Council fellowship.

Patricia Casey Emeritus Professor of Psychiatry in University College Dublin and Consultant Psychiatrist at the Mater Misericordiae University Hospital, Dublin. Her research interests include suicide, self-harm and stress disorders. She is the author of ten academic books and is currently working on another, to be published by American Psychiatric Publishing in 2015. She contributed a further twenty-seven chapters to academic and other books and is the author of over 100 peer-reviewed papers, published in academic journals. She is a peer reviewer for the major international psychiatric journals and is editor of *BJPsych-Advances*, published by the Royal College of Psychiatrists in London. She writes a weekly column ('Mind and Meaning') for Ireland's biggest-selling broadsheet newspaper (*Irish Independent*) and contributes regularly to the media (TV, radio and print).

Joe Cleary is Professor of English at the National University of Ireland, Maynooth. His publications include *Literature, Partition and the Nation-State: Culture and Conflict in Ireland, Israel and Palestine* (2002), *The Cambridge Companion to Modern Irish Culture*, co-edited with Claire Connolly (2005) and *Outrageous Fortune: Capital* *and Culture in Modern Ireland* (2007). He has most recently edited *The Cambridge Companion to Irish Modernism*, published in 2014. His articles have appeared in many leading Irish, British and American journals including *South Atlantic Quarterly, Boundary 2, Modern Language Quarterly, Textual Practice, The Field Day Review* and *Éire-Ireland*.

David Carroll Cochran is Professor of Politics and Director of the Kucera Center at Loras College in Dubuque, Iowa. His main areas of teaching and scholarship are religion and politics, racial and ethnic politics, and the morality of war. His most recent books are, as author, *Catholic Realism and the Abolition of War* (2014) and, as co-editor with John C. Waldmeir, *The Catholic Church in Ireland Today* (2015). In addition to his academic writing, he frequently writes about politics and culture for magazines such as *America* and *Commonweal*.

Michael Cronin teaches in the Faculty of Humanities and Social Sciences at Dublin City University. He is author of *Translating Ireland: Translation, Languages and Identity* (1996); *Across the Lines: Travel, Language, Translation* (2000); *Translation and Globalization* (2003); *Time Tracks: Scenes from the Irish Everyday* (2003); *Irish in the New Century/An Ghaeilge san Aois Nua* (2005), *Translation and Identity* (2006); *The Barrytown Trilogy* (2007); *Translation Goes to the Movies* (2009) and *The Expanding World: Towards a Politics of Microspection* (2012), *Translation in the Digital Age* (2013). He is co-editor of *Tourism in Ireland: A Critical Analysis* (1993); *Anthologie de nouvelles irlandaises* (1997); *Unity in Diversity? Current Trends in Translation Studies* (1998); *Reinventing Ireland: Culture, Society and the Global Economy* (2002); *Irish Tourism: Image, Culture and Identity* (2003); *The Languages of Ireland* (2003) and *Transforming Ireland* (2009). He is a Member of the Royal Irish Academy and of the *Academia Europeae*.

Louise Fuller is Associate Fellow, Department of History, Maynooth University, Maynooth, County Kildare, Ireland. She is author of *Irish Catholicism since 1950: The Undoing of a Culture* (2002, 2004) and co-editor with Eamon Maher and John Littleton of *Irish and Catholic? Towards an Understanding of Identity* (2006). She has contributed chapters to many volumes and published several journal articles on Irish socio-cultural history with particular reference to the role and influence of the Catholic Church. Her research interests include Irish political and cultural history in the nineteenth and twentieth centuries, the history of Irish education, the interplay between religion and society and its influence on socio-cultural change and the role of religion in the formation of identity.

Eamon Maher is Director of the National Centre for Franco-Irish Studies in IT Tallaght, where he also lectures in humanities. He is General Editor of the *Reimagining Ireland* book series. He has written and edited a number of books, the most recent of which, with Eugene O'Brien, are the collections *From Prosperity* *to Austerity: A Socio-cultural Critique of the Celtic Tiger and Its Aftermath* (2014) and, with Máirtín Mac Con Iomaire, *Tickling the Palate: Gastronomy in Irish Literature and Culture* (2014). Eamon is currently working on a study of the twentieth-century Catholic novel, as well as writing a monograph on the French writer, Jean Sulivan.

Catherine Maignant is Professor of Irish Studies at the University of Lille and President of the French Association for Irish Studies. After writing a PhD on early medieval Irish Christianity, she now specialises in contemporary Irish religious history. Her research interests include the new religious movements, the response of the Catholic Church to secularisation, interreligious dialogue, Celtic Christianity and the religious aspects of globalisation.

Patsy McGarry is Religious Affairs Correspondent with the *Irish Times*. He has written numerous books, most notably *While Justice Slept: The True Story of Nicky Kelly and the Sallins Train Robbery* (2006) and *First Citizen: Mary McAleese and the Irish Presidency* (2008).

Eugene O'Brien is Senior Lecturer and Head of the Department of English Language and Literature in Mary Immaculate College, Limerick, and Director of the Mary Immaculate College Institute for Irish Studies. He is the editor of the Oxford University Press Online Biography Module in Literary and Critical Theory. His recent publications include *Seamus Heaney: Searches for Answers* (2006) and *Kicking Bishop Brennan up the Arse: Negotiating Texts and Contexts in Contemporary Irish Studies* (2009). He co-edited (with Eamon Maher) *Modernity and Postmodernity in a Franco-Irish Context* (2008), *Breaking the Mould: Literary Representations of Irish Catholicism* (2010) and *From Prosperity to Austerity A Socio-cultural Critique of the Celtic Tiger and Its Aftermath* (2014). His monograph, *Seamus Heaney as Aesthetic Thinker: A Study of the Prose*, was published by Syracuse University Press in 2016, while an edited collection entitled *The Soul Exceeds Its Circumstances: The Later Poetry of Seamus Heaney*, will be published by the University of Notre Dame Press in 2016.

Sharon Tighe-Mooney works in the Centre for Teaching and Learning at the National University of Ireland, Maynooth. She completed her doctoral research on Kate O'Brien's fiction in 2010 at the School of English, Media and Theatre Studies, Maynooth University and has a Professional Certificate in Teaching and Learning (2012). She also obtained an MA in English, Sociology and Theology from Maynooth University. She is co-editor of *Essays in Irish Literary Criticism: Themes of Gender, Sexuality, and Corporeality* (2008).

Vincent Twomey was born in Cork in 1941. He attended Christian Brothers College, Cork. He entered the Divine Word Missionaries in 1963 and was ordained priest in 1970. He undertook undergraduate studies in the Societas Verbi Divini Studium, Donamon, Co. Roscommon (philosophy) and at St Patrick's College, Maynooth (theology). His doctoral studies were at University of Regensburg under the supervision of the then Professor Joseph Ratzinger. He was awarded the doctorate in 1979. He was Professor of Dogmatic Theology at the Regional Seminary of Papua New Guinea and the Solomon Islands from 1979 to 1981, and the SVD Theology Faculty at Mödling, near Vienna, Austria, from 1982 to 1983. He was Lecturer in Moral Theology on the Theology Faculty, Pontifical University, Maynooth from 1983 to 2004, serving as Professor of Moral Theology from 2004 to 2006. He was Visiting Professor on the University of Fribourg, Switzerland, in the summer semester 1984, and also Visiting Scholar, Theology Faculty, Seton Hall University, NJ. At present he is Rector of the Divine Word Missionaries Campus, Maynooth, Co. Kildare.

Eamonn Wall is Professor of International Studies and English at the University of Missouri-St. Louis. His recent books include *Writing the Irish West: Ecologies and Traditions* (2011) and *Sailing Lake Mareotis* (2011). *Junction City: Selected Poems 1990–2015* was published in 2015. Essays, reviews and articles have appeared in the *Irish Times*, *Washington Post*, *Chicago Tribune*, *New Hibernia Review*, *Criticism* and other publications. His current scholarly project is a study of transatlantic themes in Irish and Irish-American writing.

Introduction

Eamon Maher and Eugene O'Brien

Bind us together, Lord
Bind us together
With cords that cannot be broken
Bind us together, Lord
Bind us together
Bind us together in Love
There is only one God,
There is only one King,
There is only one Body,
That is why we sing.

On a sunny 30 September 1979, at Ballybrit racecourse in Galway, over 200,000 young people listened to two of Ireland's most popular clerics sing the hymn 'Bind Us Together', and the performance was given rapturous applause. One of the singers was Eamon Casey, Bishop of Galway. Casey was one of the best known and most popular members of the hierarchy: telegenic, baby-faced, funny, a man of passionate convictions and a long-time critic of the government's lack of spending on charity. In fact, as chair of the organisation Trócaire, he was adept at politicising this charity work and refused to meet President Ronald Reagan on his visit to Ireland in 1984, in protest against US policy in Central America. He was often on *The Late Late Show*, where his skills as a raconteur were showcased, and he was seen as a very human cleric at a time when the priestly vocation was often still viewed as an austere calling. In addition, Casey was known as a bon viveur who enjoyed socialising and driving fast cars. He was a major force in Irish society, especially when it came to presenting a human face of a monolithic organisation such as the Catholic Church. Casey had charisma, the common touch. He had his finger on the pulse of the Ireland of the 1980s, a time of economic free fall and increasing dissatisfaction with both church and state.

His partner on the stage in Galway was Fr Michael Cleary, a man from the working-class area of Ballyfermot in Dublin. He was known as the 'singing priest' and presented his own radio show on a station that had a very large following among young people, 98FM. He had a strong commitment to charity and to enlightening people about inner-city deprivation and was a tireless worker for people in ghetto areas of Dublin. Doctrinally conservative, as indeed was Casey, he voiced the stricter message of Church teaching, especially on matters of sexuality. In 1992, on *The Late Late Show* (he was also quite a regular contributor to this programme), while discussing the 'X Case', a situation involving a fourteen-year-old girl who travelled to England for an abortion after becoming pregnant as a result of rape, he maintained that the whole thing was an elaborate test case orchestrated by liberal groups and the media. At a time when Irish public opinion was becoming polarised between those who believed in 'the right to life' and those who were in 'the right to choose' camp, Cleary's voice was a clear one. He stood firmly behind the Church's doctrines.

So, as Ireland's most famous and media-friendly clerics sang on the open stage of the racecourse in Galway, awaiting the arrival of the most charismatic and media-friendly pontiff in the history of the Catholic Church, the eyes of the whole country were fixed on them. Later, the Pope spoke to the 200,000 young people in tones that predicted confidently that the synergy (or perhaps even collusion) between the Catholic Church and the Irish State would endure and strengthen:

> I believe in youth with all my heart and all the strength of my conviction. And today I say: I believe in the youth of Ireland. I believe in you who stand here before me, in every one of you. When I look at you, I see the Ireland of the future. Tomorrow you will be the living force of your country, you will decide what Ireland will be. Tomorrow, as technicians or teachers, nurses or secretaries, farmers or tradesmen, doctors or engineers, priests or religious – tomorrow you will have the power to make dreams come true. (John Paul II 2004: 46)

The words of the opening hymn were proleptic of this continued union, as the Church and State were, and would continue to be, 'one body', and the binding blocks did not look to be in danger of being dismantled at any point in the near future. In the dawning of a media-saturated age, these three representatives of Roman Catholicism had taken control of the medium and made it their own. Much of Ireland only had a single TV channel, and the audience figures for the Pope's visit were huge. The tone of all of the broadcasts was reverential and sombre, and the images that remain from the visit are ones of mass celebrations, a sense of community at worship and no real deviation from this monological message from a pastor to his flock.

During his visit, the Pope went to Dublin, Drogheda, Clonmacnoise, Galway Knock and Limerick, and, some thirty years later, in 2009, a report was issued that made reference to the Limerick stage of the papal visit. Here the Pope spoke about the family and children, and, particularly, the importance of the latter in the Christian vision of the family: 'And here, I want to say a very special word to all Irish parents. Marriage must include openness to the gift of children. Generous openness to accept children from God as the gift to their love is the mark of a Christian couple' (John Paul II 2004: 85). However, the report did not refer to the full content of the Pope's speech, even though it was concerned with the treatment of children in Church-run institutions. Instead, it referred more generally to the special occasion that was the papal visit. In volume 2, chapter 3 of the Ryan Report, the colloquial name for the findings of the Commission to Inquire into Child Abuse, published on 20 May 2009, we find reference to a more sinister side of Irish Catholicism, and to the period of the Pope's visit in particular. In this section, the subject is St Joseph's Industrial School, Ferryhouse, Clonmel ('Ferryhouse'), from 1885 to 1999. The part of the report that is of particular relevance to us is dated 1 October 1979, and makes for harrowing reading:

> The other boy was sent for, and Fr Stefano described how *'the two boys sat in my office and unfolded to me a most horrific story of what had been happening to them'*. The boys told Fr Stefano story after story of cruelty and abuse. The worst, as far as he was concerned, was the abuse of one of the boys during the Pope's visit to Ireland in 1979. The whole school went to see the Pope in Limerick, except for one of the two boys who was not allowed to go because of his record of absconding. Br Bruno volunteered to stay back and supervise him. The boy told Fr Stefano that, when the rest of the boys left, *'this Brother came and raped me in my bed'*. (Ryan 2009: II, 2, 87; italics in original)

Therefore, while the Pope was speaking about the value of children in the Catholic world view, some forty miles away, a Rosminian brother was raping two boys who had been placed under his care by both the Catholic Church and the State.

This provides a sharp contrast to the euphoria engendered by the papal visit and adds an ironic touch both to the hymn, 'Bind Us Together' and to the words of the Pope to the youth of Ireland: 'Young people of Ireland, I love you.' Indeed, it also points a finger at the fraudulent character of the two singing clerics. In 1992, Bishop Eamon Casey admitted that he had had an affair with a woman, Annie Murphy, and that he was father to her son, Patrick. In his turn, one year later, after his death in 1993, it was revealed that Michael Cleary had a sexual relationship with his housekeeper Phyllis Hamilton for a number of years. Their son, Ross, lived with the couple without ever being acknowledged as Fr Cleary's offspring. It was also stated that they had another child who had been given up for adoption. Needless to say, there were massive denials of these stories, and, once more on the ever-influential *Late Late Show*, in April 1993, Annie Murphy was given a very hostile reception by the host, Gay Byrne, and by a number of Casey's relatives who were in the audience. There was still a strong hegemonic attachment to Catholicism as 'our' religion and as a social cement that bonded most Irish people together. It was less a devotional or religious affiliation than an ideological and cultural identification that was unthought and unthinking. There was a cultural and ideological symphysis between Church and State that was taken for granted by all.

These two events shook the credibility of the Church to the core, and, interestingly, in both cases it was the media that broke the stories. The Dublin magazine *The Phoenix* was the source of the revelations about Michael Cleary while the *Irish Times* reported initially on the Annie Murphy story. Thus, it was the cultural sphere within which the initial stages of unbinding began to take place. Newspapers, documentaries, television and radio reports, along with literary depictions, began to take issue with the received views of the Church, and the reverential tones of the premier television current-affairs reporter Brian Farrell as he intoned a descriptive narrative of the papal visit in 1979 was gradually replaced by more critical voices with respect to the actions of the clergy and the organisation and system as a whole. Thus, for example, 'in November 1994, RTÉ devoted to it a special edition of *Tuesday File*, which included one of the earliest televised interviews with a victim of clerical sex abuse' (Kenny 2009: 64), which discussed the case of Fr Brendan Smyth, who was wanted for child abuse in Northern Ireland but whose extradition had been delayed in the Republic. A year later, in October 1995, a special edition of *Counterpoint*, entitled *Suffer Little Children*, broadcast on UTV, caused shock and consternation in the Republic (Kenny 2009: 65).[1] These programmes put clerical sexual abuse in the public sphere, a sphere that was gradually loosening the binding connection with the Church. A number of clerics came before the courts as people who had repressed memories of abuse now found the courage to come forward. Names such as Fr Ivan Payne, Fr Seán Fortune and Fr Paul McGennis became part of an ongoing list of proven abusers. The media focus on this issue continued the following year. Kenny notes that:

> Nuns as well as priests were occasionally implicated in allegations of sexual abuse. On 22 February 1996, RTÉ screened *Dear Daughter*, a documentary by Louis Lentin that revealed through interviews what life had been like during the late 1950s and early 1960s for some children at the Goldenbridge Orphanage, Dublin, run by the Sisters of Mercy. (Kenny 2009: 65)

This caused the Mercy order, which ran this institution, to apologise publicly, an unthinkable act only a few years earlier.

However, the beginning of the real crisis in Irish Catholicism was Mary Raftery's trilogy of documentaries, *States of Fear*, broadcast on 27 April, 4 and 7 May 1999, where sexual, physical and psychological abuse across a range of industrial schools was analysed and brought into the open on a grand scale. In the wake of this programme, significantly more people came forward to detail instances of abuse, and the Taoiseach, Bertie Ahern, apologised on behalf of the

State. The Commission to Inquire into Child Abuse was established a year later and delivered its report in May 2009. Much worse was to come in the exposure of clerical abuse scandals contained in the Ferns (2005), Ryan (2009), Murphy (2009) and Cloyne (2011) reports, which revealed an institutional mindset that bears all the hallmarks of 'groupthink' (Kenny 2011; Murphy et al. 2005; Murphy 2009; Ryan 2009). These reports concretised a gradual process of secularisation, influenced heavily by access to a global media, the Internet and hundreds of television channels.

On 20 July 2011, the Taoiseach, Enda Kenny, made a strong speech on the relationship between Church and State in a manner that would have been unthinkable in the 1970s, especially as Kenny is probably an average and conservative Catholic in his personal life. In this speech, he went on to excoriate the Catholic Church and to make a telling point in terms of a separation of Church and State in Ireland. Kenny spoke of what he termed 'clericalism' and stressed how the 'rape and torture of children were downplayed or "managed" to uphold instead, the primacy of the institution, its power, standing and "reputation"' (Kenny 2011). More tellingly, he went on to stress that the Church was just one organisation within the State and that it could no longer see itself as politically and culturally hegemonic. The standards that the Church saw as appropriate for its own governance 'cannot and will not, be applied to the workings of democracy and civil society in this republic' (Kenny 2011). When one looks back to how the nation as a whole stood still in 1979 for the papal visit, there has clearly been a sea change in attitudes in Ireland, and it is a change not only voiced in the very heart of government but also, even more importantly, broadcast on RTÉ. Indeed, on researching (or googling as it is now known) the speech on the Internet, the RTÉ website is the first site that appears, and, indeed, it is the source of these quotations. This means that the country as a whole heard this speech, or at least the significant sections, and it made the front page of all the papers in the Republic of Ireland the following day. Kenny's articulation of a twenty-first-century Ireland as a 'Republic of laws, of rights and responsibilities, of proper civic order, where the delinquency and arrogance of a particular kind of "morality" will no longer be tolerated or ignored' (Kenny 2011) was a moment that encapsulated the fall from grace of an institution which had hitherto been culturally indistinguishable from Ireland as a nation. It is this fall from grace of the Church as a cultural phenomenon in Irish society that will be the focus of this book.

It is clear from this brief rehearsal of events that between 1979 and 2009 a sea change (one could even say 'unbinding') occurred in the perception of the Catholic Church and in the relationship between Church and State. The representation of the Pope's visit as a type of spiritual homecoming in 1979, as a bringing together of a pastor and his people, and of a church and its state, and the report in a state document, thirty years later, of an act of child abuse in a Church-run institution, are two very significant highlights in this process. The medium and the message are inextricably connected, and, as Church control over the cultural sphere

was gradually attenuated, that sphere became more critical of the Church as institution and as system. The power of the Church was in many ways a soft power, one
which was set out in legalistic canon law and enforced through control over health
and education, but which maintained and replicated its power through ideology.
Like all ideology, it was culturally mediated through education, writing, television
and radio. As Terry Eagleton has observed, 'an ideology exists because there are
certain things which must not be spoken of' (Eagleton 1986: 90), and in Ireland,
during that period, this was definitely the case. The Church had an undue influence over how Irish society educated its young, treated the sick and wrote its laws.
Even the Constitution of Ireland had been shown to the hierarchy before it was
passed in parliament to make sure that Church and State spoke with one voice on
topics that were seen to impact on the Church's role as moral custodian of a nation.

The journey from Galway to Cloyne, spanning over thirty years, was a journey
of separation and of delegitimisation of the Church and its role in Ireland. A gradual process of disintegration took place as the media, whose deferential tone to the
Church was clear in the number of times priests and bishops were given very positive coverage on television and in the newspapers, had their own radio shows and
were often presented and interviewed in a deferential manner. Censorship, which
remained strong in terms of what was allowed to be read in Ireland up to the 1980s,
was a further controlling factor in mediating the position of the Church and creating that 'one body' of which the aforementioned hymn speaks. Louis Althusser,
writing about the maintenance and renewal of power, speaks of how soft power,
or ideology, is the means by which a ruling elite maintains itself in power and also
maintains the hierarchy of relationships that acknowledge that power apparatuses
may teach 'know-how' but in forms that ensure *subjection to the ruling ideology* or
the mastery of its 'practice' (Althusser 2001: 133). Althusser's studies of ideology at
work are especially pertinent to this book, which looks at how culture helped to
reinforce, and also deconstruct, Catholic hegemony in Ireland while also examining how, in many ways, the Irish unconscious can be seen to be strongly influenced
by the remnants of Catholic rituals and beliefs. Althusser noted that during the
Middle Ages in Europe, 'the Church' was the 'religious ideological State apparatus'
and that 'alongside the Church there was the family Ideological State Apparatus,
which played a considerable part, incommensurable with its role in capitalist social
formations' (Althusser 2001: 151). In this period of European history, the Church
set out the laws and codes of society, and these were communicated to the next
generations through the medium of family: it is interesting to note that in his sermons on his Irish trip, the Pope mentioned the family sixteen times, an index of its
importance to Catholic ideological practice. This is central to Althusser's thesis: 'In
the pre-capitalist historical period which I have examined extremely broadly, it
is absolutely clear that *there was one dominant Ideological State Apparatus, the Church*,
which concentrated within it not only religious functions, but also educational
ones, and a large proportion of the functions of communications and "culture"'
(Althusser 2001: 151, italics in original).

In Ireland of the late 1970s, this was still largely true, mainly as a result of its island status and its colonial history, which meant that intellectual movements such as the Renaissance, the Reformation and the Enlightenment were largely offset in an Irish context by the stifling rule exercised over it by the United Kingdom. While Europe was moving through ideological revolutions, Ireland was mired in colonial and political struggles, following the almost paradigmatic Third World colonial narrative of ethnic revivalist movements, revolution and then partition, followed by civil war. Through all of this strife, the power of the Church was never questioned, and, indeed, Church and State entered into a symbiotic relationship on the achievement of independence in 1922. So, while one of the key achievements of the French Revolution was the 'creation of new ideological State apparatuses to replace the religious ideological State apparatus in its dominant role' (Althusser 2001: 152), there was no such parallel process in Ireland. Here the Church and State were bound together, although, as we will point out, these tight cords were becoming looser by 1979. When we say church and state, what we mean is the ruling classes of the time, as 'the class which is the ruling *material* force of society is at the same time its ruling *intellectual* force', a point made by Marx and Engels in *The German Ideology* (1998: 67, italics in original). In the Irish context, these intellectual ideas were dominated and shaped by Catholic doctrine, which resulted, quite logically, in a Catholic ethos permeating Irish intellectual and cultural life.

Catholic culture was Irish culture, and it is again no accident that there were twenty-six mentions of 'society' in the papal sermons of 1979, none more exemplary than this one:

> Yes, Ireland, that has come overcome so many difficult moments in her history, is being challenged in a new way today, for she is not immune from the influence of ideologies and trends which present-day civilisation and progress carry with them. The very capability of mass media to bring the whole world into your homes produces a new kind of confrontation with values and trends that up until now have been alien to Irish society. Pervading materialism imposes its dominion on man today in many different forms and with aggressiveness that spares no one. The most sacred principles, which were the sure guides for the behaviour of individuals and society, are being hollowed-out by false pretences concerning freedom, the sacredness of life, the indissolubility of marriage, the true sense of human sexuality, the right attitude towards the material goods that progress has to offer. Many people now are tempted to self-indulgence and consumerism, and human identity is often defined by what one owns. Prosperity and affluence, even when they are only beginning to be available to larger strata of society, tend to make people assume that they have a right to all that prosperity can bring, and thus they can become more selfish in their demands. (John Paul II 2004: 6)

The fear of the mass media and consumer culture is a fear of the very processes sketched by Althusser in Continental Europe. The adequation between church and state is clearly under threat when capitalism and consumerist culture offers a complication of the hitherto dyadic relationship of the two traditional power blocs of Irish life. In the face of these threats, a later sermon by John Paul II harks back to a time when:

> Ireland … displayed a remarkable interpenetration of her whole culture, speech and way of life by the things of God and the life of grace. Life was in a sense organised around religious events. The task of this generation of Irish men and women is to transform the more complex world of modern industrial and urban life by the same Gospel spirit. (John Paul II 2004: 83–4)

The ideology of this sermon corresponds to what Roland Barthes terms 'mythology'. In this eulogising of a simpler time, a time where the choices were not as difficult for a person with religious convictions, myth, as Barthes puts it, 'acts economically' in that it 'it abolishes the complexity of human acts, it gives them the simplicity of essences, it does away with all dialectics, with any going back beyond what is immediately visible, it organises a world without contradictions' (Barthes 1986:143). What these sermons show is an awareness of the power of culture and ideology as a means of maintaining power and hegemony, and also a fear of counter-cultural perspectives that would dilute and deconstruct such hegemonic positions by offering alternatives. A mass media, not subject to Church control, could cause serious unbinding between Church and State, and this concern would prove to be proleptic of what would transpire in Ireland over the next thirty to forty years, as the ideology of the Church and State was gradually deconstructed by a more secular and pluralistic ideology. In these sermons, and in the visit as a whole, there was an attempt being made to bring Ireland back from the brink of a more pluralistic and secular culture and to espouse instead a more traditional one. Like all ideological imperatives, this one attempted to 'establish and sustain relations of power which are systematically asymmetrical', because 'ideology, broadly speaking, is meaning in the service of power' (Thompson 1990:7).

We have stressed how the Catholic version of 'meaning' was the only one available in the Ireland of the 1970s, but this book will trace the gradual pluralisation and globalisation of the transmitters of meaning in this period. From 1955, British television channels were available in Belfast and along the east coast of Ireland. RTÉ, the Irish television network, was set up in 1961, and a single channel, very much in keeping with the broadly Catholic ethos of the country, was available from that year, with a second channel becoming available in 1978. However, the British and commercial channels were available on the east coast, albeit with very poor reception until the setting up of a cable service, RTÉ Relays, in 1963 that provided clearer images. In 1974, Waterford set up a cable service and, by the early 1980s, Limerick and Cork were part of this new multi-channel service. The importance of these channels in the dismantling of Catholic socio-cultural hegemony cannot be overstated, as perspectives on social and moral issues, which were non-Catholic, and in some cases, non-religious, became part of the conversation in living rooms and in public houses, and the parameters of debate were gradually broadened. Thus, what had been taken as orthodox opinions on homosexuality, contraception, divorce and abortion, were now called into question, and the process had begun of liberalising social legislation to bring Ireland into line with the other secular European countries in the EU. What was especially significant was that opinions, which were contrary to Catholic doctrine, were not seen as aberrant or radical on BBC or ITV but were discussed as just another in a series of options. This defamiliarisation of non-Catholic perspectives had an accretive effect, as younger people especially often turned to the media for their opinions whereas heretofore they had looked to the Church.

Cultural, ethical and moral issues, especially those dealing with sexual morality, became the cultural battleground in these years, with the media offering a more secular, European and Anglo-American perspective on dealing with these issues. Also, increasing mobility between countries through the Erasmus exchange of students and academics, allied to media representations, demonstrated that the Catholicism of France, Spain and Italy was very different to that of Ireland, where Church and State were closely allied. The availability of films, books, discussions and newspapers that took more secular positions on issues that had been seen as firmly within the Catholic Church's purview gradually eroded the hegemonic certainties and offered alternatives. The hierarchy, habituated to obedience, were neither intellectually nor ideologically equipped to engage in debate, and this further lessened the respect in which they were held. One could see the respective falls from grace of Casey and Cleary as emblematic figures of a more gradual and accretive process wherein respect for the Church was gradually but inexorably eroded in the cultural sphere. We are stressing the cultural nature of this battleground, as it was in this arena that the debates were held, and it was culturally, rather than through any issues of belief or ritual, that the influence of Catholicism became subject to critique.

It is difficult to capture in a brief introduction the full dismantling of the once-dominant force that was Irish Catholicism. Even in 1979, which some wrongly view as the apogee of the Catholic Church in this country, secularism was on the rise, as more and more young people availed of free education and, as a result, managed to secure better-paid jobs that ensured their economic independence. Attending university, while still largely the purview of the privileged classes, became far more accessible to the general population. It is likely that the startling fall in vocations to the priesthood and religious life, and the increasing challenge to the Church's stances on issues pertaining to human sexuality, were among the main reasons that prompted the Pope to visit Ireland in 1979. Rather than being a triumphalist visit, it was an attempt to lessen the tide of secularism and to re-energise the faithful. However, in spite of the personal success enjoyed by Pope John Paul II during his time in Ireland, the situation of the Church did not improve in the 1980s and 1990s, which were characterised by divisive referendums on contraception, divorce and abortion. A more educated, liberal, urban population found it increasingly difficult to obey submissively Catholic teaching when it came to what happened between consenting adults in the privacy of their bedroom. In this regard, the opinion expressed by the novelist Roddy Doyle (born in 1958) in an interview with Caramine White, is indicative of a resentment of the Church's attempt to set the agenda on areas that went beyond its remit, in the writer's view. When asked why there is such an absence of religion in his books, Doyle replied:

> There's no religion in me own life, for certain, I've no room for it at all. It's difficult in a country like Ireland because you do have to put your face out and tell it to go away – 'Fuck off.' You have to be quite blunt to allow yourself your own agnostic space. (White 2001: 168)

Creating his 'own agnostic space' was clearly a priority for Doyle, who, as a private citizen, fervently supported the 'Yes' campaign for divorce in 1996. Because the Church's influence was all-pervasive in Irish society, the only way to free oneself from its shackles was, in Doyle's forthright phrase, to tell it to 'Fuck off'. In his view, the referendum on divorce was not simply about the right to dissolve marriage legally; instead, it was more concerned with the Catholic Church's desire to dictate what it meant to be Irish. He noted in an interview with Liam Fay: 'It basically was the Catholic Church against everyone else. It was the insistence that if you're Irish, you're white and you're Catholic as well, and if you're not both of these things then you're not fully Irish. Ultimately, that is what it was all about' (Fay 1996: 19). This perspective offers a stark contrast to some of the main canonical figures in Irish literature of the previous generation such as Friel, McGahern and Heaney, all of whom, although they had long ceased practising their religion, had a reverence for the rituals and ceremonies of the Catholic Church, which they saw in some ways as the language of their youth, as part of a shared cultural consciousness. It is interesting that both McGahern and Heaney were buried in their local parish cemeteries with all the trimmings, including the funeral mass and a decade of the rosary at the graveside. Brian Friel chose to be buried in Glenties, Co. Donegal, the setting of many of his works, but he did not opt for a mass. Instead, there were prayers said at his graveside by the parish priest of Glenties, Fr Pat Prendergast, and then his family and others closely associated with the writer heard tributes from his close friends Tom Paulin and Thomas Kilroy. The reason for the writers choosing such traditional rituals had as much to do with their respect for local custom as any deeply held religious belief, but it is significant for all that. In his memorable essay, 'The Church and Its Spire', McGahern summed up his relationship with the Catholic Church in the following manner:

> I was born into Catholicism as I might have been born into Buddhism or Protestantism or any of the other isms or sects, and brought up as a Roman Catholic in the infancy

of this small state when the Church has almost total power: it was the dominating force of my whole upbringing, education and early working life. (McGahern 2009: 133)

McGahern's position was that, for all that the Church was by times patriarchal, authoritarian and responsible for promoting an unhealthy attitude to human sexuality, it also had these wonderful religious ceremonies that brightened up his otherwise humdrum life growing up in Leitrim and Roscommon. His great regret was that Irish Catholicism opted for the Romanesque spirit, 'the low roof, the fortress, the fundamentalists' pulpit-pounding zeal, the darkly ominous and fearful warnings to transgressors' (McGahern 2009: 145), rather than embracing the Gothic form, with its impressive spires that raised man's look from the avaricious earth and helped him to imagine the transcendent. A member of a later generation of writers, Anne Enright, describes a starkly different reaction to religious ceremonies than one finds in McGahern. Take the following extract from the award-winning novel, *The Gathering*:

> The drab days of Lent are over, the Legion's mission has been triumphant, the brothels have been raided by the police, sprinkled with holy water, brought off by Frank Duff, and closed down. A great religious procession has been held and a cross raised in Purdon Street by the man himself, who stood up on a kitchen table and drove in the nail with a surprisingly large hammer. Twenty girls had been decanted into the Sancta Maria hostel and dried out at either end. Everyone has been praying day and night, night and day, until they are fed up with it, the whole city has had it up to here, they have suffered the ashes and kissed the rood and felt truly, deeply, spiritually *cleaned out*: Easter dawns, thanks be to the Jay, and when they have eaten and laughed and looked at the daffodils they go up to bed to make love (it's a long time, forty days) and have a big sleep and, the next morning, they all go off to the races. (Enright 2008: 105)

What is noticeable in this passage is the scepticism and drudgery that are associated with the ceremonies of Lent. It was a period one had to go through, because as a Catholic it was mandatory. The great champion of the Pioneer Total Abstinence Association and the Legion of Mary, Frank Duff, is given honourable mention for nailing a cross into a kitchen 'with a surprisingly large hammer' – the irony is not lost on the reader – and bringing alcohol-addicted women into a hostel to dry out. There is no hint of an appreciation of the positive side of Catholicism in this passage: everything is couched in an imposed type of mechanical religiosity, which, once the services are over, will not have left any spiritual imprint. It strikes us that it is no coincidence that both Doyle and Enright are primarily novelists concerned with Dublin and its environs, something that has imbued them with a different perspective on Catholicism than that of the rural-based Friel, McGahern and Heaney. They are also the first generation of writers to emerge from the shadow of these giants, and their experience of Catholicism is noticeably different. Whatever the position they adopt in relation to Catholicism, however, it is clear that they provide an invaluable gauge as to what the public reaction is to religion at a certain period and in a certain milieu.

In her defining study, *Irish Catholicism since 1950: The Undoing of a Culture*, historian Louise Fuller pointed out that the 1960s encyclical *Humanae vitae* galvanised public opinion in a way not previously witnessed in Ireland, something which she attributes to a society that was becoming more exposed to liberal values through the arrival of the television set in many homes and through increased access to foreign travel. She continues:

> The questioning of Church authority has to be seen against the backdrop of a worldwide phenomenon characterised by many people's desire to break free of the shackles of authority. The gloom of the post-war era was past. Man was about to reach the moon. Economic affluence, educational opportunities, the communications revolution and increased mobility made his horizons seem limitless. It was the era of individualism, 'flower-power', 'free love' and 'hanging loose'. (Fuller 2004: 198)

Until then, the voice of authority was singular; it came from the pulpit on a Sunday, and papal and episcopal letters could be read in every church, which achieved an almost saturation effect in terms of the dissemination of Roman Catholic ideology. New voices of authority now competed with the Church, and these voices, from educated presenters and panellists, were all-pervasive in the corners of Irish living rooms. A couple of decades later, the 'baby boomer' generation would have come into its own, which spelled trouble for the continued hegemony of the Church. Clearly, people who during their youth had challenged the ruling elites were not, in middle age, going to succumb to their ongoing interference.

While we have spent some time looking at the effects of change on Irish society, it is also necessary to examine how secularism and the delayed advent of modernity to Ireland affected those who were priests or who were training to become priests. The turmoil in the national seminary in Maynooth in the period pre- and post-1979 is a useful indicator of how things were evolving. In his 1986 novella, *The Seminary*, Michael Harding gives us an insider's view of the confusion that beset many young male seminarians at this time. The eighty-year-old fictional spiritual director, Fr George Skewer, who had spent the majority of his life in Maynooth, notes:

> If he met a seminarian at the gate, wearing a red shirt and denim jeans, or chatting intently to a young first-arts girl, he looked the other way and preferred to remember what seminarians used to look like: lonesome figures, tortured faces, untypical of youth; all individuality submerged under the long dress-like black cassock. In his view, as it was and should be in the making days of a priest. (Harding 1986: 36)

If we are to believe the report of the apostolic visitation set up in the wake of the Murphy Report by Pope Benedict, Fr Skewer's view of what constitutes a proper seminary training is the correct one. In 2012, one of the findings of the visitation team was that the formal segregation of seminarians from lay students was to be reinstated in Maynooth. The underlying premise of this action is that somehow interaction with those not studying for the priesthood (particularly women) might prove distracting in relation to the life of prayer and reflection that should characterise seminary training. However, one wonders what is to happen to newly ordained priests when they go to work in parishes, where the majority of those attending religious ceremonies will be women. Will donning the once more fashionable clerical garb somehow insulate them from temptation? Will their hypothetical consideration of the potential dangers posed by concupiscence in the seminary assist them in their future careers? In addition, will spending time in an all-male environment help those of a homosexual orientation to live fulfilled celibate lives? The final-year student in Harding's story, Peter Maguire, describes the special treatment he receives when home on holidays from Maynooth:

> He assisted on the altar in his parish that Easter, and wore his black suit and collar everywhere. People would approach him at the church gate and shake his hand. At home his mother began fussing over him and telling his sisters to move from the chair and let him watch what he wanted on the television … And he felt good at last that something had come of his six years and his mother's prayers. (Harding 1986: 78)

Peter perseveres with his vocation, although it is clear that he has at best a sceptical view of religion and regularly doubts his suitability for the priesthood. His friend Mel Kavanagh falls by the wayside, however, because of an inability to accept the arid spiritual example that he sees ingrained in someone like Peter. The latter has nothing but disdain for his fellow seminarians, seeing them as misguided and inept. In an uncharacteristic outburst, Kavanagh exclaims:

> 'Y'see, most guys in here, I believe, are maligned, and if the truth were known, have a lot going for them. Because they have one thing you don't have, and it's called faith. That's your problem Peter … you have no faith … in God … or people … it makes no difference … it's all the one. And true, I kept very quiet about it. I keep very quiet about a lot of things … so that bastards like you won't be going around … pontificating about it.' (Harding 1986: 86)

As a former priest, Harding presents a damning critique of the type of life lived by many who did their training in the national seminary of Ireland in the 1970s and 1980s, some of whom are now relatively senior clerics. Pope John Paul II was visibly displeased when he visited the beautiful Gunn Chapel in Maynooth in 1979 and was greeted with the triumphalist chant, 'He's got the whole world / In his hands; / he's got the whole world.' The Pontiff's reaction on television showed that he felt this type of welcome to his arrival was better suited to a pop concert than to the hallowed surrounds of the chapel.

Undoubtedly, the decades we have chosen to cover in this book were significant ones in the 'undoing' (to use Fuller's phrase) of the dominant Catholic
culture in Ireland. From Pope John Paul's visit to the publication of four damning reports in relation to callous mistreatment of young people in industrial
schools and Magdalene laundries, the reputational damage to the Church was
huge, but it is possibly true to say that even without the revelations that came
to light in the 1990s and 2000s, the die was cast in terms of people's move
away from organised religion. The title of journalist Mary Kenny's 1997 book,
Goodbye to Catholic Ireland, shows an awareness that Catholicism as she knew
it during her youth was gone, a disappearance that was no cause for rejoicing
in her view. She refused to succumb to total pessimism, however, as she wrote
towards the end of her study:

> Catholicism in Ireland, as it was, is dead, but of course a spirituality remains, as indeed
> it does for all Celtic peoples: the annual pilgrimages, the visitations to holy places,
> and the funeral rites according to Mother Church remain. One seldom sees anyone
> saying the Angelus now – the Angelus bell is still rung on national radio and televi-
> sion, though its days are numbered, being widely criticised as 'sectarian' – or bless-
> ing themselves while passing a church, but there are snatches of Catholic Ireland in
> daily life. (Kenny 1997: 392–3)

What Kenny is saying really is that there has been a serious decline in traditional
Catholic culture in Ireland, a lost legacy the consequences of which we seek to
explore in this collection. There have been a number of books that cover the
various scandals of the past few decades and their impact on the position of the
Catholic Church in Ireland. The purpose of *Tracing the Cultural Legacy of Irish
Catholicism* is to employ a multidisciplinary approach in an attempt to bring to
light how and why this process took place, and to explore the consequences it has
had for Irish society. Vincent Twomey, Professor Emeritus of Moral Theology in
St Patrick's College, Maynooth, offered some excellent explanations in *The End
of Irish Catholicism?* about how Ireland's fragile Catholic identity found it impossible to deal with the combination of increasing secularism and the clerical abuse
scandals because of its lack of an intellectual tradition that encouraged free and
open debate about theological and philosophical issues, as happens in a country
like France, for example. Twomey observes:

> The lack of a rich tradition of systematic (self)-questioning and searching, which is
> what theological scholarship is, coupled with the way whatever little writing on the
> subject to appear in Ireland has been effectively ignored, may well be the price we are
> paying for the assumption that, since we were a chosen nation, we would never lose
> the faith; we did not have to think things through. (Twomey 2003: 40)

The chapters that follow are a way of 'thinking things through', of assessing how
we have come to the present impasse and what approach Irish society might

adopt as it seeks to come to terms with what is effectively a post-Catholic culture. Our main objective is to map how the early monolithic connection of Irishness and Catholicism evolved into the more pluralistic public sphere in which we now live. In doing this, we want to avoid the trap into which many commentators fall by adopting a stance that is pro- or anti-Catholicism. In tracing the important cultural legacy that is Irish Catholicism, we have assembled a multidisciplinary group of authors who are all experts in their field and who provide intriguing lenses through which to explore the phenomenon.

The collection's opening part seeks to provide a context for the book's major theme. Patsy McGarry draws on the knowledge of the changed role of religion in Irish society that he has accumulated as religious affairs correspondent of the *Irish Times* through the troubled recent decades in an attempt to illustrate how 'the times are a changin'' in terms of Catholic hegemony in Ireland. He opens with a comment made by the Church of Ireland Bishop of Cork, Most Reverend Paul Colton, who stated just after the publication of the Ryan Report that Ireland was undergoing 'a national trauma'. McGarry traces the causes of this trauma and points out that until the Church hierarchy is prepared to acknowledge responsibility for their poor handling of the abuse scandals, and the pain inflicted on the survivors, there will be no healing. His treatment of the various scandals and the role of Irish bishops – many of whom were following clear instructions from Rome – in trying to limit reputational damage to the Church, illustrate McGarry's contention that things will continue to get worse for the foreseeable future in Ireland, because of a failure to come to grips with systemic failures within the organisation. Taking up from where McGarry leaves off, Louise Fuller claims that there can be no doubt that Irish Catholicism is in serious decline. The decline itself is no huge surprise: it is the extent of the implosion and the consequences this has had on Irish society that require explanation. The 'aggressive secularism' that is now commonplace has led to a situation where it has become extremely difficult to express a Catholic viewpoint in the public arena, a situation that is unhealthy in its own way as the theocracy that dominated for far too long in Ireland. Major changes in how it communicates the Word of God will be necessary if the Church is to have any hope of re-engaging the minds and hearts of a population that is becoming theologically illiterate and indifferent to religious observance of any type.

Using Charles Taylor's *A Catholic Modernity?* as its starting point, David Carroll Cochran's essay explores the evolving role of Catholicism in Ireland over the past half century and concludes that the disentangling of the Church from the dominant political and cultural institutions of society has paradoxically extended many of the very values Catholicism celebrates. Due to the severing of its close traditional connection to the State, the Church has rediscovered its original mission to provide a prophetic spiritual voice, especially in favour of the poor, and to align itself more closely with the concerns of its founder, Jesus Christ. Justin Carville draws on recent debates in relation to photography and the everyday in order to examine the role of street photography in the cultural politics of religion as it was played out in the quotidian moments of social relations within Dublin's urban and suburban spaces during the 1980s and 1990s. The essay argues that photography was important in giving visual expression to the social contradictions within the relations between religion and the transformation of Irish social life, not through the dramatic and traumatic experiences that defined the nation's increased secularism but in the quiet, humdrum and sometimes monotonous routines of religious ceremonies and everyday social relations.

The opening section concludes with Vincent Twomey's thought-provoking essay, which sees reasons for hope in the midst of all the problems currently besetting Irish Catholicism. He opines that people's faith has withstood the turmoil within and without the Church and argues that there are signs of the kind of renewal that was recommended by some of the documents of Vatican II. Detecting these signs is important in revealing the newly opened-up possibilities (and risks) for a more humble church that seeks to fulfil its God-given mission to bring joy to the world of today. The re-evangelising of Ireland will not happen easily: it requires placing more emphasis on the beauty of lived Christianity and, by extension, of everyday sanctity.

Part II contains essays that concentrate largely on the written word and its relationship with Catholicism. Eamonn Wall's discussion of Irish-American Catholic experience reveals many similarities on either side of the pond, and some differences also. The Irish-American authors and commentators provide unique perspectives on many facets of Irish life, including the unique role played by the Catholic Church. Among the authors discussed are Frank McCourt, whose account of a poor Catholic childhood in Limerick is so memorably captured in the best-seller, *Angela's Ashes*, Colum McCann, Colm Tóibín and Mary Gordon – the latter may not be well known to an Irish audience, but she has some intriguing insights into her Catholic upbringing and beliefs. Similarly, the theologian Richard P. McBrien, journalist and writer Maureen Dezell and sociologist Andrew Greely combine to illustrate the impact that the Irish Church has had on its American equivalent. Wall maintains that looking towards Ireland from the USA and drawing on American notions of egalitarianism and individual freedom sometimes allows for a more dispassionate view of Ireland's Catholic heritage and enables envisaging its future with a far greater clarity than can be achieved when change is all around you.

Eamon Maher's contribution takes a number of priests with a public profile and examines the extent to which they are prophetic voices or complicit functionaries. Choosing the French priest-writer Jean Sulivan (1913–80) as a comparator, Maher examines the published work of Joseph Dunn, Vincent Twomey, Mark Patrick Hederman and Brendan Hoban, before concluding that they all share the prophetic tendency of raising uncomfortable and often unpopular issues while remaining within the institution. He further argues that being so closely aligned to the Church makes it difficult, and professionally dangerous, for priests to criticise certain practices within the institution. However, while retaining a huge love of, and devotion to, the main tenets of Catholicism, these men never-theless feel obliged to point out things that are going wrong, even when express-ing such views can often involve them in conflict with their superiors at home and in Rome. Catherine Maignant's chapter deals with another Irish priest, Tony Flannery, whose writings and liberal media pronouncements led to a caution from the Congregation for the Doctrine of the Faith, which disqualifies him from pub-lishing work or accepting invitations to express his views at public events without seeking prior permission from Rome. Maignant argues that Flannery has all the traits of a Christian witness, in that he is a prophet who appears to be reviled by certain forces within his own church for daring to express unpalatable truths. Notwithstanding his censure, he has continued to write and to air his sometimes daring opinions, all the while knowing that they could eventually lead to his excommunication.

Eugene O'Brien concludes Part II with a discussion of the implications that the 'Yes' vote in the May 2015 referendum on same-sex marriage may have for the social and cultural position of the Catholic Church in contemporary Ireland and in the future. His analysis channels the thinking of Ferdinand Tönnies, an early German sociologist and a contemporary of Durkheim and Weber, who used the German words *Gemeinschaft* and *Gesellschaft* to distinguish between two fundamentally different structural paradigms for social relations. O'Brien sees marriage as a core ideological signifier of ideological hegemony, and, using the fantasy fiction of Terry Pratchett's satire on religion entitled *Small Gods* as a lens, he looks at the referendum as a significant turning point in the definition of marriage and, by extension, in the transformation Irish society from the organic community of the *Gemeinschaft* to the more postmodern and pluralist notion of the *Gesellschaft*.

Part III focuses on the main challenges to Catholicism in contemporary Ireland. Michael Cronin opens the section by observing that the greatest threat to Irish society has been the dominant discourse of neo-liberalism and the Market, which has come to be the deity to which all must bend. The Irish Church has traditionally been associated with a regime of fear and punishment, which is somewhat paradoxical given that the founding message of Christianity is one of hope, of the end of fear. In Cronin's view, a more radical move for a church which has been brought to its knees by a multiplicity of cultural factors would be to embrace empathy and a politics of hope, which might consist of no longer saying 'No' but 'Yes'. The affirmation of justice for all, a more equal sharing of wealth, the creation of a climate where difference is embraced: these are the life-affirming and Christian principles on which the future of Irish Catholicism should be based.

Patricia Casey makes the point that up until recently there was no tradi-tion of a questioning laity, or, indeed, clergy, in the Irish Church. Centuries of persecution had brought priests and laity closer, even though they were never viewed as equals. A coalescence of events at home and abroad in the form of the sexual revolution, the rise of Communism, the reforms of Vatican II, created a Western church where personal choice took precedence over the dictates of Rome. In Ireland, certain myths such as Catholic guilt, the links between celibacy and paedophilia, the death of God, and the delusional nature of all religions, began to gain traction. The clerical abuse scandals served to reinforce hostility towards the Church and to add weight to the aforementioned myths, which has resulted in a society that is becoming increasingly impervious to the Word of God. Casey sees the need for Irish people to become educated about their faith so as to be in a position to speak to a secular audience and to find space for their Christian faith.

A group that is often considered to be marginalised and discriminated within the Church are women. Sharon Tighe-Mooney sees the divorce, contraception and abortion referendums of the 1980s and 1990s as a watershed for Irish women, as these were issues that impacted directly on their lives. Tighe-Mooney examines the events of the past four decades in Irish society in the context of the weakening hegemony of the Catholic Church juxtaposed with the growing realisation by women, especially when the child-abuse scandals broke, that their lives had been framed by a celibate male-dominated institution that displayed serious double standards in the area of human sexuality. She argues that in order to survive into the future, the Church will be increasingly dependent on women remaining active within the institution. As Irish women Catholics are demanding a central role in the running of a church that has shown itself allergic to change, especially when it comes to gender equality, Tighe-Mooney wonders what the future holds for both groups.

The collection closes with Joe Cleary's questioning of what the future of the Catholic Church is now that one of the great threats to its hegemony during the twentieth century, communism, has fallen largely into abeyance. Will the Church continue to align itself with capitalism and ignore the steady grip of the associated neo-liberal agenda that favours secular, material values over religious ones? In contemporary Ireland, it often seems as though a blind adherence to religion has been replaced by an equally blind embrace of neo-liberalism. Cleary asks what psychological price the Irish will pay for their submissive compliance with the fashionable ideas of the moment and explores how a healthy relationship with the Church might be developed in such a changed cultural environment.

From this brief discussion of the contents of the collection, we trust that the importance and relevance of its subject matter will be clear to all. The editors deliberately sought out contributors who adopt varying positions when it comes to Irish Catholicism, and we feel that what you are about to read provides an excellent exposé of the much changed face of Irish Catholicism, whose cultural legacy, regardless of where one stands on the subject, is beyond doubt.

Note

1 In 1999, Eoin O'Sullivan and Mary Raftery published a book with the very similar title, *Suffer the Little Children*, a hugely damaging exposure of the abuse that character-ised Ireland's industrial schools. The title is an ironic reference to the Bible's mention of the special place of children in God's heart: 'Suffer the little children to come unto me and forbid them not: for of such in the Kingdom of God.'

Works cited

Althusser, Louis (2001) *Lenin and Philosophy, and Other Essays*, New York: Monthly Review Press.

Barthes, Roland (1986) *Mythologies*, London: Paladin.

Eagleton, Terry (1986) *Criticism and Ideology*, London: Verso.

Enright, Anne (2008) *The Gathering*, London: Vintage.

Fay, Liam (1996) 'What's the Story?', *Hot Press*, 3 April, pp. 18–20.

Fuller, Louise (2004) *Irish Catholicism since 1950: The Undoing of a Culture*, Dublin: Gill & Macmillan.

Harding, Michael (1986) *Priest: A Fiction*, Belfast: Blackstaff.

John Paul II (2004) *The Pope in Ireland: Addresses and Homilies*, Dublin: Veritas and the Catholic Communication Office.

Kenny, Colum (2009) 'Significant Television: Journalism, Sex Abuse and the Catholic Church in Ireland', *Irish Communications Review*, 11, 63–76.

Kenny, Enda (2011) 'Speech on the Cloyne Report', Dáil Éireann, Wednesday, 20 July, available at www.rte.ie/news/2011/0720/303965-cloyne1 (accessed 28 April 2015).

Kenny, Mary (1997) *Goodbye to Catholic Ireland*, London: Sinclair-Stevenson.

Marx, Karl and Friedrich Engels (1998) *The German Ideology: Including Theses on Feuerbach and Introduction to the Critique of Political Economy*, Amherst, NY: Prometheus Books.

McGahern, John (2009) 'The Church and Its Spire', in Stanley Van Der Ziel (ed.), *Love of the World: Essays*, London: Faber and Faber, pp. 133–48.

Murphy, Francis D., Helen Buckley and Laraine Joyce (2005) *The Ferns Report Presented by the Ferns Inquiry to the Minister for Health and Children*, Dublin: Government Publications.

Murphy, Yvonne (2009) *Commission of Investigation: Report into the Catholic Archdiocese of Dublin, July 2009, Part 1*, Dublin: Government Publications.

Murphy, Yvonne, Ita Mangan and Hugh O'Neill (2011) *Commission of Investigation Report in the Diocese of Cloyne*, Dublin: House of the Oireachtas, available at http://debates.oireachtas.ie/dail/2011/07/20/00013.asp#N17 (accessed 28 April 2015).

Raftery, Mary and Eoin O'Sullivan (1999) *Suffer the Little Children*, Dublin: New Island Books.

Ryan, Seán (2009) *Commission to Inquire into Child Abuse Report*, 5 vols., Dublin Government Publications.

Thompson, John B. (1990) *Ideology and Modern Culture: Critical Social Theory in the Era of Mass Communication*, Cambridge: Polity Press.

Twomey, D. Vincent (2003) *The End of Irish Catholicism?* Dublin: Veritas.

White, Caramine (2001) *Reading Roddy Doyle*, New York: Syracuse University Press.

PART I

Tracing change and setting the context

1

'The times they are a changin'': Tracing the transformation of Irish Catholicism through the eyes of a journalist

Patsy McGarry

It was towards the end of May 2009 that the Church of Ireland Bishop of Cork, Most Reverend Paul Colton said that Ireland was in the midst of a 'a national trauma'. That followed publication of the Commission to Inquire into Child Abuse report. Chaired by Mr Justice Seán Ryan, it followed a decade of investigations by the Commission and contained revelations of truly shocking and systemic sexual, physical and emotional abuse of tens of thousands of children in residential institutions run by eighteen Catholic religious congregations during the twentieth century. To date, over 15,500 of those children (now adults) have been compensated by the Irish State, receiving an average €63,000 each.

The Ryan Commission heard evidence covering the period from 1914, but the bulk of its work addressed the period from the early 1930s to the early 1970s. Accounts of abuse by over 1,700 witnesses, given in relation to 216 institutions, were detailed in the report, which ran to over 2,600 pages. More than 800 priests, brothers, nuns and lay people were implicated. The commission's report, popularly known as the Ryan Report, was published on 20 May 2009.

What Bishop Colton said then was true, but there was more to come. The Ryan Report was followed by two further published statutory reports into the handling of clerical child sex-abuse allegations by authorities in Dublin's Catholic archdiocese (published in November 2009) and Cloyne diocese (published in July 2011), as well as the interdepartmental inquiry into the Magdalene laundries (published in February 2013), and an ongoing statutory inquiry into mother-and-baby homes which is expected to report in 2018. What Bishop Colton described as 'trauma' in 2009 was mid-way between four such statutory reports. The first two were the Ferns Report of October 2005, which investigated the handling of clerical child sexual-abuse allegations in that diocese and the Ryan Report of May. Many of the abuse revelations, which precipitated such trauma, predated the visit of Pope John Paul II to Ireland in 1979, and by many decades. However, some were actually coincident with the papal visit and continued afterwards.

One such abuse incident during the papal visit even occurred at Dublin's Pro-Cathedral when Fr Patrick McCabe abused a boy, as emerged during the priest's trial in March 2013. Moreover, the Ryan Commission's investigation committee was told of another incident at a public hearing in September 2004, referred to in the introduction of this book, where a young boy was raped by the Brother left in charge of him. Rosminian priest Fr Patrick Pierce, manager in 1975–91 of St Joseph's Industrial School at Ferryhouse in Co Tipperary, told the committee that the boy had not been allowed accompany his colleagues to the Pope's mass as punishment for absconding. The brother who raped him had been a prefect at the school and volunteered to stay back with the boy. It was the early 1990s before the assault was reported to the Gardaí, and the abuser was convicted twenty years after the event in 1999. He was sentenced to nine years' imprisonment, three suspended (Ryan 2009: III, 2, 87).

Then, of course, Pope John Paul's warm-up act at Galway comprised the then Bishop of Galway Eamon Casey and well-known Dublin media priest Fr Michael Cleary, both of whom, as would emerge in later years, were themselves already fathers in 1979. What these matters reinforce is the view that Pope John Paul's visit to Ireland in 1979 did not, and could not, stem those forces already at play, which would undermine the influence and authority of the Catholic Church in Ireland. Such dark currents as revealed over recent decades would visit catastrophe on his beloved Church in Ireland, beginning just eight years later in 1987, when the Irish Catholic bishops' sole response to a warning from the USA that clerical child sexual-abuse allegation could be imminent was to take out insurance in their dioceses.

The Ryan Report, the Ferns Report and subsequent reports would, collectively, be a source of great national shame at Ireland's treatment of its children and vulnerable adults throughout most of the twentieth century. A consequence of such reports has been a fundamental shift in Irish attitudes to the Catholic Church, an institution that was at the centre of them all. It was also an institution which had been central to the identity of millions of Irish people who for generations had unquestioningly revered it and its personnel. Suddenly and shockingly it had become a suspect outsider, so much so that even Rome itself would get in on the act. In his March 2010 pastoral letter to Irish Catholics, following publication of the Ryan and Murphy reports the previous year, Pope Benedict XVI told the Irish bishops that 'some of you and your predecessors failed, at times grievously' when it came to child protection. What the Irish Church allowed 'obscured the Gospel to a degree that not even centuries of persecution (in the penal laws era) had succeeded in doing' (Benedict XVI 2010). Pope Benedict sent seven high-powered teams of cardinals, archbishops and bishops to conduct apostolic visitations on the Irish Church and see how things could be put right. However, there was not a word about Rome's role in any of this. Not a word about prefect of the Congregation for the Clergy Cardinal Castrillón Hoyos who was responsible for the 1997 letter to the Irish bishops dismissing their 1996 framework document on child protection as 'merely a study document' because it recommended that all abuse allegations against priests should be reported to the civil authorities. That letter, the Cloyne Report said, 'gave comfort and support' to those who 'dissented from the stated official Irish church policy' on child protection (Commission of Investigation into Catholic Diocese of Cloyne 2011: 6). This was the same cardinal who infamously, in the letter dated 8 September 2001, congratulated French bishop Pierre Pican who received a three-month suspended sentence for not cooperating with French authorities in their investigations into a priest who was later sentenced to eighteen years in jail for repeated rape of a boy and sexual assaults on ten others. 'I congratulate you for not denouncing a priest to the civil administration', Cardinal Castrillón Hoyos wrote in his letter to Bishop Pican, a letter which he insisted had been approved by Pope John Paul II (Castrillón Hoyos 2001).

In 1999, when the Irish bishops were visiting Rome, they were reminded by a Vatican official that they were 'bishops first, not policemen' when it came to reporting clerical child sex abuse. But there was worse to come. In May 2001, when he was prefect of the Congregation for the Doctrine of the Faith, Cardinal Joseph Ratzinger (later Pope Benedict XVI) sent two letters to every Catholic bishop in the world, in Latin (Ratzinger 2001). One insisted that the contents of both letters be kept secret, while the other directed that all clerical child sex abuse allegations 'with a semblance of truth' be sent to the Congregation for the Doctrine of the Faith, and it would decide whether they be dealt with at diocesan or Vatican level. Such letters were sent to the Irish Catholic bishops too, of course, and were therefore of keen interest to the Murphy Commissions in Ireland that investigated the handling of clerical child sexual-abuse allegations in the Dublin archdiocese and Cloyne diocese.

Rome did not even acknowledge correspondence from the commission in September 2006 when it was investigating the handling of clerical child sex abuse allegations in the Dublin archdiocese. Instead, Rome complained that the commission did not use proper channels. So, in February 2007, the Murphy Commission wrote to then Papal Nuncio to Ireland, Archbishop Giuseppe Lazzarotto, requesting he forward 'all documents in his possession relevant to the Commission' (Murphy 2009: I, 37). He did not reply. In early 2009, it wrote to then nuncio, Archbishop Giuseppe Leanza, (in office since April 2008), enclosing a draft of its report for comment. He did not reply either. The nunciature in Dublin was the conduit for clerical child abuse reports to Rome, while Archbishop Leanza was personally involved in talks that led to Bishop Magee standing aside as bishop of Cloyne in February 2009. When it was investigating that diocese, the Murphy Commission asked Archbishop Leanza: asked Archbishop Leanza to 'submit to it any information which you have about the matters under investigation'. He felt 'unable to assist' it 'in this matter'.[1]

Such lack of cooperation was a source of profound annoyance where the Irish authorities were concerned. This was most acutely illustrated in 2011. On 20 July, days after publication of the Cloyne Report, Taoiseach Enda Kenny (a practising Catholic), addressing the Dáil, said of the Church that 'The rape and torture of children were downplayed or "managed" to uphold instead, the primacy of the institution, its power, standing and "reputation"' (Kenny 2011). The Vatican's reaction to such abuse 'was to parse and analyse it with the gimlet eye of a canon lawyer … This calculated, withering position being the polar opposite of the radicalism, humility and compassion upon which the Roman Church was founded.' Kenny continued, saying that the Cloyne Report 'excavates the dysfunction, disconnection, elitism … the narcissism … that dominate the culture of the Vatican to this day'. It told 'a tale of a frankly brazen disregard for protecting children'. Revelations in Cloyne 'have brought the Government, Irish Catholics and the Vatican to an unprecedented juncture', he said, concluding that 'This is not Rome. This is the Republic of Ireland 2011, a republic of laws' (Kenny 2011).

By any reckoning, this speech was a watershed in Catholic Ireland's relationship with Rome, and it was enunciated by an Irish Catholic prime minister. It was very far removed from a statement to the same chamber sixty years previously by Mr Kenny's predecessor, John A Costello, then also Taoiseach and leader of the same political party, Fine Gael. In April 1951, during debate on the ill-fated Mother and Child Scheme, opposed by the Catholic bishops led by Archbishop of Dublin John Charles McQuaid, Costello felt impelled to announce, 'I am an Irishman second: I am a Catholic first and I accept without qualification in all respects the teaching of the hierarchy and the church to which I belong.' He told the Dáil, 'I, as a Catholic, obey my church authorities and will continue to do so' (Keogh 1994: 208).

Following that July 2011 address by Enda Kenny, things were to get even worse in Ireland's relationship with Rome. In November 2011 then Tánaiste and minister for foreign affairs, Eamon Gilmore, announced that Ireland's embassy to the Holy See was to close for financial reasons. Few believed, even in the midst of the worst recession of modern times, that financial reasons were the only ones leading to closure of that embassy in that year.

What all of these events mean today is that Irish people are beyond shock when it comes to scandalous behaviour by Catholic Church authorities in denying and attempting to conceal the truth. It is also a matter of national shame that the Irish State, through its 'deferential and submissive attitude' (to use Justice Ryan's words) to religious congregations and the Church generally, failed in its primary duty to children (Ryan 2009: IV, 451). Further, the sense of betrayal of an innocent people's trust by the Church goes deep. Yet it was statutory agencies of the Irish State that exposed that shame, despite the Church. Indeed, as we now know, those same religious congregations – with one exception – were drawn into deeply reluctant cooperation with the Ryan Commission and proved recalcitrant to the end, as those of us who reported on public hearings of the commission's investigation committee can testify. In fact, one congregation persisted in its denial of all abuse in its institutions up to 15 May 2009, just five days prior to publication of the Ryan Report. On that date, Br Kevin Mullan, provincial of the Christian Brothers in Ireland, sent a letter to the Residential Institutions' Redress Board denying all such abuse following contact by the board after it had received an application from a former resident at the O'Brien Institute in Dublin's Marino. The former resident had alleged abuse there. The institute had been run by the Christian Brothers. Not alone did Br Mullan deny any abuse had happened there, he asserted he had not been aware of any complaint of abuse from the applicant prior to receipt by the Christian Brothers of the letter from the Redress Board. The insinuation was clear: that the applicant had been tempted to make the complaint by the existence of the board (McGarry 2009).

It transpired that the letter sent by Br Mullan to the Redress Board on 15 May was one of a type which he always sent to that board on receipt of similar letters from it following applications for redress received from the very many others who had been residents as children at institutions run by the Christian Brothers in Ireland. The same formula was followed by Br Mullan in all his replies to the board, with some adjustments to account for details specific to each applicant. The template for his letter, it is believed, was drawn up by lawyers. Even in his initial reaction on the publication of the Ryan Report, Br Mullan did not acknowledge that abuse existed in institutions run by his congregation, as seen in TV interviews that night. That position was softened in media appearances by his colleague Br Edmund Garvey over subsequent days, but it was not until 26 May 2009, six days after the publication of the report, that the Christian Brothers issued a statement through the Murray Consultants public-relations firm in which they said they accepted 'with shame the findings of the Commission to Inquire into Child Abuse' (Christian Brothers' European Province 2009).

Where the 15 May letter of that year was concerned, a statement by the brothers was issued on 3 June 2009, following a report of the letter in the *Irish Times* that day. The statement said that such letters to the Redress Board predated publication of the Ryan Report (on 20 May 2009) 'which highlighted the shocking nature and extent of abuse that occurred'. It added:

> The Brothers' subsequent apologies reflected their shame that as recently as five days prior to publication of the report their responses were still shamefully inadequate and hurtful. Since publication of the Report of the Commission of Inquiry into Child Abuse, the congregation has accepted its culpability as well as recognising its moral obligation to former residents and to present and future generations of children. (Healy 2009)

To that point, it can be said, the Christian Brothers had been relying on the moral authority of the Catholic Church in Ireland, and of their own position as a congregation in that church, to carry through their assertions that no abuse existed in their institutions. Despite the weight of evidence to the contrary, they continued to deny it had happened, expecting to be believed, simply because they said so. That type of deference was no longer in existence in the Ireland of the third millennium.

Their stance to May 2009 was characterised by no less a figure than the current Catholic archbishop of Dublin, Most Revd Diarmuid Martin, as one of unbelievable denial. There are those of us familiar with the details who would not be as charitable. 'Denial' suggests limited culpability, a psychological inability to accept the truth. The facts of the case, where the Christian Brothers and others were concerned, would indicate something much more deliberate. That would also appear to be the mind of Justice Seán Ryan. At the press conference to launch his report the judge singled out for praise just one congregation of the eighteen he investigated. They were the Rosminians (Institute of Charity). He did so, he said, because they had sought to understand and deal with the abuse that took place in the two institutions they had run, at Upton in Cork and Ferryhouse near Clonmel in Tipperary. The other congregations merely sought to explain it away, in his opinion.

The Ryan Report exposed many of the eighteen religious congregations it investigated as being morally bankrupt, some even brazenly so in a seeming cynical exploitation of what remaining moral authority the Catholic Church and its institutions retained in Ireland, as they tried to persuade people that truth was fiction and that those telling the truth were liars motivated by money or a desire to damage the Church, or both. This was so because they said so, whatever the volume of evidence suggesting otherwise, much of it coming from their own documents.

The existence of the Ryan Commission, the Ferns Commission, the Murphy Commission (whose remit was extended to include Cloyne diocese), the committee that reported on the Magdalene laundries and, now, the Commission of Investigation into Mother and Baby Homes, all investigating institutions of the Catholic Church, are the most profound illustration of the revolution in moral authority that has taken place in the Irish State over recent decades. Not so very long ago, the very idea of any Irish State agency investigating the Catholic Church or any of its institutions in Ireland was beyond the strangest imagination of any among the great majority or many minorities of people in Ireland. That there should have been so many, and almost all within a decade, suggests something seismic.

This current phase of intense, traumatic fallout could be said to have begun in 1999, almost two decades after John Paul II visited Ireland. It was in May 1999 that former Taoiseach Bertie Ahern apologised on behalf of the State to former residents of institutions run by the eighteen congregations. On 11 May 1999, he said in Dáil Éireann, 'On behalf of the State and of all the citizens of the State, the Government wishes to make a sincere and long overdue apology to the victims of child hood abuse for our collective failure to intervene, to detect their pain, to come to their rescue.' It was an extraordinary moment in Irish Church–State relations. Implicit in it was an acknowledgement that children had been abandoned to 'their pain' in Catholic Church-run institutions by a state that did not 'come to their rescue'. Extraordinary language too and from another Taoiseach who was a practising Catholic (Ahern 1999).

Following on from that apology, the Commission to Inquire into Child Abuse was set up, as was the Residential Institutions Redress Board. The commission was the first such body in the history of the State: a statutory body headed by a judge of the High Court charged with investigating how Catholic Church agencies had dealt with citizens, in this case children, placed in their care. It would be three years later, in April 2002, before moves to set up the Ferns Inquiry were initiated. The Dublin investigation was set up in March 2006 and the Cloyne inquiry in 2009.

So what prompted Bertie Ahern to apologise to former residents of institutions run by religious congregations? He himself gave an explanation on 25 March 2009 at an event to mark the tenth anniversary of the Aislinn Centre in Dublin. This centre helps people who have been in the institutions. One of its founders was Christine Buckley, who was herself in Dublin's Goldenbridge orphanage as a child, which was run by the Sisters of Mercy. She was featured in *Dear Daughter*, a television documentary broadcast in 1996, in which she gave a graphic account of the abuse she and other children suffered at Goldenbridge. It was the first such TV programme about abuse in residential institutions for children in Ireland.

Bertie Ahern recalled at the Aislinn event:

I suppose Christine first entered my consciousness, in February 1996, the year before I became Taoiseach, when RTÉ broadcast the *Dear Daughter* programme on abuse in Goldenbridge. When we met, Christine made a big impression on me and as I got to know her over the years we worked closely together. She was a great source of knowledge and counsel to me as my Governments sought to do the right thing by those who had the terrible misfortune to suffer child abuse. (Ahern 2009)

He went on then to make some interesting observations:

The issue of child abuse in institutions in our society is a scandal of appalling proportions. The more we have learnt about these sickening activities in certain places, the greater our anger at those who perpetrated abuse and the greater our disappointment at those who allowed it to happen. The existence of this abuse is not a recent development. The greatest proportion of abuse occurred many decades ago, prior to the reforms of the 1970s. However, for a number of reasons, the full extent of abuse in institutions has only in more recent years become apparent. (McGreevy 2009)

He speculated as to why this was the case:

> One of the reasons for the cloak of secrecy that surrounded this abuse was the failure of successive Governments to face up to the extent to which organs of the State have responsibility for abuse. There was a reluctance to admit that as a State and as a society we failed many of the children of the nation by allowing them to be incarcerated in places where they were not cherished, but poorly treated. (McGreevy 2009)

Then he became even more interesting:

> I know that we are fast approaching the 10th anniversary of Government's apology to victims of child abuse. I can assure people here that there were plenty of people telling me not to do it, that there was compelling reasons – financial and legal – why we should say nothing but that did not hold water for me. I had heard the victims' distress, I had listened to the sincerity and logic of people like Christine and I knew it was the right thing to do. (McGreevy 2009)

He continued:

> It was one of the best decisions I made as Taoiseach. It was something I felt deeply about and I thank God I did it. There are many brave but vulnerable survivors of childhood abuse, whose young lives were shattered by terrible wrongs that were perpetrated upon them. The reality is that much of the abuse that occurred in the past was directed towards children who were pupils in residential institutions that were regulated and supervised by the State. An apology and a recognition of the wrong that was done to them in the State's care was the very least they deserved. (McGreevy 2009)

He went on to quote from that apology he delivered in the Dáil, on 11 May 1999. But what he failed to say in his comments at Aislinn in March 2009 was that the immediate reason for his apology on behalf of the State was a three-part series broadcast on RTÉ television about what went on in residential institutions for children, the last edition of which was broadcast just hours after Mr Ahern made his apology in the Dáil, on 11 May 1999.

The first programme in that series, titled *States of Fear* and produced by Mary Raftery, was broadcast on 27 April 1999. On 28 April, in the Dáil, then Labour party leader Ruairi Quinn suggested that the party whips meet to agree that time be taken in the house to allow members, on behalf of successive and previous governments, to offer the minimum of a word of apology and give an undertaking that such abuse would not happen again. Taoiseach Bertie Ahern said the matter could be discussed by the party whips: 'What went on in these institutions over the years was inhuman and degrading. All of these children were isolated and without help.' He said he hoped such abuse was not happening today: 'We have never, as a society, dealt with these things' ('State Apology' 1999). This was a pivotal moment, but, you will note, there was no talk of an investigation into what went on in those institutions as of then. That came later. Such was the cumulative effect of the series, broadcast on 27 April, 4 May and 11 May 1999, that, before its final broadcast, the Taoiseach had announced the intention to set up the Commission to Inquire into Child Abuse, as well as plans for a redress board to compensate survivors of the institutions. However, if Mary Raftery's journalism was key in all of this, it begged a question: what of journalism in Ireland before then where this awful scandal was concerned?

The answer to that was probably best explained by Brian Quinn, editor of the *Evening Herald* from 1969 to 1976, in a letter to the *Irish Times*, which was published on 11 May 1999, the morning prior to the last part of *States of Fear* being broadcast. He wrote:

> It was with mounting shame that I viewed Mary Raftery's TV documentary *States of Fear*. Journalists of the 1940s and 1950s had their suspicions about the industrial schools. We knew, in particular, that a stay with the Christian Brothers was to be avoided, the main reason being the brothers' reputation for excessive corporal punishment.
>
> Even in a climate of acceptance that brothers and nuns were beyond repute, we should have tried harder to find out the real truth. In the defence of journalists of that time, we would not have been believed and managements and editors would never have held out against a massed attack by the all-powerful Irish Catholic Church.
>
> From first-hand experience I witnessed one of the worst of the Christian Brothers break into the office of the manager and demand that a court case that mentioned Artane (the largest industrial school in Dublin) should not be used. Before the manager could lift a phone he would push open the editorial door to tell us the manager had instructed that the case be dumped. He got away with this just one more time.
>
> On the third time of demanding, the manager, who was most honourable and dedicated to ethics, said 'no', as he was not going to interfere with the editors any more on behalf of Artane. Those requests should have alerted journalists to start inquiries into what was happening in Artane. That we did not is a heavy burden.
>
> There was also the matter of ignorance. That the Christian Brothers were indulging their passion for sexual abuse on their captive boys was something that I admit would not have occurred to me. In addition, the Irish Catholic Church was held in awe, particularly after the triumphalist Eucharistic Congress of 1932.
>
> Mary Raftery is to be congratulated on, at last, pulling down the edifice of lies and evasion that flourished for so long. Journalists of that time were trapped in a carefully designed plot that mixed lies with official evasion and ecclesiastical terror. Nevertheless, I for one, believe that we allowed cowardice to rule. – Yours, etc., Brian Quinn. (Quinn 1999)

To be fair to the paper where I work, in 1966 journalist Michael Viney wrote a series titled 'The Young Offenders' about children detained in such institutions that appeared in the *Irish Times*. The series was referred to in the Ryan Report. However, as my late colleague Dick Walsh wrote in the *Irish Times* on 1 May 1999,

as *States of Fear* was being broadcast, the press in Ireland at the time when Michael
Viney's series appeared in 1966 'wouldn't say boo to a goose'. He continued:

> *The Irish Independent*, a respected and authoritative newspaper, was too busy with
> Lenten pastorals. The *Irish Press* sheltered a fine collection of sacked schoolteachers,
> spoiled priests and lapsed republicans but, with Fianna Fáil in power, steered clear
> of controversy. So did Radio Éireann and the *Cork Examiner*, as they then were; and
> *The Irish Times*, selling fewer than 30,000 copies a day, hardly mattered. (Walsh 1999)

That was Ireland in the 1960s. So what happened in the intervening thirty years
plus? A minor indication comes from Mary Raftery herself. She has said that one
of the things that inspired her to do *States of Fear* was a certain humiliation in
RTÉ, where she was then a producer, at the embarrassing fact that TV documentaries outside the Republic were responsible for two of the more important events
in the early 1990s.

In May 1991, ITV broadcast a *World in Action* programme by Irish journalist Susan O'Keeffe on the Irish beef industry, which led to the establishment of
the Beef Tribunal in Ireland. It investigated questionable practices therein before
producing its report in 1994. Susan O'Keeffe had tried unsuccessfully to interest various Irish media in the story before she went to the UK. More significantly in this context, however, was the Belfast UTV *Counterpoint* programme
Suffer Little Children by Chris Moore broadcast in October 1994. It dealt with the
forty-year-long career – in Dublin, Belfast and the USA – of serial child abuser
and Norbertine priest, Fr Brendan Smyth. Smyth was jailed in Dublin in 1997 and
died in prison one month after his sentence began. The Norbertine order which
Fr Smyth had joined in 1945 was aware of his crimes as early as the late 1940s
but failed to report him to either the Gardaí in the Republic or the Royal Ulster
Constabulary in Northern Ireland. Instead, he was moved from parish to parish
and between dioceses whenever allegations were made against him. In some cases,
his congregation did not inform relevant diocesan bishops that Smyth had a history
of child sex abuse and should be kept away from children. The UTV documentary
had a profound effect in the Republic. The arrest of Fr Smyth in 1994 led indirectly to the collapse of the then Fianna Fáil/Labour government in Dublin when
it emerged that an application for the priest's extradition to Northern Ireland had
been delayed for eight months at the attorney general's office in Dublin.

Rumours of Church–State collusion spread like wildfire. Then Labour party
TD Pat Rabbitte spoke in the Dáil of the State being rocked to its foundations
by what would emerge. An unstable government fell, and an investigation found
no grounds for conspiracy theories, just incompetence – that profligate father of
rumour and conspiracy. A senior official at the attorney general's office was retired.

The story of Fr Brendan Smyth and the cover-up by Church authorities of
his crimes dented still further a wider Church leadership barely in recovery from
the May 1992 revelations in the *Irish Times* that one of their number, Bishop of

Galway Eamonn Casey, had a seventeen-year-old son. He was by then working out his penance in the humid jungles of South America. It was in this climate that Mary Raftery decided to produce a programme on residential industrial schools in Ireland. Her immediate inspiration was some print journalism she had done on the first Dublin criminal gang to deal in drugs. She established that at its core was a family of brothers, all of whom had been in the Artane industrial school as children. She was also sick of outside television companies doing what Irish journalists should be doing. So she set about working on *States of Fear*. She followed that up with *Cardinal Secrets* which looked at how allegations of clerical child sex abuse had been handled in Dublin's Catholic archdiocese. It was broadcast in October 2002 and led to the setting up of the Dublin Archdiocese Commission of Investigation, better known as the Murphy Commission, as its chair was Ms Justice Yvonne Murphy. It reported in November 2009 (Murphy 2009).

However, it was another TV programme from abroad that led to the first investigation by the Irish State into how a Catholic diocese handled allegations of clerical child sexual abuse. The BBC's *Suing the Pope*, broadcast in March 2002, led to the resignation of then bishop of Ferns, Most Revd Brendan Comiskey, and prompted the setting up of the Ferns Inquiry. It reported in October 2005. There can be no doubt that the media has played a role in the shift of moral authority in Ireland from Church to State agencies. But it is by no means the whole story. And it was the media, this time the *Irish Times*, which, again in 2002, exposed the damning fact that the first and only reaction of Irish bishops on being warned in the late 1980s about the possibility of clerical child abuse emerging as an issue in Ireland was, as previously mentioned, to take out insurance in each diocese.

Yes, it was the media, again the *Irish Times* and also in 2002, that exposed how the former president of the Catholic Church's main seminary in Ireland, St Patrick's College, Maynooth, Monsignor Micheál Ledwith, had been discreetly removed by the bishops in 1994 from that post following allegations of child sexual abuse made against him. It emerged then too that a former senior dean at Maynooth, Fr Gerard McGinnity, had been removed – eventually to a remote rural Armagh parish – when he conveyed the concerns of senior seminarians about Monsignor Ledwith to the bishops. Monsignor Ledwith has since been laicised.

But if such exposure was hugely significant to the shift in moral authority from the Church in Ireland, this was not solely down to the media, however tempting it might be for a journalist to conclude otherwise. Irish Catholicism had been undergoing profound change since the 1960s. That decade represented the twilight of old certainties where Catholicism in Ireland was concerned. Changes, prompted by Vatican II, had an unnerving effect on a people who had rested for generations on the seemingly solid rock of unchangeable Catholic teaching in a world seemingly at sea. Younger people then, like my own father, were thrown by what began to emerge. He was a traditional Catholic, not given to great piety, but he attended mass every Sunday and clearly respected the clergy.

In 1961, the Vatican announced that St Philomena was being removed from the Calendar of Saints. He was traumatised. His mother, who died when he was in his teens, had been devoted to St Philomena. Through a slow lingering death, and in great pain with stomach cancer, her only consolation was St Philomena. She had St Philomena scapulars, which she had left my father, her youngest son, when she died. And now he was being told, as he saw it, that St Philomena never existed. He stopped going to mass, a shocking thing to do in a rural West of Ireland parish in the 1960s and in an Ireland where, ten years later, in the early 1970s, 91 per cent of Catholics attended weekly mass. He never resumed the practice on a regular basis before his death in 1999.

Meanwhile, the mass was no longer in Latin, and the priest now faced the people. The comfortable gloom of old in churches was replaced with brash, bright colours. All was soon changed, changed utterly. Then in 1967 free education was introduced in Ireland, up to and including third-level. It produced a questioning generation which was dissatisfied with old answers. This generation of young Catholics had been fed on the debates of Vatican II and what followed. They were awestruck by the revolt against Pope Paul VI's *Humanae vitae* encyclical of 1968, not that they disagreed with those who opposed the Pope's reiteration of the Church's traditional teaching banning artificial means of contraception so much as that Irish Catholics would publicly oppose the Pope at all. The sky didn't fall after this revolt, and reason seemed to be on the side of those who disagreed with the Pope.

This was the generation that would soon lead the so-called moral civil wars of the 1980s, 1990s and beyond in Ireland, favouring freely available contraception, decriminalisation of homosexuality, availability of divorce, same-sex marriage and availability of abortion services. Where contraception was concerned, the first significant breakthrough, despite Catholic Church resistance, was the 'Irish solution to an Irish problem' legislation introduced by then Minister for Health Charles Haughey in 1979, when he had a Bill passed that allowed for artificial means of contraception to be available on prescription to married couples. The relevant Act was passed in July 1979, two months before Pope John Paul II visited Ireland. That this Catholic Church hegemony was shown to be broken such a short time before the papal visit is hugely significant in that it illustrates a beginning to a rising tide of irrevocable change in relations between Church and society in Ireland which would not be slowed by those charming three days in September 1979 when Pope St John Paul graced the country's shores. In reality, that visit was but an interlude.

This Haughey measure, however, was frustrated for a time because some Catholic pharmacists had a crisis of conscience and refused to stock the contraceptives, establishing a pattern of conscientious objection that would follow every liberalising measure in Ireland as elsewhere. It was 1985 before contraceptives were made freely available by law in the Republic. In 1993, homosexuality was decriminalised. Through the 1980s and 1990s, there were three abortion referendums and two divorce referendums, each very bitterly opposed by the Catholic Church. In a 1995 referendum, it was agreed by a slim majority that divorce should be available in the Republic. In 2013, the Protection of Life during Pregnancy Act allowed for abortion in strictly controlled circumstances where the mother's life was at risk, including through suicide. Again this was vigorously opposed by the Catholic Church, with some bishops taking to the streets in protest, a first in Ireland.

The Church also strongly opposed the referendum of May 2015 that extended the right to marry to gay people. The vote of over 62 per cent in favour of same-sex marriage despite such opposition was another illustration of the waning influence of the Catholic Church in Ireland.

In all of this process of change, a powerful, articulate element among that generation pushing the liberal agenda have been outspoken determined women who became the driving force for much change that took place as a result of those moral civil wars in the 1970s, 1980s, 1990s and since. There can be little doubt that this has been influenced by the diminished roles allowed women in the Catholic Church, at all levels.

Among the ranks of such women have been former presidents of Ireland, Mary Robinson and Mary McAleese. In the 1970s, both had been involved with the Campaign for Homosexual Law Reform at Trinity College where they had been, successively, Reid Professor of Law. As a senator in the 1970s and 1980s, Mary Robinson campaigned on a wide range of women's issues, including the right of women to sit on juries. She opposed the then requirement that all women, upon marriage, resign from the civil service, and campaigned for the right to the legal availability of contraception.

One of the most forceful and commanding campaigners for same-sex marriage in Ireland during the lead-up to the May 2015 referendum was Mary McAleese. Since her term as president of Ireland ended in November 2011, she has been publicly and fiercely critical of the Catholic Church's attitude to gay people, and to women.

It is also significant that among those journalists in Ireland who did most work in exposing clerical child sex abuse, women have been very prominent. We have already spoken of Mary Raftery. *Suing the Pope* in 2002 was the work of BBC journalist Sarah Macdonald, and it was based on the book *A Message from Heaven* by Alison O'Connor, which was published in 2000 (O'Connor, 2000). It was among the first to detail clerical child sexual abuse in an Irish Catholic diocese.

Ireland's moral civil wars of recent decades have been bitter and full of attrition, as is the character of civil war. They still go on, if with less intensity. Another abortion referendum looms which may resurrect those old intensities. The Labour party made it part of its manifesto for the 2016 election in Ireland that, if re-elected to government, it will hold a referendum to remove the 8th Amendment to the Constitution that respects the equal right to life of pregnant mother and child. This was inserted into the Constitution following the first abortion referendum in 1983. Then there is education, where, at primary level, the Catholic Church controls 93 per cent of schools. It was expected that education could be the bloodiest battlefield of all between the Church and liberalising forces, but that now seems less likely. Despite the emergence of a new Ireland where the Catholic Church seems to many to be on the margins, there is little real demand for change in the management of schools. Where most parents are concerned, whether Catholic or not, the apparent view is 'the system ain't broke, why fix it?' In addition, the Catholic Church has shown that it is willing to divest itself of schools to accommodate a more diverse mix.

But one outcome of these moral civil wars is no longer in question, and that is the revolution that has taken place in moral authority in Ireland. It no longer rests with the bishops nor is it likely to again following on what we now know of their past exercise of that authority when they blatantly placed their reputation, and that of the Church, before the welfare of children. We can only hope those agencies of state with which that authority now rests will use it more responsibly, and with a greater compassion and wisdom than was so in the past. At least in this changed circumstance the people of Ireland now have the power to hold the holders of that authority to account.

In the long journey to this point, 1979 and the visit of Pope John Paul II was of little significance. Indeed, the most significant year in the journey to today was twenty-one years earlier. In 1958, the First Programme for Economic Expansion was published by the Irish government, leading to the State's first real period of prosperity in the 1960s which allowed it to introduce free education at second and third levels later in that decade. And 1958 was the year Pope John XXIII was elected pope, he who established the Second Vatican Council that set the Catholic Church in Ireland, as elsewhere, on a new path. The times, they have certainly changed, and they will, in all likelihood, continue to do so as far as the Catholic Church in Ireland is concerned.

Note

1   *Irish Times*, 28 July 2011, p. 7.

Works cited

Ahern, Bertie (1999) 'Official Government Apology to the Victims of Child Abuse', 11 May, available at www.caranua.ie/useful_resources/government_responses (accessed 15 April 2015).

Benedict XVI (2010) 'Pastoral Letter of the Holy Father Pope Benedict XVI to the Catholics of Ireland', *Libreria Editrice Vaticana*, available at http://w2.vatican.va/content/benedict-xvi/en/letters/2010/documents/hf_ben-xvi_let_20100319_church-ireland.html (accessed 19 January 2016).

Castrillón Hoyos, Darío (2001) 'Letter to Bishop Pican', 8 September, available at www.documentcloud.org/documents/243768–5a-pican-letter-english-translation.html (accessed 21 January 2016).

Christian Brothers' European Province (2009) 'Media Statement in Response to the Findings of the Ryan Commission', 26 May, available at http://edmundrice.net/images/stories/pdf/Mrdia_report_ryan.pdf (accessed 19 January 2016).

Commission of Investigation into Catholic Diocese of Cloyne (2011) *Report by Commission of Investigation into the Handling by Church and State Authorities of Allegations and Suspicions of Child Sexual Abuse Against Clerics of the Catholic Diocese of Cloyne*, Dublin: Government Publications.

Healy, Alison (2009) 'Brothers Sorry for "Shameful" Abuse Denials', *Irish Times*, 4 June, available at www.irishtimes.com/news/brothers-sorry-for-shameful-abuse-denials-1.776366# (accessed 15 January 2016).

Holy See Press Office (2011) 'Response to Mr Eamon Gilmore, Tánaiste and Minister for Foreign Affairs and Trade of Ireland, Concerning the Cloyne Report', *News VA Official Vatican Network*, September, available at www.news.va/it/news/43267 (accessed 15 April 2015).

Kenny, Enda (2011) 'Speech on the *Cloyne Report*', Dáil Éireann, 20 July, available at www.rte.ie/news/2011/0720/303965-cloyne1 (accessed 15 April 2015).

Keogh, Dermot (1994) *Twentieth Century Ireland: Nation and State*, Dublin: Gill & Macmillan.

McAleese, Martin (2013) *Report of the Inter-departmental Committee to Establish the Facts of State Involvement with the Magdalen Laundries*, Dublin: Government Publications.

McGarry, Patsy (2009) 'Order Denied Abuse Five Days before Report', *Irish Times*, 3 June, available at www.irishtimes.com/news/order-denied-abuse-five-days-before-report-1.775558 (accessed 28 April 2015).

McGreevy, Ronan (2009) 'Apology to Victims of Child Abuse Was Right', *Irish Times*, 26 March, available at www.irishtimes.com/news/apology-to-victims-of-abuse-in-institutions-was-right-says-ahern-1.730434# (accessed 15 April 2015).

Murphy, Francis D., Helen Buckley and Laraine Joyce (2005) *The Ferns Report Presented by the Ferns Inquiry to the Minister for Health and Children*, Dublin: Government Publications.

Murphy, Yvonne (2009) *Commission of Investigation: Report into the Catholic Archdiocese of Dublin, July 2009 – Part 1*, Dublin: Government Publications.

O'Connor, Alison (2000) *A Message from Heaven: The Life and Crimes of Father Sean Fortune*, Dingle: Brandon.

Quinn, Brian (1999) 'Journalism and Child Abuse', *Irish Times*, 11 May, available at www.irishtimes.com/opinion/letters/journalism-and-child-abuse-1.18 3378 (accessed 28 April 2015).

Ratzinger, Joseph (2001) 'Letter to Catholic Bishops', available at www.bishop-accountability.org/resources/resource-files/churchdocs/EpistulaEnglish.htm (accessed 15 April 2015).

Ryan, Seán (2009) *Commission to Inquire into Child Abuse Report*, 5 vols., Dublin Government Publications.

'State Apology for Victims of Abuse Discussed', *Irish Times*, 21 April 1999, available at www.irishtimes.com/news/politics/oireachtas/state-apology-for-victims-of-abuse-discussed-1.178991 (accessed 30 April 2015).

Walsh, Dick (1999) 'A Shameful Silence as the Children Suffered', *Irish Times*, 1 May, available at www.irishtimes.com/opinion/a-shameful-silence-as-the-children-suffered-1.179940 (accessed 28 April 2016).

2

Revisiting the faith of our fathers … and reimagining its relevance in the context of twenty-first-century Ireland

Louise Fuller

Much has been written in recent years about the declining influence of the Catholic Church in Ireland. Clearly this is a fact not in question. There is no shortage of data in relation to religious practice and the decline in vocations; political decisions are no longer influenced by Catholic Church teaching as is evidenced in legislation and constitutional change since the 1970s. The evidence speaks for itself; there is no need to rehearse it in detail. While the most recent census recorded 84 per cent of the population as Catholic (Census of Population of Ireland, 2011), surveys have shown that this does not mean that Catholics adhere to Church teaching in relation to how they live their private lives, in particular with regard to principles of sexual morality, which are central to Church teaching. What is remarkable is that all of these fundamental changes happened in such a short period of time in a country that was as traditionally Catholic as Ireland. This has resulted in endless speculation as to how, and why, this has happened so dramatically, whether it could have been avoided and the consequences it has had for Irish society as a whole. These are the areas which this chapter seeks to address.

The timespan covered by this book has obvious resonance for Irish people. Pope John Paul II visited Ireland in September 1979, and Galway was the venue for the youth mass. The Masters of Ceremony for the event were the Bishop of Galway Eamon Casey and Fr Michael Cleary – two of the most high-profile clerics in Ireland at that time. Revelations in the early 1990s that they both led secret private lives not in keeping with their clerical callings caused convulsions in Irish society. This was followed seemingly relentlessly with revelations in relation to clergy and religious and the sexual abuse of children in parishes and in religious-run institutions over the years. This led to several State-commissioned investigations and reports, one of which was the report on the diocese of Cloyne, published in 2011. Its findings were damning, and the Bishop of Cloyne, John

Magee, who had been secretary to Pope Paul VI, Pope John Paul I and John Paul II, resigned as a result. In 1979, all had seemed well in Irish Catholicism, and the enthusiasm surrounding the Pope's visit would have conveyed that to any outside observer. A comprehensive survey of values and attitudes in the mid-1970s recorded that 91 per cent of Irish Catholics attended mass weekly (Catholic Communications Institute of Ireland 1975: 71). But cracks were beginning to appear as early as the 1950s and certainly in the 1960s. However, the period addressed here, 1979 to 2011, a matter of thirty-odd years and one generation later, saw radical change in every way: in values, attitudes and, not least, in Sunday mass attendance, which now stands at about 35 to 37 per cent of Irish Catholics, depending on what survey material one consults. In addition, this is an overall percentage. In some parishes in Dublin, the attendance is at 5 per cent and lower (Martin 2014). The title of this book and the timespan covered might suggest that the answers to the tectonic changes lie in the scandals that have been uncovered, and, while undoubtedly they have profoundly undermined the authority and credibility of the Church, this is by no means the whole story. The full answers to questions about the collapse of Irish Catholicism are far more complex, lie further back in time and sometimes go beyond the Irish context.

Philosophical, scientific, technological and economic changes brewing over the past few centuries and coming to fruition in the twentieth century ultimately played the most significant role leading to the secularisation we have seen in recent decades in Ireland. The change simply came later to Ireland. The question that confounds both clerical and lay Church members is, given that Irish Catholics' strong allegiance to the faith over the centuries, the copper-fastening of this allegiance by social legislation in the post-Independence era and the loyalty of Irish Catholics to religious practice and Catholic moral teaching, not so much why it happened, but rather, why it came about so rapidly. Were there indications of change to come, or were Irish Catholics, bishops, priests and lay people taken by surprise? What was the response of the Church to secularising trends? What preparations were put in place to preserve what was of value in Catholic Christianity? Given the profound changes in society in the mid twentieth century, how did the Church as an institution respond and try to integrate the positive attributes of a more secular culture while at the same time, given its enormous influence, ward off the more negative aspects of that culture? Why did a way of life so ingrained practically disappear? Was it in some way flawed from the outset?

The enormous power and influence of the Church in the 1950s is reflected in the following statement issued by the bishops at the close of their Plenary Council held in Maynooth from 7–15 August 1956, in which they observed:

It is our privilege to serve a community whose love of God, loyalty to His Church and devotion to its head, the Vicar of Christ, are worthy of the highest praise. High standards of morality and of fidelity to religious duties, cordial relations between clergy and laity, sanctity of family life – these traditional features of Irish Catholicism are as manifest now as they have ever been. (National Synod 1956: 555)

Irish Catholic family life was largely as described in the bishops' summary. There is no shortage of supportive first-hand evidence from those who grew up in this all-pervasive Catholic atmosphere. Journalist T. P. O'Mahony's account of his upbringing would doubtless resonate with Catholics throughout the country:

> I had come through the grim, grey decade of the 1950s, and witnessed the end, in 1958, of the long pontificate of Pius XII. I was the product of a working class Catholic home on the northside of Cork city. I had grown up in a household where 'the faith' was a daily reality. A picture of the Sacred Heart had pride of place in our living room, and every evening we knelt, under the watchful eye of our grandmother, to recite the family Rosary. Weekly confession and Holy Communion were par for the course. Lent was a time of strict fasting and daily Mass, and the clergy were treated with awesome respect. (O'Mahony 2008: 23)

Notwithstanding the bishops' satisfaction with this state of affairs, there were, even in the 1950s, already challenges to this traditional Catholic way of life, as I have outlined elsewhere (Fuller 2002), and bishops' pastoral letters of that time were replete with apprehensions and warnings about dangers to faith and morals (2002: 38–51). They had a sense that this happy state of affairs in terms of their hegemonic religious position was beginning to be vulnerable. As a consequence, their pastoral approach was negative in its thrust; they were extremely dogmatic, consumed with fears that Irish Catholics would fall prey to secular trends developing in Continental Europe since the turn of the century. Consequently, they were at pains to preserve and protect the status quo. This provides a clue to the demise of Irish-style Catholicism. Essentially, it could only survive in the safe hothouse type atmosphere that epitomised Ireland at that time. The bishops worried about those who emigrated to England, and about threats to their faith, and possible loss of faith, when they were no longer in their own safe protected environment. But that safe environment even at home could no longer insulate or protect because, as the bishops went on to point out in their 1956 statement, 'through the development of modern means of communication our people at home as well as abroad are today in more direct and frequent contact with influences hostile to the faith than they have been in former times' (National Synod 1956: 556). Change was even then seeping through, and the media were to be the harbingers of that change, but the paternalistic approach adopted by the Church was not the answer. In the 1960s, the changes accelerated and thereafter became a tidal wave for which Irish Catholicism was not in any way prepared.

Catholicism in traditionally Catholic countries in mainland Europe had been in decline since the turn of the nineteenth century. In the post-war period, political, social and philosophical developments led to a questioning of traditional Catholic theology and a sense that it was not responsive to the kind of challenges posed by a rapidly changing world. In many more secularised countries, reforms in liturgical practice and new initiatives in church architecture were undertaken to address these changes. For the most part, the Irish Church saw little necessity to engage with such initiatives because Irish Catholics were very loyal to their religious practice. Theology was legalistic, and rules and regulations were the order of the day. In his memoir, published two years after retiring as Cardinal Primate of Ireland, Cahal Daly acknowledged the faults of the past, notably 'the excessive clericalism, the caution, the fussiness about rubrics, rules and petty regulations' and what he termed 'the complacencies of the early and middle twentieth century' (Daly 1998: 521). Born in 1916, his career as priest, bishop and cardinal spanned the century, and he was witness to seismic change in Irish Catholicism. Because Catholic moral teaching was upheld by law and in the Constitution, this cultivated a coercive moral climate rather than a morality based on conscience, conviction and free choice. Legal prohibitions and a rigid censorship regime prevented Irish Catholics from engaging in activities which were against the teaching of their church and from engaging with ideas that would undermine their faith and threaten allegiance to Church teaching. Such was the preoccupation with protecting people that the message became skewed. The approach certainly led to conformity by many, which lasted most of the twentieth century, but it did not provide the spiritual sustenance required to fend off the more secular climate that came to prevail from the 1960s. In addition to that, the authoritarianism and legalism ultimately gave rise to resentment and downright hostility, particularly from the 1990s forward, when the Church's position was severely compromised, because many of its representatives were shown not to have practised what they preached.

In the earlier part of the twentieth century in Ireland, there was little resistance to the status quo apart from intellectuals and writers. Because Catholicism was so interwoven with Irish culture, some of the most eloquent reflections and critiques, both positive and negative, of Catholic religious experience have come from writers. Capturing the spirit of Irish Catholicism as he experienced it, John McGahern identified very succinctly the fundamental reasons why it ultimately fell apart:

> Childishness was nurtured and encouraged to last a whole life long. Foolish pedantry took the place of thought and feeling … Faith and obedience were demanded … As well as the substitution of empty observances for reflection, thought or judgement, there was an obsession with morality, especially sexual, which resulted in an almost complete exclusion of the spiritual. (McGahern 2009: 146)

In the context of such a climate, he rightly points out, that 'when change happened it was certain to be rapid' (McGahern 2009: 147). Similar critical observations in relation to the quality of Irish Catholicism were made by some clergy as early as the 1950s. In 1951, Professor J. G. McGarry of St Patrick's College, Maynooth, one of the founding members of *The Furrow*, pointed to the prevailing spiritual climate, which lacked a 'sound foundation and substance' and saw a 'general need for a spiritual life founded more securely on doctrine' (McGarry

1951: 189). In 1959, Fr John C. Kelly SJ, writing in *Doctrine and Life*, was critical of what he referred to as a 'peasant religion' (Kelly 1959: 120). However,
the deficit in Irish Catholicism was not realised at that time by mainstream
clergy and bishops, who, generally speaking, had a very exalted picture of Irish
Catholic culture and were very grateful that their flock were not going down
the wayward track of their less fortunate fellow churchmen in mainland Europe.
Cardinal Daly, who studied in France in the early 1950s, recalled the 'smugness
and superiority' that marked his early reactions to the problems of the French
Church in the post-war era (Daly 1998: 115). He and many Irish clergy at the
time saw Ireland as a model Catholic country: churches and seminaries were
full, and doubts and questioning were little in evidence, but this situation would
not last.

Time had run out for this model of Catholicism – and this was recognised
by Pope John XXIII. He had been Nuncio in France from 1944 to 1953 and
witnessed the efforts of theologians there who were trying to rework traditional
Catholic theology to make it more responsive to cultural change. Pope Pius XII
condemned the new directions in theology in his encyclical *Humani Generis* in
1950. Theological debate and questioning were not features of the Irish Church
– theologians essentially followed the line set by Rome. As Daly pointed out, this
was a time in Ireland when things were expected 'to remain more or less the same
and which did not anticipate radical change in society or in the Church' (Daly
1998: 111).

But when John XXIII, shortly after his election as pope, indicated that he
was going to convene an ecumenical council of the Church, he was thinking
along different lines. Irrespective of what was happening in Ireland, the world was
changing, and Catholicism had to respond to these changes. The Second Vatican
Council document, *The Church in the Modern World*, recognised the major cultural
upheavals that were taking place: 'Today, the human race is passing through a new
stage of its history. Profound and rapid changes are spreading by degrees around
the whole world .... Hence we can ... speak of a true social and cultural transformation, one which has repercussions on man's religious life as well' (Abbott 1966:
202). Essentially, the council documents provided the Church with a rationale and
a blueprint for change. While the substance of the ancient doctrine of the deposit
of faith could not change, the way in which it was presented could change in
order to make it responsive to modern life. This meant a fundamental ground shift
in Catholic thinking, which was to have momentous implications for Catholics
throughout the world, and even more so in Ireland, where religious matters
were seen as set in stone and not open to debate. Church teaching was defined,
handed down by bishops in a manner that did not invite debate. However, the
social and cultural changes ushered in by the 1960s meant that this approach was
no longer viable. While the universal Church in Council reflected on its position in the modern world and proposed changes to make it more responsive
to change, the Irish Church found itself in the extraordinary position of being

somewhat frozen in time. This was typified for many by Archbishop McQuaid's admittedly extreme position (Fuller 2002: 112). Nevertheless, the bishops for the most part accepted the changes instigated by the Council, but not with a lot of enthusiasm, given the healthy condition of Irish Catholicism as they perceived it. By the time the Council was over, the process of change could no longer be halted. Many developments – political, economic, educational and cultural – were all catalysts of change, but undoubtedly the most important was the opening of an Irish television station in 1962. By 1966, over half the homes in Ireland had a television set (Central Statistics Office 2000: 58). Television provided a forum for discussion of all manner of views, whether the Church approved or otherwise; it was democratic, egalitarian and pushed back the frontiers of what was acceptable to debate incrementally over time. The Second Vatican Council finished in 1965. The Church still wielded enormous power, but it was being challenged gradually. A reference to Bishop Michael Browne of Galway as a moron, by a participant on *The Late Late Show* on RTÉ television in 1966 was indicative of the changing times (Byrne 1972: 86–91).

In the 1960s, religious practice was practically universal, as was adherence to Catholic teaching, although there is some evidence that birth control was beginning to be an issue. That said, the 1960s ushered in a very different era, where the emphasis was on autonomy and freedom – freedom of expression, freedom of thought, freedom of worship. The Pastoral Constitution on the Church in the Modern World recognised that 'the Church has always had the duty of scrutinising the signs of the times and of interpreting them in the light of the gospel' and pointed to the necessity to 'recognise and understand the world in which we live, its expectations, its longings, and its often dramatic characteristics' (Abbott 1966: 201–2).

The Church in Ireland had, to a great extent, been very successful in holding back the tide – unlike on mainland Europe – but from the 1960s this was no longer possible. Now the universal Church was reviewing its position to bring about *aggiornamento*, or updating. As the 1960s progressed, it was quite clear that the Council had been timely. But there were many signs by the late 1960s that, revolutionary as the Council had been, the pace of change was so rapid that it outstripped the capacity of the Church to keep up, as evidenced by defections from the priesthood and religious life and the decline in vocations that began in the late 1960s.

But the most important sign of all, both from a lay and clerical point of view, was the reaction to the promulgation by Pope Paul VI of the encyclical on birth control, *Humanae Vitae*, in 1968. Pope Paul's delay in promulgating the encyclical and his decision to go against the majority opinion of the commission originally set up by Pope John XXIII caused a crisis of confidence for the papacy which has had lasting effects on Catholicism worldwide. It was a major turning point for the Church and the papacy and a sign that the spirit of the council had been imbibed by both laity and clergy. The days of accepting anything on the basis of a decree by any authority figure were over. This was compounded by the fact that Church personnel no longer spoke with one uniform voice. Many theologians roundly condemned the encyclical. An Irish moral theologian, Fr James Good, who described the encyclical as 'a major tragedy', was banned from preaching and from teaching in University College Cork by his local bishop. Bishop Lucey of Cork, like McQuaid of Dublin and Browne of Galway, was another iconic figure in Irish Catholicism of the time. While there may have been disagreements in the past, they tended not to be voiced publicly. From the 1960s on, the communications media ensured that contested issues and disagreements were in the public domain. Essentially this placed responsibility on people to follow their consciences – make up their minds according to their own lights – something Irish Catholics were not accustomed to doing.

Even so, the high level of religious practice continued in the 1970s and into the 1980s. The really dramatic decline did not occur until the 1990s, which is why many attribute it to scandals that emerged from the early 1990s. Essentially, what was happening, though, was that practice was holding firm but Irish Catholics were following their consciences and making up their own minds about Catholic teaching – in particular teaching in relation to sexual morality, which was the area that Church authorities emphasised more than any other. From the 1960s, traditional views were increasingly questioned. Appeals to authority and dogma were decidedly passé. The Council had faced up to the spirit of the times, and many Catholics – priests, nuns and lay people – felt liberated. But there were also those who felt confused and marginalised in the new dispensation. They had grown up with a devotional Catholicism, where one did not question, where nothing changed and where a legalistic theology with hard and fast rules applied, and there were no grey areas between right and wrong. Suddenly many priests and religious sisters were discarding their clerical clothes in favour of lay styles of dress, and others were abandoning seminary and convent altogether. Whereas the emphasis in the past was very decidedly on sacrifice and self-denial for the glory of the kingdom of God, now the emphasis fell on self-fulfilment. The emphasis on fear, Hell and sinful humanity shifted perceptibly to that of love and the essential goodness of human nature, and rules seemingly set in stone such as Lenten fast could be set aside. Peter Hebblethwaite, an English Jesuit, who himself left the priesthood at that time, wrote a book entitled *The Runaway Church* (1975) – and that was certainly how it appeared to many Catholics. The encyclical *Humanae Vitae* was seen as Pope Paul VI attempting to 'rein in' the Church in 1968. But the spirit of the encyclical was out of keeping with the *Zeitgeist*, and this, combined with the mood of Vatican II and the optimism generated by the reforms of the Council, made this an impossible task.

Essentially, the model of Catholicism in Ireland – with its emphasis on mass, confession, communion, devotions, obedience – put in place in the historical-political conditions of the nineteenth century, was no longer suitable to the times. The Church, because of its vested interest in controlling education, was central to the struggle for self-rule in the late nineteenth century. The nationalist cause and Catholicism coalesced, which resulted in the Church having enormous power in the newly independent state. It was a model of church that depended on compulsion, fear of transgression and conformity to rules and regulations seen as immutable. While it seemed to serve the Church well, looking back, it is very clear that it has not been to the advantage of Catholicism in Ireland. The fact that Catholicism was so all-pervasive, and that education was primarily the responsibility of religious, and that the law of the land upheld Catholic morality, to some extent relieved Church personnel of the task of teaching and preaching the Good News of the Gospel. A private devotional-type religion of obligations was cultivated along with a rules-dominated morality under pain of sin. This resulted in a compliant laity, who were undoubtedly loyal practitioners of the faith, but of a faith which, in many cases, was not securely founded and therefore could not withstand the winds of change when they came. For the generation that came of age in the 1960s and 1970s, religious education in school was primarily apologetical – expounding the truths of the faith – a legacy from the Council of Trent. This approach to knowledge and education was not solely of the Irish Church's making; this was Roman policy since the Council of Trent, a policy that emphasised defence of the truths of the faith at all costs. In due course, the Syllabus of Errors was drawn up, and the Index of Forbidden Books. The Church was fearful of what were considered to be dangerous ideas, and censorship was a way to block access to them.

Pope Pius XII gave many addresses through the 1950s on the dangers inherent in the film industry, and in Ireland the bishops were constantly preoccupied with the dangers of films, plays and 'evil literature'. Books by Irish writers such as Walter Macken, Kate O'Brien, John McGahern, Edna O'Brien, John Broderick, to mention but a few, were banned under state legislation. Writers in their different ways explore the human condition in all of its complexity, which of necessity involves exploring themes with which the Church may not be comfortable, primarily to do with sex, relationships, struggles of conscience, good and evil. In the 1950s, Fr Peter Connolly, Professor of English in Maynooth, was critical of a 'juvenile standard of censorship' that aimed to protect people, pointing out that only the 'morally naïve' were not 'aware that there are controversial areas in moral theology'. Comments by Connolly in relation to a 1954 film, *Le Defroqué*, give a sense of the climate of the time. It portrayed the 'fall and resurrection of a priest', which depicted 'human sin and weakness'. He reckoned that cinema managers would probably be 'chary' of it – and he himself felt that it probably could not be shown to a general audience on the basis that not everybody would be equipped 'to face a priest as [a] tragic hero' (Connolly 1956: 111). The Church, with its paternalistic approach, tried to shield its followers from the facts of life, and success in this regard depended obviously on people's level of education and the cultural climate of the country they lived in, something that was set to change radically in the 1960s.

The role of any church in whatever context is to interpret human life in all of its contradictions, to show why it is meaningful in spite of pain, suffering and evil and to make a case for an ultimate destiny beyond that of the present world. Brian Friel's play *Philadelphia, Here I Come!*, published in 1965, was a touchstone for the more challenging times ahead for the Church when the main character Gar angrily confronted the Canon: 'you could translate all this loneliness, this groping, this dreadful bloody buffoonery into Christian terms that will make life bearable for us all. And yet you don't say a word. Why, Canon? Isn't this your job? – to translate? Why don't you speak, then?' (Friel 1965: 96). The muting of the critical intellectual voice in Ireland was short-sighted and ultimately unhealthy and damaging. As long ago as 1947, Sean O'Faolain reflected bitterly that, in Ireland, 'one group is held at arm's length, the writers or intellectuals'. He continued, 'the priest and the writer ought to be fighting side by side, if for nothing else than the rebuttal of the vulgarity that is pouring daily into the vacuum left in the popular mind by the dying out of the old traditional life' (O'Faolain 1980: 118–19). It was a prophetic opinion to voice at that time. Almost seventy years later, when 'the old traditional life' is no more, the Church now finds itself in an age when not only do many contest the idea of a God and the idea of an ultimate human destiny beyond this life but also, paradoxically, there is a new emphasis on spirituality, as witnessed by the plethora of books published on both of these themes. So the ground has shifted totally. What is certain is that Catholicism as we knew it is now an anachronism. There are currently many interpreters of the signs of the times, and the Church has to make its own case in the marketplace of ideas. While in the past the Church presented itself as having all the answers to the mystery of life, it is clear in the postmodern era that we are living in an age of uncertainty and that most people are groping their way towards some limited forms of understanding. People are reinterpreting their lives, and metanarratives are highly suspect in this atmosphere. For many, the notion of transcendence is unproblematic; for some, it is tenuous; and for more it is unsustainable. The task of the pastor in this cultural climate is to help people to recognise the immanence of God in the world, while equally confronting honestly the fact that faith ultimately means living with uncertainty, mystery and doubt. Many commentators over the years have pointed to the rich resources which could have been tapped in Irish writing to explore complex issues.

While religious practice has declined very significantly in Ireland, this has to be measured relative to the somewhat inflated and perhaps unrealistic figures recorded in the 1970s. These were based on a model of Catholicism which was no longer fit for purpose and what is most remarkable is that it limped on for as long as it did. It no longer provided the kind of spiritual sustenance needed in a vastly changed cultural context, nor did it provide adequate answers to the complex moral dilemmas that many Catholics were grappling with. The Church in Ireland still operated on the basis of laying down the law and expecting Catholics to conform. It persisted with this approach until the contraception issue in the 1970s forced a change of style, but it did not change willingly. There were many prelates who persisted with the old-style authoritarian approach. While the older generation had accepted the authoritarianism of the Church, this was no longer acceptable to those coming of age from the 1960s onwards. The fact that the Church did not read the 'signs of the times' has weakened its authority and position, and the real resentment bubbled to the surface from the nineties when the scandals were seen as the Church not practising what it had preached all along, and preached in a very dogmatic way. A backlash was inevitable. From the 1960s on, people's opportunities, whether it be for educational/economic development and/or how to spend their leisure time, were greatly expanded, which meant that they began to have higher expectations and to question more in relation to all aspects of their lives, including their experience of religion.

While religious practice has declined significantly, sociologists point to the fact that Catholics in Ireland are still seen as relatively loyal to their faith in comparison with other countries, and they have attributed this to cultural factors which, over the centuries crystallised into the symbiotic relationship between Catholicism and nationalism, which became the defining characteristic at the foundation of the Irish state. However, this loyalty of Catholics to their faith has been commented upon by observers in other cultures also. In 1994, Andrew Greely, commenting on American Catholicism, wrote: 'For the last thirty years the hierarchy and the clergy have done just about everything they could to drive the laity out of the Church and have not succeeded' (Greely 1994: 497). He argues that, 'Catholics remain Catholic because of the Catholic religious sensibility, a congeries of metaphors that explain what human life means, with deep and powerful appeal to the total person' (Greely 1994: 495–6). He argues that the dictum 'once a Catholic always a Catholic' is based on the fact that 'the religious images of Catholicism are acquired early in life and are tenacious. You may break with the institution, you may reject the propositions, but you cannot escape the images' (Greely 1994: 498). This has been borne out by many Catholics, be they ordinary Catholics who have fallen away from practice and writers like McGahern for whom belief had 'long gone', although he missed the rituals. This is clearly illustrated also in the case of Seamus Heaney, whose poetry is suffused with religious imagery. In his poem, 'Out of This World', dedicated to the memory of Czesław Miłosz, he writes of the paradox which lies at the heart of his own loss of faith:

> There was never a scene
> When I had it out with myself or with another.
> The loss occurred off-stage. And yet I cannot
> Disavow words like 'thanksgiving' or 'host'
> Or 'communion bread'. They have an undying
> Tremor and draw, like well water far down.
>   (Heaney 2006: 47)

The power of imagery is also echoed in the writing of Eamon Duffy, Church historian, who grew up in Ireland in the 1950s. In his book, *Faith of Our Fathers*, he writes: '... Catholicism was also mystery: the competent mutter and movement of the priest at the altar, the words of power half-understood, the sense of being in touch, literally in touch, with holy things, with Holiness itself (Duffy 2004: 15).

But as early as the 1970s, when mass attendance was at 91 per cent, some more aware clerical commentators were concerned that the disconnect between liturgy – the language of religion – and life was becoming so wide that it was almost impossible to bridge. Fr P. J. Brophy, looking back on his youth, pointed out that in those days 'pulpit and people talked the same language'; it was a time when 'there were very few rival spectacles' and devotions like Benediction satisfied people's 'modest longing for pageantry of some kind' (Brophy 1974: 215). Fr Eamon Bredin in 1979 observed that the new liturgy seemed to 'have left the inner core of people's lives untouched' (Bredin 1979: 45). The difficulty was that people were now 'searching for something in the liturgy', whereas in the past they had been content to be silent observers (Bredin 1979: 53). In the following decade, there was a resurgence of Marian devotion throughout the country. Fr Gabriel Daly OSA saw it as a replica of the 'old style evening devotions', but he viewed the phenomenon as a failure of pastors and teachers in presenting the Good News, 'when people have to turn to moving statues in order to satisfy their spiritual needs' (Daly 1985: 6). The important point highlighted here is spiritual need and while a nostalgic return to the past was the path for some, for the vast majority under forty, this had little resonance and would have less and less as time went by. That sense of the sacred when religion permeated culture – as conveyed by Heaney, McGahern and Duffy – would have to be redrawn to respond to the consciousness of a new generation in a more secular culture. For the most part, the Irish Church failed to fully appreciate, let alone respond to, this challenge. As one looks back, the Church authorities in the 1970s were preoccupied with issues of control in education and with the contraception issue and in the eighties and nineties with the abortion and divorce issues.

A writer who picked up the mood of the times was John O'Donohue. Writing as a priest in 1995, he captured the failures of the past and the dilemma that this led to for the Church in 1990s Ireland:

> A religious system which immunises itself against critical questioning becomes either dangerous or irrelevant. In a more uniform culture where it can dominate, it can be oppressive ... In a postmodern and pluralistic culture such a system becomes irrelevant and increasingly isolated. Once it has lost the authority of domination, it is dependent on the inner authority of its own truth. If immunised against reflection and critique, it is reduced to cliché and posture. These evoke the nostalgia of a vanished world, but lack all substance to engage the actual world of the present. (O'Donohue 1995: 137)

In what many now describe as a post-Catholic Ireland, characterised by questioning, doubt and unbelief, the Church can no longer impose its version of the truth. This is of course what it sees as its God-given mission, but it must be realised by 'proposing' its values and world view – a word that Pope Francis repeatedly uses to describe his desired teaching style. Religion has to do with values and belief in a transcendent reality beyond this life. Whereas in the past these went hand in hand, in postmodern society this is no longer necessarily the case. For many who no longer believe in an afterlife, the notion of salvation, so central to Church teaching, may be an anachronistic concept. While perhaps, this is not a very high percentage in Ireland, doubt is much more prevalent than in the past. In a fundamentally changed cultural context, free of traditional pressures to conform, the onus today is on Irish Catholics to make a fair evaluation of their cultural legacy, acknowledging the undoubted weaknesses of the past but also weighing up its considerable strengths and overall potential to give meaning, or otherwise, to their lives. This is a radical challenge that the Irish Church and Irish Catholics have hardly begun to face.

At a time when ready-made answers are no longer trusted, this challenge requires most of all a thoughtful and imaginative approach. In a recent article, Eugene O'Brien has, to my mind, caught the mood. 'Given that there is now contestation, as opposed to unqualified acceptance, with regards to the pre-existence of an afterlife or spirit world', he suggests:

> the more cryptic and sporadic insights of poetry may be the discourse best-equipped to deal with this, because it is the discourse where thinking can go beyond its normal boundary … Poetised thinking allows for a different perspective on the immanent so that glimpses of the transcendent can be captured. (O'Brien 2014: 132)

In an Ireland which has gone in a matter of sixty years from poverty and economic stagnation to the materialism of the Celtic Tiger and recently to economic meltdown, in addition to a collapse of confidence in all major institutions of the State as well as the Church, and which is noted internationally for its artists and writers, perhaps it is time for the Church to look to the artist to retrieve the religious imagination, because he or she, more than most, is in tune with the *Zeitgeist*. Poets such as Seamus Heaney, and recently John F. Deane and Pádraig J. Daly, provide an opportunity to reflect on questions of belief, doubt, meaning, pain, loss, good, evil and the numinous. Deane has written 'that a good religious poem is the final argument against nothingness' and feels that 'in our time the corrosion of the religious imagination is therefore the more depressing' (Deane 2006: 12). He points out that in our 'secular society so much at odds with deep human and universal rights and yearnings, it is the Christian artist who stands non-conformist rebel, challenge to such secularism' (Deane 2006: 9).

Pádraig J. Daly, himself a ministering priest, has captured very eloquently the bleak situation for religious and the Catholic Church in Ireland today in his poem 'Holding Away the Dark':

> Have mercy on us, O Lord,
> Who have lived beyond our time of usefulness
> And totter round the empty edifices of our glory,
> Looking towards our end.
>
> (Daly 2015: 77)

The mood is grim, and, undoubtedly, the Church is fighting a rearguard battle in Ireland, but in the matter of religious allegiance, absolute conclusions can never be drawn. The religious instinct is deeply ingrained in human nature. Sociologists have pointed to the resilience of the Catholic cultural legacy in Ireland, and there are many signs of this. The 2013 European Social Survey data for Ireland shows that larger numbers of Catholics record that they are religious as opposed to not very religious. On a scale of zero to ten, 70 per cent place themselves on the upward side of the scale (O'Mahony 2013). This is in spite of the very public failures of the institutional Church over the past few decades. Irish Catholics have historically demonstrated the ability to act independently of the institution when they see fit. Equally, in spite of what many have seen as a scandalous betrayal of ideals by the Church authorities in recent decades, there is much evidence that Catholics at parish level remain loyal to their local clergy. At a time when many might apply the term 'post-Catholic' to Irish society, the Church and its clergy can take some comfort from the fact that, in the event of any tragedy occurring throughout the country, the local clergyman is still called upon by the media to comment, an obvious recognition of his role at the centre of community life in Ireland. The clergyman will always have a role to play at the cutting edge of life, precisely because many people will still call on clergy of whatever denomination, in Friel's words, to 'translate'. Daly captures the anguish that all humans feel at some stage when 'infants wail, mothers weep, fathers bury sons' and 'those without hope look to us for hope, who have no hope' (Daly 2015: 78). But this is not the kind of raw honesty, empathy, humility, doubt that one associated with clergy in the past, when commands came from on high and the idea was conveyed that the Church had all the answers. This epitomises the kind of authenticity that Church personnel must communicate if they are to rebuild on what remains of the cultural legacy and re-engage the twenty-first-century mind and heart.

Works cited

Abbott, Walter M. (ed.) (1966) *The Church in the Modern World*, in *The Documents of Vatican II*, Dublin and London: Geoffrey Chapman.

Amárach (2012) *Contemporary Catholic Perspectives*, available at www.associationofcatholicpriests.ie/2012/04/contemporary-catholic-perspectives (accessed 10 December 2015).

Bredin, Eamon (1979) 'The Liturgy: Problems and Prospects', *The Furrow*, 30:1, 45–53.

Brophy, P. J. (1974) 'Whatever Happened to Our Liturgical Dreams?', *The Furrow*, 25:4, 213–18.

Byrne, Gay (1972) *To Whom It Concerns*, Dublin: Gill & Macmillan.

Catholic Communications Institute of Ireland (1975) *Survey of Religious Practice, Attitudes and Beliefs in the Republic of Ireland 1973–4, Report no. 1 on Religious Practice*, Dublin: Catholic Communications Institute of Ireland, available at www.catholicbishops.ie/2010/11/05/feature-40-years-of-social-research (accessed 10 December 2015).

Census of Population of Ireland, 2011.

Central Statistics Office (2000) *That Was Then, This Is Now: Change in Ireland, 1949–1999*, Central Statistics Office: Dublin.

Commission of Investigation into Catholic Diocese of Cloyne (2011) *Report by Commission of Investigation into the Handling by Church and State Authorities of Allegations and Suspicions of Child Sexual Abuse Against Clerics of the Catholic Diocese of Cloyne*, Dublin: Government Publications.

Connolly, Peter (1956) 'Films', *The Furrow*, 7:2, 108–11.

Daly, Cahal B. (1998) *Steps on My Pilgrim Journey: Memories and Reflections*, Dublin: Veritas Publications.

Daly, Gabriel (1985) 'Message of the Statues: The Theologian's View', *Sunday Independent*, 22 September, p. 6.

Daly, Pádraig J. (2015) 'Holding Away the Dark', in *God in Winter*, Dublin: Dedalus.

Deane, John F. (2006) *In Dogged Loyalty: The Religion of Poetry, the Poetry of Religion*, Dublin: Columba.

Duffy, Eamon (2004) *Faith of Our Fathers: Reflections on Catholic Tradition*, London: Continuum.

Friel, Brian (1965) *Philadelphia, Here I Come!* London: Faber and Faber.

Fuller, Louise (2002) *Irish Catholicism since 1950: The Undoing of a Culture*, Dublin: Gill & Macmillan.

Greely, Andrew (1994) 'Why Do Catholics Stay in the Church?' *The Furrow*, 45:9, 495–502.

Heaney, Seamus (2006) *District and Circle*, London: Faber and Faber.

Ipsos MRBI (2012) *Changing Ireland: Irish Attitudes and Values Survey*, results published in the *Irish Times*, 26 November, p. 10.

Kelly, John C. (1959) 'Solid Virtue in Ireland', *Doctrine and Life*, 9:5, 116–23.

Martin, Diarmaid (2014) Speaking notes of address to the priests and members of the Parish Pastoral Council of the North City Centre deanery, 'Fostering Faith in the City Centre', at Holy Cross College, Clonliffe, 27 February, available at www. Catholicbishops.ie/2014/02/27/speaking-notes-archbishop-diarmuid-martin-holy-cross-college-clonliffe (accessed 31 October 2015).

McGahern, John (2009) 'The Church and Its Spire', in Stanley van der Ziel (ed.), *Love of the World: Essays*, London: Faber and Faber, pp. 133–48.

McGarry, J. G. (1951) Review of *Doctrine and Life*, 1:1, in *The Furrow*, 2:3, 189.

National Synod (1956) Statement, *The Furrow*, 7:9, 555–6.

O'Brien, Eugene (2014) '"An Art That Knows Its Mind": Prayer, Poetry and Post-Catholic Identity in Seamus Heaney's "Squarings"', in Eamon Maher and Catherine Maignant (eds.), *Études Irlandaises*, 39:2, 127–43.

O'Donohue, John (1995) 'The Irish Church: Beyond the Bleak Landscape', *The Furrow*, 46:3, 135–43.

O'Faolain, Sean (1980) *The Irish*, London: Penguin Books.

O'Mahony, Eoin (ed.) (2013) *Religion and Belief among Catholics in Ireland: A Short Review of Recent European Social Survey Data*, Council for Research and Development of the Irish Bishops' Conference, available at www.catholicbishops.ie/wp-cont ent/uploads/2013/10/Religion-and-belief-among-Catholics-in-Ireland-round-5-ESS. pdf (accessed 10 December 2015).

O'Mahony, T. P. (2008) *Has God Logged Off? The Quest for Meaning in the 21st Century*, Dublin: Columba.

Paul VI (1968) *Humanae Vitae*, available at www.papalencyclicals.net/Paul06/p6humana. htm (accessed 10 December 2015).

Pius XII (1950) *Humani Generis*, available at www.papalencyclicals.net/Pius12/P12HUMAN. HTM (accessed 10 December 2015).

3

Dethroning Irish Catholicism: Church, State and modernity in contemporary Ireland

David Carroll Cochran

In his essay *A Catholic Modernity?*, the Canadian Catholic philosopher Charles Taylor reflects on how modern secularism's process of 'dethroning' Catholicism, of gradually disentangling the Church from the dominant institutions of societies where it long held political and social power, has paradoxically extended many of Catholicism's core commitments and liberated it to find a new and creative voice within modernity.

Taylor is reacting to a general pattern unfolding over centuries, but the Republic of Ireland represents an intriguingly compressed version of it in action. Taylor's theoretical framework offers a lens through which to examine dramatic changes in the public role of Catholicism over the country's relatively short history, as well as how a different vision of its place in Irish life can emerge in the wake of these changes. This vision is a compelling one, but one that also faces important challenges.

Taylor, Catholicism, and modernity

The background to Taylor's *A Catholic Modernity?* is the notion of 'Christendom', which he defines as 'a civilisation where the structures, institutions, and culture were all supposed to reflect the Christian nature of the society' (Taylor 1999: 17). In its purest form, this was the confessional state, long the norm across Europe, in which throne and altar were united so that the law privileged a particular Christian Church and enforced its moral teachings. Over several centuries, however, secularism weakened this arrangement and eventually 'dethroned' Christendom, a process that often involved violence, especially in Catholic countries such as France (Taylor 1999: 18).

Some Catholics lament the fall of Christendom with the attendant loss of the Church's power and prestige. Taylor is not among them. He argues that modernity has brought significant gains for humanity, ones that were 'unlikely to come about without some breach with established religion' (Taylor 1999: 29). Indeed, on his account, modernity has brought an extension of gospel principles not possible within the old structure of Christendom:

> The notion is that modern culture, in breaking with the structures and beliefs of Christendom, also carried certain facets of Christian life further than they ever were taken or could have been taken within Christendom. In relation to the earlier forms of Christian culture, we have to face the humbling realisation that the breakout was a necessary condition of the development. (Taylor 1999: 16)

These benefits include the idea of 'universal human rights' that affirm the equal moral status of all persons regardless of their particular communities or circumstances, as well as a modern humanitarian impulse based on the 'affirmation of ordinary life' that seeks to alleviate suffering and uphold the dignity of everyday persons around the world (Taylor 1999: 16, 25). In Taylor's view, 'we live in an extraordinary moral culture, measured against the norm of human history, in which suffering and death, through famine, flood, earthquake, pestilence, or war, can awaken worldwide movements of sympathy and practical solidarity' (1999: 25). These moral achievements have deep Christian roots, but they needed secularisation's dethroning of Christendom to become more fully realised and universalised. Taylor argues that 'we have to agree that it was this process that made possible what we now recognise as a great advance in the practical penetration of the gospel in human life', something that is 'a humbling experience, but also a liberating one' (1999: 18).

For Taylor, the dethroning is 'liberating' because the Church is no longer locked into a distorting alliance with political authority. Christendom's problem was always 'the attempt to marry the faith with a form of culture and a mode of society', because this always 'involves coercion' and the 'pressure of conformity'. History shows that 'where the sacred was bound up with and supported the political order' it became corrupted (Taylor 1999: 17). By setting aside alliances with political power, believers are free to live their faith more authentically. Taylor writes:

> This kind of freedom, so much the fruit of the gospel, we have only when nobody (that is, no particular outlook) is running the show. So a vote of thanks to Voltaire and others for (not necessarily wittingly) showing us this and for allowing us to live the gospel in a purer way, free of that continual and often bloody forcing of conscience which was the sin and blight of all those 'Christian' centuries. The gospel was always meant to stand out, unencumbered by arms. (1999: 18)

For Taylor, what is liberating is 'the freedom to come to God on one's own or, otherwise put, moved only by the Holy Spirit, whose barely audible voice will often be heard better when the loudspeakers of armed authority are silent' (1999: 19).

Taylor also suggests an additional liberating dimension of Christendom's fall. This is the possibility of a less restrictive and hierarchical Catholicism. The moral language of modernity can undermine Catholic clericalism and move the Church away from the kind of narrowness that attempts to enforce a sameness that is 'bought at the price of suppressing something of the diversity in the humanity that God created' (Taylor 1999: 22, 14). Liberation is also a form of new openness within the Church itself.

If Taylor's essay argues that there is much good in the modernity secularism has brought, good that Catholicism should welcome, including its own loss of political power, it also warns that a modernity increasingly closed off to the transcendent has its own 'dangers', ones that create an ongoing need for Catholics and other believers to address (Taylor 1999: 19). He contends that modernism's universal humanitarian concern places high moral demands on people, ones that are difficult to sustain. It can easily corrode into a shallow, selfish philanthropy that says more about the helper than the helped. He writes, 'A solidarity ultimately driven by the giver's own sense of moral superiority is a whimsical and fickle thing' (Taylor 1999: 31). This can tip into resentment towards those helped, seeing them as objects of pity and even contempt, contrasting their flaws with the goodness and self-reliance of their benefactors. Taylor sees this process behind 'the present hardening of feeling against the impoverished and disfavoured in Western democracies' (1999: 31). Indeed, he points to an anti-humanist strain in modernity's 'affirmation of ordinary life', one he traces to thinkers such as Nietzsche. Here, affirming one's own life and fulfilment means throwing off constraints such as compassion, mercy or solidarity with others. This becomes a wilfulness and sense of individual power that 'chafes at the benevolence, the universalism, the harmony, the order' of a just society (Taylor 1999: 27). Religious traditions that emphasise transcendence, radical self-gift and humility can help mitigate these dangers. Taylor emphasises in particular the antidote of 'a love or compassion that is unconditional' at the heart of Christianity (1999: 35).

The rise of trends such as expressive individualism and consumerism in modern secular societies to fill a void left by the loss of transcendence is a theme Taylor pursues more fully in his later *A Secular Age*. One of modernity's discontents is 'the spectre of meaninglessness' (Taylor 2007: 717). What Taylor calls the 'buffered self', one closed to enchantment and transcendent significance, experiences a sense of 'loss' or 'flatness' or 'malaise' (2007: Chapter 8). This provides an opening for religious traditions to play a vital and continuing role in such societies. A search for meaning and authenticity can bring some people back to traditional religious traditions such as Catholicism, though now in a pluralist context in which it is just one option among many rather than in a way that restores Christendom (Taylor 2007: Chapter 14). This is a reduced but more creative role for religion in societies that are becoming 'post-secular'; ones where 'the hegemony of the master narrative of secularisation will be more and more challenged' by the continuing pull of the transcendent (Taylor 2007: 534).

Taylor, then, neither completely rejects nor completely embraces modernity. Instead, he argues that Catholics should 'find our voice within the achievements of modernity' in order to embrace what is good but, at the same time, prophetically respond and offer alternatives to what is not (1999: 36). Secularisation has done the Church a service by dethroning it from political power, but it also creates the opportunity for the Church to take on a new character with a new role in the wake of this dethroning.

Enthroning Irish Catholicism

Given Ireland's history of British rule, the rise of the Catholic Church to political and social power was relatively recent, happening while Christendom's dethroning was already well under way elsewhere. With the British State's long favouring of Protestantism, culminating in the notorious Penal Laws, Catholics faced discrimination and marginalisation into the nineteenth century. Rather than quashing Catholicism, however, this only made it a vehicle for political resistance (Finnegan 2013). While the Church did view some revolutionary and violent strands of Irish nationalism with suspicion, Catholicism also emerged as a critical 'oppositional force' to British rule (Fuller 2006: 70). As Peadar Kirby points out, unlike countries such as France where the Church was tied to the old order, in Ireland it was tied to the emerging one through its participation in a 'project of anti-colonial cultural nationalism' (Kirby 2008: 28–9).

Closely related to its nationalist role was the rise of the Church's institutional presence in the century before Irish Independence. Emerging out of Catholic emancipation and the trauma of famine, the Church gained significant influence over the everyday lives of the Irish people by the latter half of the nineteenth century through newly built churches, plentiful and disciplined clergy, rigorous devotional practices and social welfare efforts (Larkin 1984, part 2; Inglis 1998, part 2). Perhaps most significantly, it helped undermine the British State's plans for a national system of religiously mixed, non-denominational primary schools. Instead, such schools were eventually co-opted and run on denominational lines, with local Catholic clergy acting as patrons for the vast majority of them and Catholic religious orders running most secondary schools (Coolahan 2003; Kieran 2008).

This emergence of Catholicism as a powerful political and social presence positioned it, in the words of Louise Fuller, to 'wield extraordinary influence in the new State' that emerged after the break with Britain (Fuller 2006: 70–1). Indeed, for Fuller, post-Independence Ireland was marked by an alliance between Church and State that benefitted both, helping to heal the wounds of civil war and also to validate the new political order (Fuller 2002: Chapter 1). Jean-Christophe Penet echoes this analysis, arguing that the new state 'took Catholicism as its main ideology', an arrangement in which the Church received political influence while the young state gained legitimacy by drawing on Catholic ideals, rituals and nationwide celebrations such as the 1929 Catholic emancipation centenary and the 1932 International Eucharistic Congress (Fuller 2013: 308; McDonagh 2003: 44; Penet 2008: 72–3).

The State, for example, was happy to let the Church continue its prominent role in education, health care and social welfare, both seeing this role as proper and not especially interested in the cost and complexity of taking it on itself (Barrington 2003; Coolahan 2003; Kiernan 2008). It also adopted legislation and a new constitution in 1937 that recognised the 'special position' of the Church in Irish life and codified in law Catholic values on matters such as divorce, contraception, the role of women in the home and workplace, censorship and alcohol sales on certain Holy Days (Carroll 2015; Dillon 2014; Fuller 2013; McDonagh 2003; Whyte 1971: Chapters 1–2). As J. H. Whyte puts it, in his landmark study, 'from its early days, the government proved willing to use the power of the State to protect Catholic moral values' (1971: 36).

The close relationship between Church and State would last for decades. In 1948, a new government, following its first cabinet meeting, sent a telegram to Pope Pius XII giving him 'the assurance of our filial loyalty and our devotion to your August Person, as well as our firm resolve to be guided in all our work by the teaching of Christ, and to strive for the attainment of a social order in Ireland based on Christian principles' (Keogh 2007: 103). Even as late as the 1960s, Taoiseach Seán Lemass bowed to pressure from Dublin's Archbishop McQuaid not to extend the National Library onto the grounds of the Protestant Trinity College (McDonagh 2003: 47). Perhaps the most famous Church–State example of this kind came in 1951, when Noël Browne, Minister for Health, resigned in the wake of opposition by the Church hierarchy to a proposed health-care reform known as the Mother and Child Scheme. A chastened Browne declared, 'I as a Catholic accept unequivocally and unreservedly the views of the hierarchy on this matter', and Archbishop D'Alton of Armagh stated that 'we have a right to expect that our social legislation will not be in conflict with Catholic principles' (Fuller 2006: 75–6).

This Church–State alliance was rooted in a shared vision of Irish exceptionalism as a distinctively pure Catholic nation holding out against corruption from abroad, a vision that helps explain the country's policy of both economic and cultural isolation during its first four decades (Dillon 2014: 189; Fuller 2013: 208). Mary Kenny points out that Irish life in the early 1920s was marked by intense anxiety about moral decay caused by jazz, dance halls, crime fiction, new women's fashions and similar foreign influences so that 'when the new Irish Free State was born in 1923, a desire to start afresh, to build this pure and unsullied society was born with it' (Kenny 2000: 123; see also Whyte 1971: Chapter 2). This same impulse was behind the 1937

Constitution's fusion of Church, State and Nation, a document that its author, Eamon de Valera, called 'the spiritual and cultural embodiment of the Irish people' (Hederman 2010: 61). As late as 1952, a writer in the *Irish Rosary* stated, 'Perhaps the Republic of Ireland, as it is constituted today, is the only integral Catholic State in the world; a Catholic culture as it existed in the Middle Ages' (Fuller 2006: 72).

The close relationship between Church and State in this period can, however, be overstated. The Church was never formally established or endowed; there was no official concordat; and the State did not incorporate canon law. Bishops did not seek power over ordinary legislation or government operations, and even on larger state matters, the Church hierarchy did not always get its way (Whyte 1971: Chapters 1–2, 12). For instance, not long after Noël Browne's resignation, a new government headed by de Valera passed a health-care reform similar to the Mother and Child Scheme over the hierarchy's objections with little problem (Barrington 2003; Bartlett 2002). Furthermore, the kinds of morals legislation enacted in the early years of the Republic were often supported by Protestant churches as well, and such laws were not unusual in other countries (Hannon 2003: 126–7; Kenny 2000: Chapter 6; McDonagh 2003).

With these caveats in mind, however, it is clear that the Church exercised a great deal of influence on the shape and direction of Irish politics. While not formally an established church, the reality was what Enda McDonagh calls 'informal establishment', one that still amounted to a powerful instance of 'Christendom' (McDonagh 2003: 58). Even without a hand in day-to-day decision-making, the Church was able to shape the political context in which decisions unfolded. Its power lay in setting the political agenda and signalling that certain lines should not be crossed: 'The power of the Church in the political field survived more on the threat of censure rather than its actual implementation' (Inglis 1998: 75). The Church did not have to intervene directly in politics very often since its values were ones shared by institutions and actors across Ireland. In Whyte's words, 'Churchmen and statesmen were moulded by the same culture, educated at the same schools, quite often related to each other' (1971: 366).

The Church's political power, then, was an extension of its social, cultural and economic power. In Tom Inglis's influential formulation, the Church exercised a 'moral monopoly' in Irish life (1998). Being seen as a good Catholic was crucial to one's position in society. Extraordinarily high mass attendance, widespread devotional practices, regular confession, control over education and health care and frequent home visits by clergy sustained an especially controlling form of Catholicism in Ireland, one that dominated the ordinary lives of its people like no other institution. In a 1964 survey, 90 per cent of respondents agreed with the statement 'The Church is the greatest force for good in Ireland today' (Kenny 2000: 216).

Dethroning Irish Catholicism

If the rise of Taylor's 'Christendom' came late to Ireland, so too has its fall. This has created what Michele Dillon calls a process of 'compressed secularism' as Ireland has experienced rapid social change (2015a). Indeed, those who have witnessed Irish Catholicism's declining political and social power at first hand have often been struck by its relative speed. Brendan Hoban writes that 'part of our difficulty in Ireland is that centuries of change were telescoped into a few decades' (2012: 15). In addition, for former Taoiseach Garret FitzGerald, 'Ireland had for so long been sheltered by the conservative influence of the Roman Catholic Church from changes that had occurred elsewhere, over a long period', making the Church a 'kind of dam', but when these changes did come, they were 'squeezed into a single quarter of a century' and produced a 'storm flood' once the dam failed (2003: 105, 120).

The dynamics that have knocked the Church from its formally dominant position in Ireland had their roots in the 1960s and 1970s, but the process accelerated in the decades after Pope John Paul II's landmark trip to Ireland in 1979 (Fuller 2002, 2006; McGarry 2006). Beginning in the early 1960s, the State's economic policy of openness to the rest of the world, eventually leading to membership of the European Union, undermined the earlier ideal of Catholic rural frugality as it brought rising prosperity, urbanisation, foreign travel and educational attainment. Similarly, a new cultural openness followed the arrival of television in the early 1960s and the rise of the media as a rival to the Church for the hearts and minds of Irish people. Inglis writes, 'It was the media, and in particular television, which brought an end to the long nineteenth century of Irish Catholicism' (1998: 93). These changes were linked to shifts in social attitudes and practices around gender and sexuality that were increasingly at odds with Church teaching and that were especially important in breaking the traditional alliance between married women and Catholic clergy, while mass attendance and other visible markers of Catholic devotion became less important in securing one's social position in Irish life (Inglis 1998: Chapter 9).

A series of bruising legislative, judicial and constitutional battles has marked this dethroning process (Fuller 2002, 2006). Referendum victories reaffirming prohibitions on abortion and divorce in the early to mid 1980s represented what Dillon calls 'a high point before the emerging end of the Church's cultural hegemony in Ireland' (2014: 198). Indeed, these victories actually signalled the breakdown of the Church–State consensus on a range of issues since the law was now considered open to debate and change, leading to the irony of religion's seeming more central to Irish politics just as the country was becoming more secular; religious norms once widely accepted now faced serious political challenges (Penet 2008: 85–6; Twomey 2003: 128). While abortion restrictions have only seen some loosening and may represent an exceptional case (see Dillon 2015b), successful efforts to legalise contraception, divorce, homosexuality and, most recently, in

2015, same-sex marriage all point to the unravelling of the Church–State alliance on moral regulations forged in the early years of the country. Indeed, even before the same-sex marriage vote, Diarmuid Martin, the Archbishop of Dublin, wrote in 2011:

> The place of the Church in the current political discussion in Ireland is increasingly marginal. I would say that none of the political parties even thought of seeking the views of the Church around their policies for the current General Election. If anything they would seem to prefer not to be seen in any way to be associated with the Church. (Martin 2011)

The average political leader now feels 'much freer to oppose the hierarchy openly and to propose laws that they know will certainly please the electorate and displease the bishops' (Penet 2008: 81). The Irish State is now a long way from telegrams to the Pope pledging fidelity. Of course, overshadowing all of this are the abuse scandals. While the Church's loss of political and social power was already under way, their emergence soon became central to the process. While Catholicism in other countries has seen similar scandals, the impact in Ireland has been especially dramatic in two ways. First, as Lawrence Taylor points out, given how central 'clerical authority and antisexuality' were to Irish Catholicism, abuse revelations were perfectly targeted to highlight its hypocrisy (2007: 156). Second, since much of the abuse took place in educational and social-welfare institutions outsourced to the Church by the State, and also in view of the tendency of local officials to quietly refer abuse allegations to Church leaders for hushing up, these revelations have cast the alliance between Church and State as a particularly destructive one.

The drip-drip nature of the scandals, detailed in agonising report after agonising report, only magnifies their impact. Dillon writes, 'the grim details in any one of the reports would have been sufficient to stimulate dismay and anger among a loyal faithful. But the succession of reports and the systematic patterns of similar malfeasance documented in each case, cascaded into everyday Irish consciousness' (2014: 205). The sense of betrayal and anger directed at the institutionalised Church and its power in Irish life has been significant: 'It was as though everything the Catholic establishment stood for had turned out to be wrong, and everything it had opposed turned out to be right' (Kenny 2000: 322). The majority of survey respondents now report having 'no' or 'not very much' confidence in the Catholic Church (Oldmixon and Calfano 2015: 69). The State has not escaped censure either, which perhaps explains why its leaders have both apologised for its role in the abuse scandals and channelled public anger at its former ally, most famously in 2011, with Taoiseach Enda Kenny's unprecedented public condemnation of 'the dysfunction, disconnection, elitism … the narcissism that dominate the culture of the Vatican to this day' (Kenny 2011; Keogh 2007: 143).

Taylor's Catholic modernity in Ireland

Clearly, then, it has been a rough few decades for Irish Catholicism. American Catholics facing problems in their own church often comfort themselves with comparisons to their Irish counterparts: 'we've got it bad, but at least we're not the Irish Church!' This is a common way to read the situation from within the Church, lamenting its decline, its empty pews, its falling vocations, its marginalisation, its loss of public legitimacy. Nevertheless, reading the situation through the lens of Taylor's Catholic modernity framework uncovers a different interpretation, one that sees the painful process of dethroning Irish Catholicism as ultimately necessary and positive, not only for Ireland but also for the Irish Church itself. It is possible to see in the work of many who observe Irish Catholicism an emerging vision of a dethroned church renewing itself, atoning for past sins and finding a new and vital role in modern Irish life.

This vision begins with the flaws of enthroned Catholicism as it emerged in the years following Irish Independence. While the Church did much good – educating children, caring for the sick, marking life's stages through sacraments, forging communal bonds, linking people to the transcendent – its close relationship with the State was, as Linda Hogan writes, 'detrimental to both' (2003: 111). Political power was corrupting. For Mark Patrick Hederman, the fusion of Church and State created 'something of a police state' with an 'authoritarian' character, one that tried to enforce a distorted version of human life that was 'so narrow and so pure that it left out a large number of our population and a vast proportion of our humanity' (2010: 11, 54). This style of Catholicism – severe, puritanical, marked by hierarchical power and clericalism, enforcing its dictates through fear and coercion – actually represents a negation of the mercy, humanity and affirmation of incarnation, beauty and deep mystery found elsewhere in the Catholic tradition, a contrast that often struck Irish novelists and poets from the period (Hederman 2010: 109; Maher 2015: 6–8). A rule-based form of Catholic practice based on social pressure and habit amounted to a 'childish' faith rather than one rooted in real conviction and spiritual maturity, a problem a survey commissioned by the Irish bishops themselves in 1974 confirmed (Fuller 2006: 81; Kirby 2008: 30).

Given its flaws, Irish Catholicism's fall from political and social power represents progress towards a more open and humane society, which in Taylor's formulation amounts to a paradoxical extension of gospel values made possible by that very fall. It also liberates the Church itself. Free from an entanglement with state power and its coercive practices – from Taylor's 'forcing of conscience' – the Church can become more authentic to its mission. Mary Kenny argues that Irish Catholicism is stronger when not part of the State since 'it does better when it is not a monopoly, but holds the hearts of the people' (2000: 335). Dethroning turns the Church's focus away from those in power and towards those the gospel itself prioritises. Kirby writes that, 'being less embedded in the power structures of Irish society, the Church is being freed to stand with those on the margins of that society…to show the face of Christ more clearly' (2008: 41). Echoing Taylor's praise for modernity's 'affirmation of ordinary life', some observers see the potential of a chastened Irish Church to shift its concern from power and influence to pastoral care for the 'everyday life' of persons (Maignant 2008: 103). Commenting on how the vote to legalise same-sex marriage means 'Constantinian Christianity as a model for church-state relations is at an end', Oliver Rafferty writes that 'Irish Catholicism can perhaps emerge as a more caring, less overtly dogmatic and oppressive feature of the Irish landscape … more concentrated on ministering to peoples' actual needs than on wielding power in Irish society' (Rafferty 2015).

Even Catholic institutions such as hospitals and schools can benefit from stepping back from their formerly cosy relationship with the State. Archbishop Martin himself argues that such a relationship has often come at the expense of distinctiveness in the Church's social-welfare efforts, that these have 'lost something of the Christian concept of gratuitousness' and unique 'witness to Jesus'. On his account, domination of the education sector has also become bad for the Church and is 'no longer tenable today'. The Catholic ethos of many schools has become watered down, and too much religious education is just going through the motions, meaning Ireland's 'young people are among the most catechised in Europe but among the least evangelised' (Martin 2010). A more open and pluralistic education system can liberate Church-run schools to be more authentically and distinctively Catholic, even if this means a reduction in their number, which some Church leaders may find painful (Martin 2010 and 2011; see also Coolahan 2003).

These reactions to Irish Catholicism's dethroning suggest that, as in Taylor's framework, modernity's impact on the Church's political and social power might be reflected in the Church's internal structures and practices as well. This is why many are hopeful that a church humbled by the loss of its dominant position in Ireland will be liberated to reform itself. For Hoban, the time has come for the 'arrogance' and 'oppressiveness' of 'the ecclesiastical aristocracy with its pomps and pretentions' to end (2012: 17). The hope here is that a former culture of clericalism, secrecy and centralisation will give way towards more lay involvement, transparency, collaboration, dialogue and ecumenism. A dethroned church can be a more open, humble and pastorally engaged one, one more consistent with the example of Pope Francis (Littleton 2015; Maher 2015; O'Hanlon 2013; Whelan 2013).

Not surprisingly, the abuse scandals loom large in all of this; for many, it was the very character of enthroned Catholicism that enabled patterns of abuse. Those abused were victimised by 'a collusion of the Irish State with the monarchical Catholic clerical system – wedded as the latter was to authoritarianism, clericalism and secrecy' (O'Conaill 2010: 75). The Church used its claim to teach transcendent truth without second-guessing from those under it, as well as its political influence, to cover up and duck accountability for abuse in its institutions (O'Brien 2010). In Taoiseach Kenny's condemnation of the Church's failings revealed by abuse revelations, he labels them as 'the polar opposite of the radicalism, humility and compassion upon which the Roman Church was founded' (2011). An authentically Gospel-inspired response to the abuse crisis, then, required a dethroning of Irish Catholicism. While victims had to suffer in silence for years, it wasn't 'until, decades later, a different and more humane kind of Irish society discovered a capacity to open itself up to the truth about the terrible part of its past' (FitzGerald 2003: 143). This allowed both the State and the Church to move towards apology, atonement and compensation (Maignant 2014: 75–5). For Sean O'Conaill, to the extent that the 'catastrophe' of the abuse scandals helped to strip away the Church's power and prestige, it can help 'liberate and reshape all that is best in Catholicism' by lending urgency to the need for church reform (O'Conaill 2010: 74). In this view, true atonement for abuse under enthroned Catholicism requires not only healing and restorative justice for the victims but also deep changes in the Church's culture and the way it wields authority (see, for example, many of the essays in Claffey et al. 2013).

However, if modernity has been good for Ireland and Irish Catholicism by dethroning the Church, Taylor's framework is also sensitive to modernity's 'dangers' and Catholicism's capacity to respond. For Taylor, the Church does not disappear but, freed from alliances with political and social power, takes on a new character. The Irish Church is well positioned to do this since, for all the changes it has faced, it does retain an often-overlooked vibrancy. While there has been a collapse of faith in the institutional Church and its hierarchy, many local nuns, priests, brothers and lay ministers continue to find fulfilment in doing important work that is appreciated by those they serve. Most Irish still identify as Catholic; religious practice is still relatively high in comparison with other European countries; and there remains an attachment to many Catholic rituals: baptisms, first communions, weddings, funerals, pilgrimages, even novenas and other traditional devotions (Dillon 2015a; Flanagan 2015; Hoban 2012: Chapters 3 and 11; Kenny 2000: Chapter 15; Maher 2015). Therefore, while Catholicism in Ireland is, or is on its way to being, what Archbishop Martin calls 'a minority culture', it still has the potential to act as one of Pope Benedict XVI's 'creative minorities' in larger secular cultures (Coll 2013: 368; Martin 2011). Indeed, echoing Taylor, Dillon argues that the compressed period of change Ireland has undergone means the country has in some ways fast-forwarded to become a 'post-secular society', one where religion is no longer hegemonic but 'still matters and has public relevance' (2015a: 57). In this context, the Church has the potential to act as the prophetic witness in the face of modernity's discontents that Taylor has in mind.

Taylor's first major concern is the erosion of solidarity, precisely what many observers claim should be a priority for a chastened Irish Catholicism. A church freed from social and political power can offer a more radical critique of growing inequality, materialism and market power in Irish life (Kenny 2000: Chapter 15; Kirby 2008; McDonagh 2003: 60–3). With the rise of the Celtic Tiger and its collapse amidst the global financial crisis beginning in 2008, Dillon argues that by becoming a more vocal witness against social-welfare cuts, anti-immigrant policies, economic insecurity and declining 'communal solidarity' in the face of 'competitive individualism', the Church 'can articulate views that are counter-hegemonic to the dominant material and power interests in society' (2014: 204, 207–8; 2015a: 58). In this way, the Church goes from being an enthroned political power to being a dethroned critic of those who now wield political power at the expense of the common good.

Taylor's other major concern is the loss of transcendent meaning, which also resonates with observers, seeing what Kirby labels 'a profound spiritual vacuum' in modern Irish life (Kirby 2008: 41). There is a sense that drug and alcohol abuse, suicide, narcissism, loneliness and emotional emptiness signal a lost sense of the sacred, of deeper meaning, of ways to think about profound questions of life and death (Cronin 2013; Dillon 2014; Kenny 2000: Chapters 14–15; Maher 2015). This points to a deep spiritual hunger that still exists in Irish society, one the Church can minister to, not by returning to its enthroned style but by working within the dynamic pluralism of modern Ireland to find new ways, or creatively reinventing old ones to serve the spiritual needs of ordinary people (Flanagan 2015). As Inglis writes, 'We live in a disenchanted world, but it could easily be re-enchanted' (1998: 244).

Challenges and questions

There is then a vision of a dethroned Irish Catholicism emerging along the lines suggested by Taylor's Catholic modernity framework. This vision is compelling, recognising the rot within the seemingly robust enthroned Church of the past, seeing the benefits of dethroning to both the Church and the country at large and pointing with hope towards a new and more authentic presence for the Church in Irish life. It is a vision, however, that still faces some broad challenges that prompt important questions.

The first is finding effective ways to implement this vision when similar efforts have been under way for some time. As Fuller details, the kind of shifts in tone and emphasis it has in mind actually date back almost half a century. She writes of the Church following the reforms of the Second Vatican Council:

> Catholicism changed from being dogmatic to being more dialogical. It was less con-cerned with the imposition of rules and regulations than it was with what should be the spirit of Catholicism. Its tone became one of a pilgrim church seeking the truth, rather than an institution which had a monopoly on it, to the exclusion of all similar institutions. (Fuller 2002: 229)

Similarly, Irish Catholicism has been emphasising social and economic jus-tice issues such as unemployment, poverty, inequality, militarism and envi-ronmental protection since the 1970s, often accompanied by de-emphasising sexual-morality issues, at least in comparison to previous decades (Fuller 2002: Chapter 15; Kenny 2000: Chapters 10 and 12; Keogh 2007: 114–16; Lane 2003: 218–21). When Ireland voted to legalise same-sex marriage, one younger adult commented that when she went to school in the 1990s and 2000s, her religious education was not a list of 'should not's' and never included any condemnations of homosexuality but instead focused on peace and justice principles (O'Rourke 2015). Indeed, a critique of modernity's discontents such as materialism, individualism and meaninglessness was a core ideological commitment of enthroned Catholicism itself (Fuller 2006: 75, 2013: 317). Therefore, some elements of the emerging vision of a dethroned Irish Catholicism detailed above are actually not new. How, then, can such a vision best show that these elements remain important to the future of the Irish Church? Perhaps the rapid changes in Irish life and the new position the Church finds itself in as a result will give them a renewed urgency.

A second challenge centres on the question of when the law and public policy should reflect Catholic values. A big part of the critique of enthroned Catholicism in Ireland was its using the law and public policy to enforce Catholic norms on sexual behaviour, gender roles in the family and workplace, censorship and so on. Such a political alliance between Church and State was oppressive and corrupting, which is why a church losing its political influence was welcomed in the vision outlined above. Nevertheless, the same vision also urges the Church to be a prophetic voice for social and economic justice by appealing to principles such as solidarity, the common good and the preferential option for the poor. Sometimes this means individual Catholics and the Church's own institutions acting with compassion and charity apart from the State, but many observers also suggest that it includes 'advocating policy positions' and working to 'put forward alternative policy proposals to those which are currently being applied' since addressing systematic injustice requires political responses (Healy and Reynolds 2003: 195; Roddy et al. 2003: 206). While the issues may have changed, this is still an attempt to exercise political influence so that state policy more closely reflects Catholic principles. What, then, is the proper role of a dethroned Irish Church as a political advocate? How much political influence should it seek, on what issues, and what justifies such influence given the critique of its abuse in the past? It is probably now timely for the Church to address contested issues in a manner that includes all the voices within its sphere as part of a pluralistic public dialogue with its focus on consensus and the common good rather than its hierarchy being sole arbiter on all the burning issues that confront it.

Finally, a third challenge is the continuing need to address the relationship between the State and Church institutions. The critique of enthroned Catholicism argues that the relationship was too close, with the State essentially ceding control of functions such as education, health care and other social-welfare areas to the Church. Dethroning has weakened this relationship, but the process is still under way. As we have seen, the Church still plays a huge role in an education system that remains largely 'faith-based' but 'state-funded' (Kiernan 2008: 51). While not as large, its role in health-care delivery and other social-welfare services is still significant as well (Barrington 2003). What is the future of Catholic schools, hospitals and other institutions? How much state support, if any, should they receive for their work? Should they have the right to maintain their distinctive 'Catholic ethos' by, for example, giving preference to Catholic students or refusing to employ those in same-sex marriages (Coolahan 2003; Humphreys 2015a, 2015b; Kiernan 2008)? This chapter's vision of Irish Catholicism unseated from political and social dominance still sees a role for it in public life, attending to the pastoral needs of ordinary people and serving as a prophetic witness against Taylor's 'dangers' of modernity. To do this, it requires an institutional presence in civil society – not just schools and hospitals but parishes, retreat centres, homeless shelters, voluntary organisations and so on. Such a presence always brings such institutions into contact with the State through a web of regulatory, tax and subsidy policies. Just as Catholicism at its height of political influence did not mean the compete takeover of the State by the Church, the loss of that influence will not mean the end of all contact between the two. Dethroning Catholicism, then, will not eliminate difficult questions of Church and State in Ireland but will instead shift them to the new ground created by modernity, ground that Taylor helps to map and that many in a humbled Irish Church are already navigating with a sense of liberation, renewal and hope.

Works cited

Barrington, Ruth (2003) 'Catholic Influence on the Health Services, 1830–2000', in James P. Mackey and Enda McDonagh (eds.), *Religion and Politics in Ireland at the Turn of the Millennium*, Dublin: Columba, pp. 152–65.

Bartlett, Thomas (2002) 'Church and State in Modern Ireland, 1923–1970: An Appraisal Reappraised', in Brendan Bradshaw and Daire Keogh (eds.), *Christianity in Ireland: Revisiting the Story*, Dublin: Columba, pp. 249–58.

Carroll, Steven (2015) 'Fitzgerald Urged to Lift Ban on Good Friday Alcohol Sales', *Irish Times*, 28 January, available at www.irishtimes.com/news/ireland/irish-news/fitzgerald-urged-to-lift-ban-on-good-friday-alcohol-sales-1.2082973 (accessed 19 August 2015).

Claffey, Patrick, Joe Egan and Marie Keenan (eds.) (2013) *Broken Faith: Why Hope Matters*, Oxford: Peter Lang.

Coll, Niall (2013) 'Irish Identity and the Future of Catholicism', in Oliver Rafferty (ed.), *Irish Catholic Identities*, Manchester: Manchester University Press, pp. 362–76.

Coolahan, John (2003) 'Church–State Relations in Primary and Secondary Education', in James P. Mackey and Enda McDonagh (eds.), *Religion and Politics in Ireland at the Turn of the Millennium*, Dublin: Columba, pp. 132–51.

Cronin, Michael (2013) 'Fear and Loathing in the Republic: Why Hope Matters', in Patrick Claffey, Joe Egan and Marie Keenan (eds.), *Broken Faith: Why Hope Matters*, Oxford: Peter Lang, pp. 107–21.

Dillon, Michele (2014) 'The Orphaned Irish: Church and State in Neo-liberal Ireland', in Mehran Tamadonfar and Ted G. Jelen (eds.), *Religion and Regimes: Support, Separation, and Opposition*, Lanham, Md.: Lexington Books, pp. 187–211.

—— (2015a) 'Secularization, Generational Change, and Ireland's Post-Secular Opportunity', in David Carroll Cochran and John C. Waldmeir (eds.), *The Catholic Church in Ireland Today*, Lanham, Md.: Lexington Books, pp. 45–64.

—— (2015b) 'Same-Sex Marriage Not Necessarily a Harbinger of Abortion Liberalisation', *Irish Times*, 9 July, available at www.irishtimes.com/opinion/same-sex-marriage-not-necessarily-a-harbinger-of-abortion-liberalisation-1.2278948 (accessed 19 August 2015).

Finnegan, David (2013) 'Irish Political Catholicism from the 1530s to 1660', in Oliver Rafferty (ed.), *Irish Catholic Identities*, Manchester: Manchester University Press, pp. 77–91.

FitzGerald, Garret (2003) *Reflections on the Irish State*, Dublin: Irish Academic Press.

Flanagan, Bernadette (2015) 'Contemplative Strands in Irish Identity', in David Carroll Cochran and John C. Waldmeir (eds.), *The Catholic Church in Ireland Today*, Lanham, Md.: Lexington Books, pp. 143–53.

Fuller, Louise (2002) *Irish Catholicism since 1950: The Undoing of a Culture*, Dublin: Gill & Macmillan.

—— (2006) 'New Ireland and the Undoing of the Catholic Legacy: Looking Back to the Future', in Louise Fuller, John Littleton and Eamon Maher (eds.), *Irish and Catholic? Toward an Understanding of Identity*, Dublin: Columba, pp. 68–89.

—— (2013) 'Identity and Political Fragmentation in Independent Ireland', in Oliver Rafferty (ed.), *Irish Catholic Identities*, Manchester: Manchester University Press, pp. 307–20.

Hannon, Patrick (2003) 'Legislation on Contraception and Abortion', in James P. Mackey and Enda McDonagh (eds.), *Religion and Politics in Ireland at the Turn of the Millennium*, Dublin: Columba, pp. 119–31.

Healy, Sean and Bridget Reynolds (2003) 'Christian Critique of Economic Policy and Practice', in James P. Mackey and Enda McDonagh (eds.), *Religion and Politics in Ireland at the Turn of the Millennium*, Dublin: Columba, pp. 185–97.

Hederman, Mark Patrick (2010) *Underground Cathedrals*, Dublin: Columba.

Hoban, Brendan (2012) *Where Do We Go from Here? The Crisis in Irish Catholicism*, Dublin: Banley House.

Hogan, Linda (2003) 'Interpreting the Divorce Debate: Church and State in Transition', in James P. Mackey and Enda McDonagh (eds.), *Religion and Politics in Ireland at the Turn of the Millennium*, Dublin: Columba, pp. 107–18.

Humphreys, Joe (2015a) '"Catholic First" School Admissions Policies May Be Illegal', *Irish Times*, 3 January, available at www.irishtimes.com/news/education/catholic-first-school-admissions-policies-may-be-illegal-1.2053401 (accessed 19 August 2015).

—— (2015b) 'Should the State Fund Religious Schools?', *Irish Times*, 27 January, available at www.irishtimes.com/news/education/should-the-state-fund-religious-schools-1.2075990 (accessed 19 August 2015).

Inglis, Tom (1998) *Moral Monopoly: The Rise and Fall of the Catholic Church in Modern Ireland*, Dublin: University College Dublin Press.

Kenny, Enda (2011) 'Speech on Cloyne Report', *RTÉ News*, 20 July, available at www.rte.ie/news/2011/0720/303965-cloyne1 (accessed 19 August 2015).

Kenny, Mary (2000) *Goodbye to Catholic Ireland: How the Irish Lost the Civilization They Created*, Springfield, Ill.: Templegate.

Keogh, Dermot (2007) 'The Catholic Church in Ireland since the 1950s', in Leslie Woodcock Tentler (ed.), *The Church Confronts Modernity: Catholicism since 1950 in the United States, Ireland, and Quebec*, Washington, DC: The Catholic University of America Press, pp. 93–149.

Kieran, Patricia (2008) 'Embracing Change: The Remodelling of Irish Catholic Primary Schools in the 21st Century', in John Littleton and Eamon Maher (eds.), *Contemporary Catholicism in Ireland: A Critical Appraisal*, Dublin: Columba, pp. 43–68.

Kirby, Peadar (2008) 'The Catholic Church in Post-Celtic Tiger Ireland', in John Littleton and Eamon Maher (eds.), *Contemporary Catholicism in Ireland: A Critical Appraisal*, Dublin: Columba, pp. 25–42.

Lane, Dermot A. (2003) 'Irish Christians and the Struggle for a Just Society', in James P. Mackey and Enda McDonagh (eds.), *Religion and Politics in Ireland at the Turn of the Millennium*, Dublin: Columba, pp. 214–27.

Larkin, Emmet (1984) *The Historical Dimensions of Irish Catholicism*, Washington, DC: The Catholic University of American Press.

Littleton, John (2015) '*In Periculo Mortis*: Can Irish Catholicism Be Redeemed?', in David Carroll Cochran and John C. Waldmeir (eds.), *The Catholic Church in Ireland Today*, Lanham, Md.: Lexington Books, pp. 17–33.

Maher, Eamon (2015) '"Faith of Our Fathers": A Lost Legacy?', in David Carroll Cochran and John C. Waldmeir (eds.), *The Catholic Church in Ireland Today*, Lanham, Md.: Lexington Books, pp. 3–16.

Maignant, Catherine (2008) 'The New Prophets: Voices from the Margins', in John Littleton and Eamon Maher (eds.) *Contemporary Catholicism in Ireland: A Critical Appraisal*, Dublin: Columba, pp. 90–110.

—— (2014) 'Church and State in Ireland (1922–2013): Contrasting Perceptions of Humanity', *Études Irlandaises*, 39:2, 63–77.

Martin, Diarmuid (2010) 'The Future of the Catholic Church in Ireland', Address at Ely Place, 10 May, available at www.dublindiocese.ie/2010/05/10/1052010-the-future-of-the-church-in-ireland (accessed 19 August 2015).

—— (2011) '"Keeping the Show on the Road": Is this the Future of the Irish Catholic Church?', Address to the Cambridge Group for Irish Studies, Magdalene College, Cambridge, 22 February, available at www.catholicbishops.ie/2011/02/22/address-by-archbishop-martin-to-the-cambridge-group-for-irish-studies-magdalene-college-cambridge (accessed 19 August 2015).

McDonagh, Enda (2003) 'Church-State Relations in Independent Ireland', in James P. Mackey and Enda McDonagh (eds.), *Religion and Politics in Ireland at the Turn of the Millennium*, Dublin: Columba, pp. 41–63.

McGarry, Patsy (2006) 'The Rise and Fall of Roman Catholicism in Ireland', in Louise Fuller, John Littleton and Eamon Maher (eds.), *Irish and Catholic? Toward an Understanding of Identity*, Dublin: Columba, pp. 31–46.

O'Brien, Eugene (2010) '"The Boat Had Moved": The Catholic Church, Conflations and the Need for Critique', in John Littleton and Eamon Maher (eds.), *The Dublin/Murphy Report: A Watershed for Irish Catholicism?* Dublin: Columba, pp. 90–101.

O'Conaill, Sean (2010) 'The Disgracing of Catholic Monarchism', in John Littleton and Eamon Maher (eds.), *The Dublin/Murphy Report: A Watershed for Irish Catholicism?* Dublin: Columba, pp. 74–81.

O'Hanlon, Gerry (2013) 'Re-building Trust: The Role of the Catholic Church in Ireland', in Patrick Claffey, Joe Egan and Marie Keenan (eds.), *Broken Faith: Why Hope Matters*, Oxford: Peter Lang, pp. 259–78.

O'Rourke, Maeve (2015) 'There's a New Generation of "Irish Catholics" in Ireland', *New York Times*, 20 May, available at www.nytimes.com/roomfordebate /2015/05/20/same-sex-marriage-and-the-future-of-irish-catholicism/theres-a-new-generation-of-irish-catholics-in-ireland (accessed 19 August 2015).

Oldmixon, Elizabeth A. and Brian R. Calfano (2015) 'Clerical Burnout and Political Engagement: A Study of Catholic Priests in Ireland', in David Carroll Cochran and

John C. Waldmeir (eds.), *The Catholic Church in Ireland Today*, Lanham, Md.: Lexington Books, pp. 65–80.

Penet, Jean-Christophe (2008) 'From Modernity to Ultramodernity: The Changing Influence of Catholic Practice on Political Practice in Ireland', in John Littleton and Eamon Maher (eds.), *Contemporary Catholicism in Ireland: A Critical Appraisal*, Dublin: Columba, pp. 44–87.

Rafferty, Oliver P. (2015) 'Irish Catholicism Can Adapt to a New Role', *New York Times*, 20 May, available at www.nytimes.com/roomfordebate/2015/05/20/same-sex-marriage-and-the-future-of-irish-catholicism/irish-catholicism-can-adapt-to-a-new-role (accessed 18 August 2015).

Roddy, Joan, Jerome Connolly and Maura Leen (2003) 'Human Rights Have No Borders: Justice for the Stranger at Home and Abroad', in James P. Mackey and Enda McDonagh (eds.), *Religion and Politics in Ireland at the Turn of the Millennium*, Dublin: Columba, pp. 198–213.

Taylor, Charles (1999) *A Catholic Modernity?* ed. James Heft, Oxford: Oxford University Press.

—— (2007) *A Secular Age*, Cambridge, Mass.: Harvard University Press.

Taylor, Lawrence (2007) 'Crisis of Faith or Collapse of Empire?', in Leslie Woodcock Tentler (ed.), *The Church Confronts Modernity: Catholicism since 1950 in the United States, Ireland, and Quebec*, Washington, DC: The Catholic University of America Press, pp. 150–73.

Twomey, D. Vincent (2003) *The End of Irish Catholicism?* Dublin: Veritas.

Whelan, Thomas R. (2013) 'Culture of Clericalism: Towards a Theological Deconstruction', in Patrick Claffey, Joe Egan and Marie Keenan (eds.), *Broken Faith: Why Hope Matters*, Oxford: Peter Lang, pp. 175–212.

Whyte, J. H. (1971) *Church and State in Modern Ireland, 1923–1970*, Dublin: Gill & Macmillan.

4

Refracted visions: Street photography, humanism and the loss of innocence

Justin Carville

In 1999, the Belfast-based design historian David Brett published a short pithy book on the influence of what Max Weber described as 'Protestant asceticism' on architectural design and material culture in post-Reformation Europe and North America (Brett, 1999; Weber 2002: 112–22). In the preface to the expanded second edition, Brett acknowledged that the original book was written in the context of the Troubles and his interest in the possibility of a scientific enquiry into the 'historical reality of a putative "Protestant culture"' (Brett 2004: 8). As he put it in the opening pages, 'the basic argument is simple. It is, in its barest form, that the propagation of imagery in any society is directly related to the dissemination of authority. Consequently, attempts to restrict imagery relate to changes in the extent, location and exercise of power' (Brett 2004, 13). For Brett, the materialisation of the authority of Protestant theology in the material and visual culture of a society, what he termed a 'Protestant aesthetic', was visible not only in the characteristics of the built environment, architecture and pictorial traditions but also in the destruction, removal and absences of imagery from everyday social life (2004: 9). Although Brett's historical and geographical area of focus was on post-Reformation European and North American material culture, a similar argument can be put forward regarding the relationship between Catholicism and Ireland's visual culture from the nineteenth through to the twenty-first century.

Numerous scholars have observed that despite the strong influence of Catholicism on Irish society, relatively little visual art or architecture has been shaped by its theological concepts to the same extent as in other predominantly Catholic societies (Turpin 2002: 252–66). Although Gesa E. Thiessen has explored the theological influence of Catholicism on modern Irish painting (1999), and artists have contributed to the pictorialisation of Catholic faith and devotion through painting, sculpture and stained-glass window design to adorn churches, Catholicism has not embellished Irish visual culture to an extent whereby it can be said to have shaped grandiose public visual statements. Its sphere of influence has largely been concentrated in everyday civic cultural forms of visual experience. The placement and orientation of church architecture in city suburbs, rural towns and villages may have 'proclaimed the importance of Catholicism in the life of rural Ireland, its centrality in the village, and the authority of its priests' (Bourke 1999: 7), but it has been with the visual spectacle of religious events and processions such as the 1932 Eucharistic Congress, and popular visual culture, that its aesthetic affects have been most influential (Boyd 2007).

This is not to say that Catholicism has not influenced Irish pictorial traditions; rather, its authority has not materialised as a visible presence that can be easily identified through its having a distinct aesthetic codification within Irish visual culture. This is due in part to the predominance of a literary culture in Irish society whose presence has cast a shadow over its visual culture. As Lelia Doolan has observed, Irish society is 'not as literate visually as we are verbally' (1984: 116), and Marie de Paor has contended that 'Native Irish culture survived in words and traditional music' (1993: 120). In fact, the perceived 'absence of a visual tradition in Ireland, equal in stature to its powerful literary counterpart', as Luke Gibbons once described it (1986: 10), has been central to debates on the identification of culturally differentiated practices of seeing and representation that may characterise a distinct Irish visual culture (Carville 2007, 2011; Dalsimer and Kreilkamp 1993; McBride 1984; McCole 2007).

However, there are two other interrelated reasons why the Catholic Church has not influenced Irish visual culture as much as may be expected, which have a bearing on the approach I wish to take to the relations of Catholicism and the visual explored in this essay. The first is that following the foundation of the State, instead of aesthetic embellishment and ostentatious visual statements, the spirituality and faith of a distinctly Catholic Irish society was perceived to be expressed through the 'social habits' and routines of community life (Fanning 2014: 48). Grand aesthetic statements in architecture and art were not required as Catholic faith was embedded in what Pierre Bourdieu identified as 'habitus', a system of 'durable, transposable dispositions' unconsciously played out and replicated in everyday life (Bourdieu 1990a: 53, 56).

The second is that modern forms of visual culture were looked upon with suspicion. To borrow a phrase from W. J. T. Mitchell's application of Jacques Derrida to the emergence of visual studies, visual culture was a 'dangerous supplement' to traditional cultural forms (Mitchell 2005: 340–1). Visual images were open to unregulated and unsanctioned readings and interpretations as well as being a vehicle for satire and the site of social critique and cultural dissent. In this essay, I want to explore these interrelated aspects of the relationship between Catholicism and visual culture through documentary humanism and street photography. Beginning with two examples of documentary humanism and street photography from the 1950s and the late nineteenth century, the essay then explores how David Farrell's street photographs from the mid-1990s and the first decade of the twenty-first century capture the decline of the Church in the routines and flow of everyday life that frequently gave expression to Irish society's Catholic spirituality and faith.

Documentary humanism and the picturing of faith

On 24 January 1955, the New York Museum of Modern Art (MoMA) launched its most ambitious photographic exhibition, *The Family of Man* (Steichen 1955). Conceived by the then director of the museum's Department of Photography, Edward Steichen, the exhibition was comprised of some 503 photographs from sixty-eight different countries. Its positive global message of Western humanism was matched by the breadth of its international contributors. The exhibition included the work of 273 photographers, the majority of whom were of American or Western European descent, including the Dublin-based photojournalist Charles C. Fennell, whose photographs were published in *Life* magazine during the 1950s. *Life*'s archives contributed significantly to the content and formal structure of *The Family of Man* exhibition, with the magazine's modernist layout of photographs across the printed page being replicated in the innovative display of images, many of which were suspended from the ceiling or arranged in three-dimensional configurations (Szarkowski 1994: 13). Described as being designed 'as an architectural as much as a pictorial experience' by Steichen's successor as director of the Department of Photography at MoMA, John Szarkowski, between 1955 and 1962 the exhibition was toured in a number of different versions across thirty-eight countries by the United States Information Agency. The globally toured exhibition was visited by an estimated 9 million viewers, and the exhibition catalogue remained in continuous print having sold nearly 4 million copies since its initial publication in 1955 (Sandeen 1995: 95; Szarkowski 1994: 13). The enduring cultural influence of *The Family of Man* in the popular consciousness of photographic culture is such that since 1996, the last remaining version of the exhibition has been on permanent display at Clervaux Castle in Luxembourg and in 2003 the exhibition in its entirety was inscribed in the UNESCO Memory of the World register.

Yet, despite being fêted in its current incarnation, *The Family of Man* exhibition has remained a touchstone for criticism of the hijacking of documentary humanism in the interests of 'American cold war liberalism' (Sekula 1981: 19). Steichen's curation of the exhibition's vast array of photographs drawn from the personal collections of photographers and the picture archives of popular pictorial publications such as *Look* and *Life* magazines, wrestled individual photographs from their cultural and historical contexts in the service of the exhibition's idealistic universal themes of love, marriage, childbirth, family, work, religious faith and death, leading one contemporary critic to comment that the exhibition was 'essentially a picture story to support a concept … an editorial achievement rather than an exhibition of photography in the usual sense' (Deschin, quoted in Szarkowski 1994: 14 and Warner Marien 2010: 314).

Clustered around quotations from the Bible, the Hindu scripture *Bhagavadgītā*, Navajo Indian sayings, verse and the final words of Molly Bloom's monologue that concludes James Joyce's *Ulysses* (a passage that opened the section on love), the photographs were uniformly mobilised by Steichen to illustrate *The Family of Man*'s one big idea: that the human condition is one, that all human life lives out its existence and actions in a unified pattern of behaviour. It was this direction of the viewer's attention by the exhibition's arrangement of photographs to the 'ambiguous myth of the human "community"', as Roland Barthes described it (1993: 100), which has led to such trenchant criticism of *The Family of Man* in the intervening years since its first iteration at MoMA in 1955 (see, for example, Berlier 1999; Phillips 1982; Sekula 1981; Solomon-Godeau 2004). Although there has been some recent critical revisionism of *The Family of Man* exhibition which has identified with its liberal approach to ameliorate divisions in post-Second World War Europe and the tensions of the Cold War (Stimson 2006; Turner 2012), the exhibition has not been able to escape the type of cultural critique that sees in its use of documentary humanism a deliberate attempt to mask historically grounded differences of race and class by 'treating the existing class-divided world as if it were a family' (Berger 1991: 60–1). As Susan Sontag succinctly put it, the exhibition's use of humanist documentary photography was directed towards an audience who wished to 'be consoled and distracted by a sentimental humanism' (1979: 32–3).

Ireland was only depicted in three of the *Family of Man*'s 503 photographs, and Fennell's photograph was included in the small 'inhumanities' section, ironically leaving the text of Joyce's Molly Bloom monologue as probably the most prominent Irish contribution to *The Family of Man* exhibition (the passage is reproduced at the beginning of the exhibition catalogue). However, Catholic Ireland featured in this sphere of documentary humanism that has been the subject of so much critical discourse on photography at exactly the same time that *The Family of Man* was to ensure the public's awareness of the capacity of this seemingly transparent style of photography to envision the world. In the same year, and within a few short weeks of *Life* magazine's extensive coverage of the exhibition's opening, American photographer Dorothea Lange's photo-essay *Irish Country Life* was published using the same modernist layout of the picture story replicated within the space of the modern art museum (Lange 1955).

Influenced by the Harvard anthropologist Conrad Arensberg's 1937 book *The Irish Countryman*, which observed how Catholicism was beginning to suppress the influence of older folk culture such as fairy lore on everyday social life (Arensberg 1937: 184–5), Lange travelled to Ennis in Co. Clare to produce what the editors described as a 'sympathetic look' at the 'culture of a bygone day' (Lange 1955: 1). Arensberg had noted how 'religious zeal' and 'fairy belief' frequently became intermeshed in everyday life without too much conflict but made the caveat that 'the Irish countryman is a very devout man. His life is ordered in his adherence to his religion. Much of his habit of mind and his view of the world responds to his Faith. He is a devout and practicing Catholic' (Arensberg 1937: 185).

The photo-essay, which was prepared by *Life's* editors, who sent journalists to Ennis with copies of photographs after rejecting Lange's proposal to publish the photographs without any captions or editorial commentary, included a double-page spread emphasising Catholicism's influence on the routines of social life. With the sub-headline, 'the quiet life rich in faith and a bit of fun' (see Fig. 4.1), the photographs depicted church-goers purposefully strolling to Sunday mass combined with an image of the congregation spilling out of an overcrowded St Mary's church. Linked by a tightly framed photograph of a child grasping a grandparent's hand, the accompanying editorial proclaimed, 'hands linked almost in symbol of the close family relationship of the country Irish ... [*sic*] ... At their elders' side in church, at games, in work and at the market the boys are shaped to Irish ways', and underneath the photograph of the overcrowded church the caption stated that the congregation was 'full of the faith that is forever a mark of the Irish' (Lange 1955: 142–3).

Figure 4.1   Dorothea Lange, Irish country people, *Life,* 7 March 1955. 'Untitled (People)', circa 1954 (A67.137.54031.7); *Sunday, Western Ireland,* 1954 (A67.137.54066.2); 'Untitled (Fairs and Markets), circa 1954 (A67.137.54194.11); *Church,* 1932 (A67.137.54227.9).

The combination of Lange's humanist photographic gaze at rural Irish life, combined with *Life*'s editorialised discourse of religious faith and familial relations, coalesced to draw the viewer's attention to the routine social structures that give expression to how enmeshed religious devotion is within everyday Irish life. The appeal of the photographs and the editorial discourse that pulls the separate photographs together as a cohesive pictorial narrative is grounded in its capacity to universalise and mask the historical specificity of the subjects that are depicted. Much like Arensberg's *The Irish Countryman*, which, as Adrian Peace has observed, pronounced of its object of study, 'their time is not Our time, and Their Space is not Our Space' (Peace 1989: 94), Lange's photo-essay depicts Irish society as spatially and temporally dislocated from the viewer it seeks to address (Carville 2009: 213). However, the discourse of documentary humanism during this period was always overtly directed towards the overemphasising of universalism and global appeal of shared, communal human characteristics. Thus, any cultural differences are veiled through a humanistic discourse of visual appearances that naturalise and harmonise what Bourdieu identifies as the 'group or class habitus' (1990a: 56), so that historical context and specificity are elided as an obstacle to the viewer's empathetic identification with the subject. Lange's photo-essay might then be read as a transparent reflection of the social structures that embody the close affiliation between Catholicism and the routines of familial and community life to the extent that it may not even be seen as a *representation* at all. This codification of humanist documentary photography's objectivity, its function in providing a window onto the world, combined with what Allan Sekula has described as the 'universal language myth' of capitalist photographic communication (1981: 21), presented the viewer with an idealised image of Catholic Ireland that very much corresponds with how Catholic sociology envisioned faith in Ireland as being 'sustained by social habits' that remained under constant threat from urban modernity (Fanning 2014: 49).

In a close analysis of the role of Catholic sociology in the envisaging of the State from the 1930s to the 1970s, Bryan Fanning has observed that although Ireland has never been a theocratic state, the relationship between the two allowed for the Church to function as an 'ecclesiastical dictatorship' that paralleled the political democracy of the fledgling state (Fanning 2014: 51). In the 1950s, as Catholicism came under pressure due to social change, Fanning identifies how sociologists such as the Revd Jeremiah Newman, concerned about the decline of the influence of Catholic morality on Irish society, advocated legislative measures to defend Irish society against growing secularism. As he observes, Newman believed 'that spiritual life and individual faith were sustained by social habits that could be damaged by removal from a society within which religious norms prevailed. Urban life and the impersonal social structures of modernity made community intangible and faith difficult' (Fanning 2014: 49). Lange's photo-essay, with its attention focused on rural Ireland and the timeless condition of familial and communal relations oriented around the church, offered a comforting image of Catholic Ireland that corresponded with this envisioning of the routine expression of Catholic faith.

The influence of Catholicism on the social structures of rural Ireland may have been a clear signifier of difference between *Life*'s urban, cosmopolitan readers and the Irish subjects represented in the photo-essay. However, Lange's visual articulation of rural Irish life through the lowbrow aesthetic of documentary humanism (Bourdieu 1990b: 80), cemented in the public imagination by the *Family of Man* exhibition, combined with the editorial rhetoric of the harmony between religious faith and familial relations, contributed to the normalisation of the image of Ireland as a Catholic nation. As Brian Fallon has observed of this period, 'nothing impressed, repelled or simply puzzled intelligent visitors to the country so much as the atmosphere of religion which seemed all-pervading' (Fallon 1999: 183), but as a way of seeing the world, the humanistic codification of Lange's photographs depicted this pervasive characteristic that bound communities together as a positively benign feature of Irish society.

Street photography and social critique

The representation of Irish Catholicism in Lange's humanist documentary photographs presented the viewer not only with an opportunity to see how faith was enmeshed in the social fabric of familial and communal relations but also to feel it. Cold War documentary humanism was, after all, a 'way of feeling the world directly' as well as knowing it (Sekula 1981: 21). In this context, it is important to see this particular example of the global representation of Irish religiosity through the prism of documentary humanism as historically situated. Documentary humanism is not an ontological or semiotic categorisation of photography but rather a historical one. What Barthes identified as the codification of the 'myth of photographic 'naturalness': the scene *is there*, captured mechanically, not humanly' (1977: 44), distracts attention away from the ideological imperative and historical context of documentary humanism through which Lange's photographs generated much of their meaning.

As with Sontag's criticism of the use of documentary humanism in *The Family of Man* exhibition, photography allowed the viewer 'to be consoled and distracted by a sentimental humanism' (Sontag 1979: 33), the photographs unapologetically illustrating a universal *feeling* of faith and community filtered through Catholic social life rather than conveying the inequities and social realities of life in 1950s Ireland. In many respects, the benign image of Catholic Ireland depicted through Lange's humanist approach to photographing Irish society, is a betrayal of the earlier documentary forms that sought to draw attention to the inequities and social contradictions evident in capitalist social life. It is not that the humanist documentary of the 1950s was any more or less *real* than earlier or later uses of documentary photography; rather, in its naturalising of the types of patterns of social life such as those depicted in Lange's photographs of Catholic devotion, it usurped its own ability for social critique in favour of the sentimentalisation of everyday life in post-Second World War Europe (Hamilton 1997).

Some five decades earlier than the dominant visual regime of the sentimental documentary humanism of the 1950s, the barrister and anti-clerical social commentator Michael J. F. McCarthy utilised photography in the spirit of exploring social contradictions of Catholicism's influence on everyday life in his 1902 publication *Priests and People in Ireland* (1902). McCarthy was not a photographer himself but had used photographs by others in several previous publications such as *Five Years in Ireland, 1895–1900* (McCarthy 1900), to give visual expression to what he saw as the precipitous reconstruction of Irish social life by the rise in influence of the Catholic Church which he identified as an organisation that 'outnumbers the services of the imperial and local governments combined' (McCarthy 1902: xii–xiii).

In an accompanying author's note to the photo-montage frontispiece of a large Catholic church looming over a small rural village (Fig. 4.2), McCarthy states:

> while it is, of course, an ideal picture intended to emphasise a contrast which strikes every student of life in Roman Catholic Ireland, still it is only ideal in part. The church is a real church, expensive and ostentatious it is true, but not exceptionally so for Ireland; the village is real one, not many miles away from the church, and is not, by any means, an exceptionally wretched village. (McCarthy 1902: xi)

McCarthy's brief note on the frontispiece demonstrates a critical awareness of the tensions between the *real* (indexical) and *constructed* (pictorial) conditions of photographic communication which he utilised to foreground the social contradictions of Catholicism's effects on secular aspects of Irish society. Using street photographs taken by Arthur T. Ellis, McCarthy populated the pages of *Priests and People in Ireland* with photographic images of everyday social life accompanied by short passages from his own scathing commentary on what he identified as Ireland's distinctive version of Catholicism's pervasive influence on all spheres of Irish society. He termed this version of Catholicism 'Priestcraft': 'the interference and domination of the priest in the social and secular concerns of the people by virtue of his profession' (McCarthy 1902: 7).

Accompanying two street photographs of one of Dublin's poverty-stricken districts (Fig. 4.3), a text reads, 'the priests avoid the poor as if they were infected' and 'The inhabitants of this poor street are not often honoured by a visit from priest or nun … [*sic*] Nor would a poor parishioner, when in trouble, dare to accost his parish priest' (McCarthy 1902: 336–7). Accompanying a set of photographs of poor street children, another passage comments: 'The opening of a new oratory in honour of the divine child, Jesus of Prague will not serve these poor children' and 'What would Jesus think of the condition of the poor Roman Catholic children of Dublin if He were to reappear on earth to-day?' (McCarthy 1902: 376–7).

" And, were Magee alive to-day . . he might truly exclaim as he beheld the golden column of priest-money rearing its shameless yellow crest, &c." (p. 148).

Figure 4.2   Frontispiece from Michael J. F. McCarthy, *Priests and People in Ireland*, 1902.

In his portrayal of religion in Ireland, McCarthy combined text and image in a very different configuration to that utilised by the documentary humanism of *The Family of Man* and *Life* magazine's portrayal of religious faith in Ireland through Lange's photographs. Instead of drawing on a combination of lowbrow aesthetics and discursive construction of photographic naturalism to portray the

Figure 4.3 Arthur T. Ellis, *Dublin Poor, Priests and People in Ireland*, 1902.

image as a transparent reflection of everyday life, a window onto the world as it were, McCarthy's use of photograph and text contributes to a reflexive awareness of how photographic meaning is constructed. It is apparent from his commentary on the frontispiece that McCarthy was aware of photography's capacity to convey an ideological message, and his use of photography throughout the book serves to foreground the social contradictions of the influence of Catholic priests on Irish society that could not be rendered visible through the pretence of the photograph as a transparent reflection of everyday life. The types of contradictions that he observed in his survey of Catholicism's growing reach into the secular dimensions of Irish society were visibly imperceptible and impossible to encapsulate within the limitations of a single photograph. Thus, McCarthy had to create a friction between the indexicality of photographic realism and the subjective rhetoric of the text to envision the social realities of Catholicism in the everyday routines and lives of the Catholic poor.

A more recent example of street photography, which pursues this relationship between Catholicism and everyday life to draw out the contradictions of religion and secular society as a form of social critique are a series of largely unpublished and un-exhibited photographs by David Farrell. However, Farrell's visual articulations of the erosion of the bonds between the Catholic Church and everyday social life are not evident through the friction of photograph and text but by wrestling its visible presence from the ebb and flow of everyday life. A number of these photographs have been exhibited at the Royal Hibernian Gallery in the exhibition *Before, During, After ... Almost* as part of a commissioned response to 1916 and its cultural legacy, and are drawn from Farrell's personal archive of over twenty-five years of street photography. The configuration of the photographs as a collective body of work is intentionally drawn from disparate phases of Farrell's work as a photographer, with photographs from several projects dealing with the post-conflict search for the disappeared, *Innocent Landscapes* (Farrell, 2000), the decline of Catholicism and the aftermath of the Celtic Tiger (Carville 2014).[1]

Farrell has also been deliberately ambiguous in the captioning of the photographs, the absence of locations and dates a strategy to liberate the photograph from the burden of documentary certainty, with the title, 'sometime in the early nineties', frequently the only caption attached to photographs. Unlike the documentary humanism of the 1950s that anchored photographic meaning through captioning and discursive editorial commentary, the ambiguity of Farrell's photographs leaves them open to alternative interpretations and understandings beyond the didactic depiction of what is within the pictorial space of the photograph. This ambiguity allows the photographs' potential for social critique to emerge as their lack of historical specificity requires the viewer to complete the work of interpretation, leaving space for individual perspectives, prejudices and histories to fill the void between the ill-defined temporal moment of the photograph's taking and the contemporaneous moment of looking.

The chronological scope of Farrell's photographs covers an Irish society on the cusp of the emergence of the Celtic Tiger through to its spectacular collapse, a period identified as witnessing the 'moral authority' of the Catholic Church becoming increasingly 'eclipsed by materialism and consumerism', in addition to successive scandals on the moral and criminal conduct of the clergy (Keohane and Kuhling 2005: 1). If the collision between the Catholic Church and secular society during this period was structured by new forms of 'reflexive' or 'accelerated' modernisation (Keohane and Kuhling 2005: 5), the inevitable shock of the impact is not immediately visible in Farrell's photographs. The critical effect of Farrell's assemblage of discrete photographic moments wrestled from the flow of everyday social life lies not in their contemporaneous immediacy but in their delayed exposure of a social world on the precipice of dissolving into an uncertain future.

In the photograph *Priest's Graveyard, All Souls Day, Inchicore, Dublin, Some Time in the Early Nineties* for example (Fig. 4.4), the robed figures strolling among the numbered Celtic-cross headstones in quiet contemplation now appear in the hindsight and retrospection of the intervening period's questioning of the Church to be themselves lost souls wandering aimlessly in separate directions, an allegory of the fate of late twentieth-century Irish Catholicism. The impact of this image is not only in the moment of its taking, the instantaneous realisation on the part of the photographer that this particular time and place was in itself significant. Rather, it is also in the latency of the photograph and its capacity to reveal slowly what may not have been immediately perceptible to the eye that provides its potency as a form of social critique.

In his essay on the French poet Charles Baudelaire, Walter Benjamin observes that 'of the countless movements of switching, inserting, pressing, and the like, the "snapping" of the photographer has had the greatest consequences. A touch of the finger now sufficed to fix an event for an unlimited period of time. The

Figure 4.4   David Farrell, *Priest's Graveyard, All Souls Day, Inchicore, Dublin, Sometime in the Early Nineties.*

camera gave the moment a posthumous shock, as it were' (Benjamin 1992: 171). Benjamin's understanding of the 'posthumous shock' of the camera was a recognition of its capacity to retain the past moment as a fragment whose return in the present has the potential to awaken historical consciousness of that past moment as being on the precipice of disappearing.

As a latter-day or late twentieth-century *flâneur*, Farrell's photographs of this period constitute a highly concentrated series of fragments of social change in which the routines of Catholic expressions of faith in everyday life are wrestled from the ongoing passage of time and suspended within the frame of the photograph. This suspended moment conceals, but only temporarily, the 'posthumous shock' of the disappearance of the normative appearance of Catholicism in the shaping of the everyday routines of Irish social life.

The most striking examples of this are a series of photographs of public expressions of Catholic devotion and religious protest that rupture the visual appearance of the seamless immersion of Catholicism in the routines of Irish social life such as envisioned in the humanist documentary photography of Lange. If documentary humanism produced a consoling visual appearance of Irish Catholicism for a national and global viewer who wished to be moved by the extent to which religious devotion was embodied in the outward appearance of community life, Farrell's photographs of expressions of faith and devotion provide a more troubling perspective of the place of Catholic religiosity in late twentieth-century Ireland.

In the photograph *Good Friday, Ballymun, Some Time in the Early Nineties* for example (Fig. 4.5), a male figure carries a crucifix made out of mass-produced hardwood timber and cast-iron bolts against the backdrop of the high-rise concrete structures of the Ballymun housing estate. There is an obvious irony in this image, as Ballymun was the first modern urban housing development undertaken by the State, which coincided with the fiftieth anniversary of the Easter Rising and the naming of tower blocks after the signatories of the 1916 Proclamation (Kincaid 2006: 117–19). Constructed using mass-produced prefabrication of concrete to accelerate the completion of the project, Ballymun was intended as a symbolic marker of national modernisation and the shift from a rural towards an urban society; precisely the type of social engineering that Fanning identifies as of concern to Catholic sociologists who feared urban modernity's secularising effect on the routines, habits of expressions of faith and religious norms of everyday Irish life (Fanning 2014: 49). Despite the intention to establish Ballymun as a symbol of mid-twentieth-century Irish modernity, however, it has ultimately come to be symbolic of the failure not only of the application of brutalist architectural style to social housing but also of the fledgling state to adequately support the formation of communities through their own pursuit of radical social change.

Farrell's photograph conveys the alienating effects of the rational spatial configurement of the built environment of the housing estate through the skewed organisation of the pictorial space of the photograph. The rectilinear structure of

Figure 4.5   David Farrell, *Good Friday, Ballymun, Some Time in the Early Nineties.*

the tower blocks that obscure the horizon line and crucifix are pictorially out of kilter, and the camera's framing of the scene truncates the body of the figure carrying the crucifix and the crucifix itself to amplify the oppressive atmosphere of the built environment. With the rectilinear lines of the tower block and crucifix pulling in opposite directions, the skewed formal qualities of the photograph thus function to portray the scene of Catholic devotion as disjointed and out of place.

If Lange's documentary humanist photography succeeded in the portrayal of Catholic religiosity being in harmony with the routines of everyday life, Farrell's evidences a dissonance between the rituals of Catholicism and its place within late twentieth-century urban space. This sense of discord between public expressions of Catholic devotion and the observable quotidian moments on the city's streets and suburban housing estates is evident throughout Farrell's ambiguous photographs of everyday social life from the 1990s, with photographs such as *Outdoor Confession, Blessing of the Graves Ceremony, Dublin Sometime in the Early Nineties* and *Dublin, Sometime in the Early Nineties* (Figs. 4.6 and 4.7) giving visual expression to the social contradictions within the relations between religion and the transformation of Irish social life. However, Farrell identifies the disconnection between the Church and Irish society not through the dramatic and traumatic experiences that defined the nation's increased secularisation but in the quiet, humdrum and sometimes monotonous routines of everyday social relations of religious ceremonies and acts of faith. This portrayal of an Irish society that is

Figure 4.6 David Farrell, *Outdoor Confession, Blessing of the Graves Ceremony, Dublin Sometime in the Early Nineties.*

Figure 4.7 David Farrell, *Dublin, Sometime in the Early Nineties.*

slowly changing, turning by degrees towards the consumerist culture and secularisation that caused so much anxiety to Catholic sociologists who foresaw how urban modernity would erode the social habits that made Catholicism such a visible presence in everyday life, is a particularly evocative depiction of social change precisely because of its gradual, posthumous revelation of the erosion of the bonds between the Church and late twentieth-century Irish society.

Conclusion

In his outline of the theory of habitus, Bourdieu uses the term 'bodily hexis' to describe how the subjectivity of the individual combines with the cultural sphere of social life in which they participate in the embodiment of habitus: 'bodily hexis is political mythology realised, *em-bodied*, turned into a permanent disposition, a durable way of standing, speaking, walking, and thereby of feeing and thinking' (Bourdieu 1990a: 69–70; italics in original). The concept of bodily hexis not only demonstrates the significance of the body to Bourdieu's theory of habitus but also, more significantly in the context of this essay, it reinforces that the gestures, postures, deportment and movements of the body such as those associated with the routines of expressions of Catholic faith are not objective mimetic representations of learned cultural practices but, rather, enactments of the past. As he states of the difference between conscious repetition of routine actions and the unconscious disposition of the body in social spheres of interaction, the body 'does not represent what it performs, it does not memorise the past, it *enacts* the past, bringing it back to life. What is "learned by body" is not something that one has, like knowledge that can be brandished, but something one is' (Bourdieu 1990a: 73; italics in original).

It is this sense of the body as inseparable from the routines of expressions of Catholic faith and devotion in everyday life that much of the Church's authority in Irish society throughout the twentieth century was derived. As noted at the start of this essay, grand visual statements were not required by the Catholic Church in Ireland as the authority and legitimacy of Catholicism in the collective consciousness of the nation was embedded within the thoughts and bodily actions of the people, in their disposition and feelings towards each other and the physical environment in which they interacted with one another. The mid-century humanist documentary photography of Lange transparently reflected this vision of Catholicism as woven into the corporeal and social fabric of Irish everyday life. To borrow from Bourdieu's concept of 'bodily hexis', Catholicism is portrayed as not something one has, but something one is.

The use of street photography by McCarthy at the dawn of the twentieth century in *Priests and People in Ireland*, and Farrell's street photographs at the century's end, suggest, however, that this sympathetic view of Catholicism as woven into the fabric of everyday social life was deeply contrived. If the photographic form of humanist documentary evidenced an empathetic gaze on the pattern of faith and devotion embedded within the group or class habitus, Farrell's photographs offer a more cynical gaze of the place of Catholicism within late twentieth-century social change. While McCarthy's use of photography is clearly contemptuous of the influence of Catholicism in secular life, Farrell's vision is a more subtle articulation of this relationship. Their force as a form of social critique lies in their ability to quietly puncture the popular image of the role of Catholicism in the progressive movement to ameliorate the anxieties of social change through the everyday visible signs of the erosion of the bonds between religion and secular life.

Note

1 The Disappeared refers to the conflict in Northern Ireland where a number of people were killed by the Provisional IRA and their bodies were buried in unmarked graves. These people, some of whose bodies have not yet been found, have been given the collective name of 'the disappeared'.

Works cited

Arensberg, Conrad (1937) *The Irish Countryman*, New York: Macmillan.

Barthes, Roland (1977) 'The Rhetoric of the Image', in *Image, Music, Text*, trans. Stephen Heath, London: Fontana, pp. 32–51.

—— (1993) 'The Great Family of Man', in *Mythologies*, trans. Annette Levers, London: Vintage, pp. 100–2.

Benjamin, Walter (1992) 'On Some Motifs in Baudelaire', in *Illuminations*, trans. Harry Zohn, London: Fontana, pp. 152–96.

Berger, John (1991) *About Looking*, New York: Vintage.

Berlier, Monique (1999) '*The Family of Man*: Readings of an Exhibition', in Bonnie Brenan and Hanno Hardt (eds.), *Picturing the Past: Media, History and Photography*, Urbana, Ill.: University of Illinois Press, pp. 206–41.

Bourdieu, Pierre (1990a) *The Logic of Practice*, trans. Richard Nice, Cambridge: Polity.

—— (1990b) *Photography: A Middle-Brow Art*, trans. Shaun Whiteside, Cambridge: Polity.

Bourke, Angela (1999) *The Burning of Bridget Cleary: A True Story*, London: Pimlico Press.

Boyd, Gary (2007) 'Supernatural Catholicity: Dublin and the 1932 Eucharistic Congress', *Early Popular Visual Culture*, 5:3, 317–33.

Brett, David (1999) *The Plain Style: The Reformation, Culture and the Crisis of Protestant Identity*, Belfast: Black Square Books.

—— (2004) *The Plain Style*, 2nd edn, Cambridge: Lutterworth Press.

Carville, Justin (2007) 'Introduction: Popular Visual Culture in Ireland', *Early Popular Visual Culture*, 5:3, 229–30.

—— (2009) 'A "Sympathetic Look": Documentary Humanism and Irish Identity in Dorothea Lange's "Irish Country People"', in James P. Byrne, Padraig Kirwan and Michael O'Sullivan (eds.), *Affecting Irishness: Negotiating Cultural Identity Within and Beyond the Nation*, Oxford: Peter Lang, pp. 197–217.

—— (2011) *Photography and Ireland*, London and Chicago, Ill.: Reaktion and University of Chicago Press.

—— (2014) 'Topographies of Terror: Photography and the Post-Celtic Tiger Landscape', in Eamon Maher and Eugene O'Brien (eds.), *From Prosperity to Austerity: A Socio-cultural*

Critique of the Celtic Tiger and Its Aftermath, Manchester: Manchester University of Press, pp. 103–18.

Dalsimer, Adele M. (ed.) (1993) *Visualizing Ireland: National Identity and the Pictorial Tradition*, London: Faber and Faber.

Dalsimer, Adele M. and Vera Krielkamp (1993) 'Introduction', in Adele M. Dalsimer (ed.), *Visualizing Ireland: National Identity and the Pictorial Tradition*, London: Faber and Faber.

de Paor, Máire (1993) 'Irish Antiquarian Artists', in Adele M. Dalsimer (ed.), *Visualizing Ireland: National Identity and the Pictorial Tradition*, London: Faber and Faber, pp. 119–32.

Doolan, Lelia (1984) 'A Debate on Media and Popular Culture', *The Crane Bag*, 8:2, 175–95.

Fallon, Brian (1999) *An Age of Innocence: Irish Culture, 1930–1960*, Dublin: Gill & Macmillan.

Fanning, Bryan (2014) 'A Catholic Vision of Ireland', in Tom Inglis (ed.), *Are the Irish Different?* Manchester: Manchester University Press, pp. 44–53.

Farrell, David (2000) *Innocent Landscapes*, Stockport: Dewi Lewis.

Gibbons, Luke (1986) 'Alien Eye', *Circa*, 12, p. 10.

Hamilton, Peter (1997) 'Representing the Social: France and Frenchness in Post-war Humanist Photography', in Stuart Hall (ed.), *Representation: Cultural Representations and Signifying Practices*, London: Sage.

Inglis, Tom (ed.) (2014) *Are the Irish Different?* Manchester: Manchester University Press.

Keohane, Kieran and Carmen Kuhling (2005) *Collision Culture: Transformations in Everyday Life in Ireland*, Dublin: The Liffey Press.

Kincaid, Andrew (2006) *Postcolonial Dublin: Imperial Legacies and the Built Environment*, Minneapolis, Minn.: University of Minnesota Press.

Lange, Dorothea (1955) 'Irish Country People', *Life*, 7 March 1955.

McBride, Lawrence W. (ed.) (1984) *Images, Icons and the Nationalist Imagination*, Dublin: Four Courts.

McCarthy, Michael (1900) *Five Years in Ireland, 1895–1900*, Dublin, Hodges, Figgis & co., Ltd.

—— (1902) *Priests and People in Ireland*, Dublin: Hodges Figgis.

McCole, Niamh (2007) 'The Magic Lantern in Provincial Ireland, 1896–1906', *Early Popular Visual Culture*, 5:3, 247–62.

Mitchell, W. J. T. (2005) *What Do Pictures Want? The Lives and Loves of Images*, Chicago, Ill.: University of Chicago Press.

Peace, Adrian (1989) 'From Arcadia to Anomie: Critical Notes on the Constitution of Irish Society as Anthropological Object', *Critique of Anthropology*, 9:1, 89–111.

Phillips, Christopher (1982) 'The Judgment Seat of Photography', *October*, 22 (autumn), 27–63.

Sandeen, Eric (1995) *Picturing an Exhibition: The Family of Man and 1950s America*, Albuquerque, N. Mex.: University of New Mexico Press.

Sekula, Allan (1981) 'The Traffic in Photographs', *Art Journal*, 41:1, 15–25.

Solomon-Godeau, Abigail (2004) 'The Family of Man: Refurbishing Humanism for a Postmodern Age', in Jean Back and Viktoria Schmidt-Linsenoff (eds.), *The Family of Man, 1955–2001: Humanism and Postmodernism – A Reappraisal of the Photo Exhibition by Edward Steichen*, Marburg: Jonas Verlag, pp. 29–57.

Sontag, Susan (1979) *On Photography*, London: Penguin.

Steichen, Edward (1955) *The Family of Man*, New York: MoMA.

Stimson, Blake (2006) *The Pivot of World: Photography and Its Nation*, Cambridge, Mass.: MIT Press.

Szarkowski, John (1994) 'The Family of Man', *The Museum of Modern Art at Mid-Century: At Home and Abroad*, New York: MoMA.

Thiessen, Gesa E. (1999) *Theology and Modern Irish Art*, Dublin: Columba.

Turner, Fred (2012) 'The Family of Man and the Politics of Attention in Cold War America', *Public Culture*, 24:1, 55–84.

Turpin, John (2002) 'Modernism, Tradition and Debates on Religious Art in Ireland 1920–1950', *Studies: An Irish Quarterly Review*, 91:363, 252–66.

Warner Marien, Mary (2010) *Photography: A Cultural History*, 3rd edn, London: Laurence King.

Weber, Max (2002) *The Protestant Ethic and the Spirit of Capitalism and Other Writings*, London: Penguin.

5

Contemporary Irish Catholicism: A time of hope!

Vincent Twomey

So-called traditional Irish Catholicism is largely the product of historical and cultural processes in the eighteenth and nineteenth centuries, as I have tried to point out in *The End of Irish Catholicism?* (Twomey 2003). It had many weaknesses. However, it also had many strengths. New religious orders, such as the Irish Christian Brothers, the Presentation and Mercy Sisters, were founded in the eighteenth and nineteenth centuries by remarkable men and women such as Blessed Edmund Rice, the Venerable Nano Nagle and Catherine McAuley. They were augmented by the newly founded Continental congregations, male and female, that came into Ireland in droves. They were devoted to education, health care and concern for the poor. Equally astonishing was the rich devotional life that marked former generations at home and abroad in Britain, USA, Australia and New Zealand, not to mention the missionaries who went to every part of the world. Clerics were prominent in almost every level of civic society. With mass attendance of around 90 per cent, huge numbers of vocations, the educational, health-care and social-care systems being run by the Church (financially and administratively this was much to the advantage of the State), the Irish Catholic Church was a political force to be reckoned with – and politicians knew this, and, with some notable exceptions, respected it. Their own Catholic faith deepened that respect, even when more evident political motivations were present. At a time when, as a nation, we had no real political representation, the Irish Catholic Church created a sense of identity and dignity both collective and personal. To be Irish was to be Catholic, and this was even more true for people living abroad than at home.

Today, this Catholic identity is largely (and understandably) repudiated, not least because of the horrendous abuse of children, revealed initially by the media and then, with added authority, by the various reports of the government commissions set up to investigate the scandals. Traditional Irish Catholicism, for all its former achievements, which were considerable, had, by the middle of the twentieth century, clear intrinsic weaknesses, such as the absence of a critical philosophical/theological spirit: it also had a very dark side as well. Reacting in shock to the publication of the Ryan Report into abuse in state industrial schools run by religious, I wrote the following lines in the *Irish Catholic*:

> The Report [...] describes a reign of terror, where evil had become endemic. [...] Traditional Irish Catholicism exuded a sense of superiority, an arrogance that now beggars belief; we considered ourselves superior to all others. No one could teach us anything. In addition, we had a society steeped in petty snobbery, so that priesthood and religious life easily became a status symbol, while those at the bottom of the pile (the indigent poor, the parentless, farm labourers, petty thieves, etc.) were seen by Church, State and Society as non-persons – just numbers. Clerics and religious were all-powerful. They were above suspicion – and they knew it. They could act without fear of retribution. Human weaknesses of the flesh – including machismo and sadism rooted in a frustrated sexuality due to repressive Puritanism and no real vocation or spiritual training – were often combined with spiritual arrogance and narrow-mindedness. [...] The result was the perversion of Our Lord's injunction: 'Suffer little children to come unto me' (Mk 10:13). (Twomey 2009)

The Ryan Report was so shocking because it revealed what most people living in the 1950s and 1960s suspected was happening but had done nothing about. There were critics, such as Frank Duff, founder of the Legion of Mary, who protested. In 1946, after visiting some of the industrial schools in Ireland, Fr Edward Flanagan, founder of Boys Town, Omaha, Nebraska, gave a public lecture in Cork. He condemned these institutions as 'a scandal, un-Christlike, and wrong'. He accused his audience, in effect, of collaboration in the evil done. Ireland's penal institutions, he said, were 'a disgrace to the nation'.[1] During a debate in the Dáil, the Minister for Justice at the time, Gerald Boland TD, dismissed these criticisms as 'so exaggerated that I did not think people would attach any importance to them'.[2] After this authoritative judgement, silence prevailed – including, it seems, that of the journalists of the day. The most damning silence was that of the Church.

Fr Flanagan, on his return to America, said, 'What you need over there is to have someone shake you loose from your smugness and satisfaction and set an example by punishing those who are guilty of cruelty, ignorance and neglect of their duties in high places ... I wonder what God's judgment will be with reference to those who hold the deposit of the faith and who fail in their God-given stewardship of little children'. The media must be given credit for loosing us all from our smugness. And we also have some inkling of what God's judgment has been ... and yet that is only part of the story.

The Church's major strength in the past was the ability of so many faithful, nurtured by devotions such as the Rosary and the Stations of the Cross, to endure the slings and arrows of outrageous fortune (including those inflicted on them by clerics and religious), which can only be faced if one has learned to live with the acceptance of suffering and live rooted in a source that transcends the human sphere. Their faith provided them with a spirituality that was life-giving, that enabled people to live with an upright conscience and that was the ultimate source of that general sense of security that prevailed in Ireland up to the 1960s, despite economic hardship. Hope accepts the reality of the cross in our lives. But it knows at the same time that tribulation is not the last word. This awareness of the transcendent, the inner joy and confidence about future victory enable people to endure the worst. This was summed up in the phrase used in adversity: no matter what happens, 'Ah sure, God is good.' That spirituality, for example, provided the grit needed by impoverished Irish to thrive in the harsh conditions of forced emigration. It is the source of true hope and, paradoxically, inoculates people against fatalism by giving them the inner strength to overcome immediate difficulties. By way of contrast, the impression I get today is a growing inability of many contemporaries to accept and cope with the reality of suffering, as a result of which so many seek the escapist outlets we are all too familiar with: drugs, excessive drink, suicide. Already we see the shadow of euthanasia about to darken the country in the shape of the call for assisted suicide.

Economic and social changes in Ireland since the 1960s have been both radical and extensive. The transformation from a depressed economy to one of the most vibrant in the world was spectacular. It was accompanied by a renewed sense of our own identity as a people, one that is no longer linked to religion. Even though the economic bubble burst in 2008, there are signs of recovery, an achievement that has astonished many. Prosperity, no matter how welcome, inevitably gives rise to consumerism with its attendant spiritual impoverishment.

Our new self-confidence as a nation is in stark contrast with the increasing phenomenon of alienation, lack of trust in public institutions of Church and State, growing insecurity (especially on the part of the aged living alone) in the face of increasing robberies and violence and the various forms of escapism and breakdown of civilised behaviour that are creating a black hole in society. The dimming of conscience is the prelude to the police state. Security is one of the growth industries as people try to protect themselves from external threats and attacks. And yet the paradox is that, according to various European Value Surveys, we seem to be the happiest people in Europe, which is hard to square with what seems to be the slow-motion collapse of the social fabric – unless it tells us something about a factor that is rarely credited with much influence in public nowadays, namely the still more or less vibrant faith and spirituality of so many ordinary Irish people who make up the highest percentage of regular Sunday mass-goers in Western Europe.

The so-called 'Troubles' in Northern Ireland tainted the reputation of both Irish nationalism and Irish Catholicism, which were once so closely identified. The Good Friday Agreement and its aftermath in Northern Ireland coincided with the spectacular achievements of our sporting heroes at home and abroad.

The result has been a new-found recovery of Irish nationalism. The tricolour is again worn with pride. To foster a new sense of identity, this time secular (glorifying the State), the Irish Army is now touring schools to instruct the children on respect for the flag, evidently copying the American model. The state visits of the Queen of England to Ireland and of the President of Ireland to the UK also helped redefine our identity. The peacekeeping achievements of our army and police in various parts of the world, the spectacular success of highly educated Irish men and women in all fields of endeavour abroad (especially in the EU) and the remarkable worldwide aid work of such NGOs as Goal, Concern and Trócaire have all contributed to a renewed pride of place and people.

Significantly, the religious dimension of these Catholic aid agencies has faded into the background as they become in effect secular NGOs, despite their appeal to Catholics for funds, such as Trócaire's Lenten appeals, which are themselves spiritually dubious (as in using the liturgy for ideological purposes). This is all part of the secular Irish state coming of age. How did this come about? The recent scandals alone cannot explain it. It seems to this writer that the cause may be cultural in nature.

Though the majority are Catholic by birth, the general trend among our contemporaries is that of being assimilated into the dominant Anglo-Saxon world of Britain, America and Australia, thanks largely to our spoken language: English. The ethos that characterises Irish public discourse is largely determined by the mores and values of the Anglo-Saxon modern world, which is secular and liberal in outlook. The younger generation in particular, who in effect set the cultural agenda, are at home in the fast, upwardly mobile, world of business and professional life. They are articulate, charming and, even within the sphere of the flourishing world of art and sport, are forging a new identity at home and, more spectacularly, abroad. In Ireland, they tend to be found mostly in the larger urban areas, but their values have also penetrated rural Ireland, where they are even more effective because of the felt need of rural youth to be 'with it'.

What happened to the once-dominant cultural and social force that was Irish Catholicism? In a word, its inherent weaknesses were laid bare in the wake of the Second Vatican Council. The trouble is that the Irish Church was unprepared for the council – and its reception by the Church in Ireland was, at best, patchy. Although the changes introduced by the Council were all obediently implemented, the confidence of the Irish clergy in what they had once accepted so uncritically as being the unchanging truth was undermined. The confused state of Catholic theology after the council – and this was not unique to Ireland – exacerbated the situation. Everything was questioned, and few clergy felt up to the task of even understanding the questions, not to mention giving convincing answers to them. Various referendums on moral issues (abortion, divorce and more recently the redefinition of marriage) revealed a clergy that seemed to be uncertain of its stance and so incapable of firm leadership or persuasive arguments. Religious education went into a tailspin – and is still spiralling downwards.

The once-Catholic teacher-training colleges – still under the patronage of the local bishops – have been radically secularised for some time. The results of all of this was summed up in an article in the *Irish Times* (10 November 2015): 'Religious education: "I don't know anybody who teaches the RE requirement"' – a statement by a primary school teacher, who requested to remain anonymous. This is probably an exaggeration, but it is not without some plausibility, not least considering the atrocious RE programme for primary schools, Alive-O. The National Council for Curriculum and Assessment has begun 'to develop a national curriculum for Education about Religions and Beliefs (ERB) and ethics' (National Council for Curriculum and Assessment 2015). Even though Professor John Coolahan, chair of the Forum on Patronage and Pluralism, which proposed the idea, claims that all children will benefit from it, formation in the child's Catholic faith will in time be replaced by information about world religions and (presumably) secular ethics. Already, RE in secondary schools offers at best an introduction to world religions – without the pupils knowing anything substantial about their own faith. In a word, Irish schoolchildren will be systematically introduced to a superficial taste of all religions. The net result can only be religious indifference at best, total scepticism at worst. Commenting on ERB, Kevin Myers wrote, 'The march towards a secular Ireland of unprincipled values and value-free principles proceeds' (2015). The Church cannot blame the State for this. We created a catechetical vacuum that the State is filling. John Coolahan claims that the ERB and ethics programme 'was intended not least for children who received no religious education at all and as preparation for living in a modern democracy' (McGarry 2015). The intention is noble. The need for religious education and ethics is real. However, the means being proposed are at best questionable since democracy is based not on secular ethics but on a well-formed personal conscience, rooted in moral courage that responds to the moral demands of our God-given nature as created beings.

A humanist or secular ethics, which seems to be what is being proposed, may offer some help for a while, thanks to the Judaeo-Christian values it has inherited, but it is also open to being used by various ideologies and bogus 'rights'. In addition, without a grounding in faith, a secular ethics is destined to end in subjectivism ('I do what I feel is right because I feel it'). The end result will be, to quote Kevin Myers: 'The bland will lead the blind in our cultural suicide' (2015). It is part of that process of the radical secularisation of Europe that, in the long run, can only lead to Europe's self-destruction – and the possible realisation of Michel Houllebecq's dire predictions in his most recent novel, *Submission* (2015), that France (followed by the rest of secular Europe) will in time meekly submit to the only vibrant religious force in Europe: Islam. People cannot live for long without some form of religion.

Faith is caught and taught in the family, augmented by the school, and nourished by active participation in the Christian sacraments and regular attendance at mass and other religious exercises (such as pilgrimages). The council's liturgical reforms, however necessary in themselves, were carried out in a way that impoverished the celebration of the mass, the very core of Irish Catholic spirituality, and practically wiped out traditional devotions, once the lifeblood of Irish Catholic life. In more recent years, the scandals caused first by a bishop being found to have fathered a son, followed by multiple revelations of abuse of the most horrific nature by clerics and religious and the covering up of all this at the highest levels, did untold, long-term damage.

And yet again, it never fails to astonish me that so many Irish Catholics have actually remained faithful to the 'faith of our fathers'. Despite the fact that its liturgical celebrations are devoid, with notable exceptions, of either inspiration or beauty, the Irish Church, as mentioned already, still has the highest percentage of mass-goers in Western Europe. The greatest strength of the Irish Church is thus the faith of those laity and clerics who have remained faithful, despite everything. Another strength is the extraordinary charitable instinct, the sheer humanity of most people, coupled with smooth efficiency. Their concern to alleviate hunger and distress throughout the world makes such agencies as Trócaire, Concern and Goal among the most active in the universal church and beyond. These NGOs are in the tradition of the extraordinary, if unsung, missionary endeavour of the past century. There is no area of distress in the world where you will not find Irish men and women, religious and lay, deeply involved in relief efforts from Outer Mongolia to South Sudan.

Is the Catholic Church in Ireland viable today? The institutional Church is eternally viable, in so far as it is sacramental by nature. And it is important to recall this, since it is too easy to reduce the Church to a merely human institution dependent on human effort. The Church as the primordial sacrament, as taught by Vatican II, also works *ex opero operato*, that is to say, by the grace of God. This means that the weakness of the clergy cannot prevent God working out his plan of salvation in the hearts of the faithful.

The same does not apply to the human substructure (dioceses, parishes, religious orders) built on the sacramental order of bishop, priest, deacon and faithful. Much attention of late has of necessity been given to formulating an adequate legal and pastoral response to sexual abuse cases, with the result that Ireland now has possibly the most stringent guidelines in the world – and the mechanisms to achieve their effectiveness. Ireland has also suffered from one of the weaknesses of the new prominence given to episcopal conferences worldwide, namely the tendency of individual bishops to hide behind the anonymity of the conference, thus failing to act autonomously as bishops and so failing to give leadership. Among other things, the desire not to rock the boat, not to lose popularity, has made the Church here, as elsewhere, rudderless.

Hopefully, this is about to change, thanks to the appointment of a whole raft of younger priests as bishops to dioceses other than their own. It will take time for them to get to know their new dioceses, to build up the morale of their clerics and lay co-workers and to conceive courageous pastoral initiatives.

Their task is unenviable. The recent referendum redefining marriage revealed rather dramatically the actual state of Irish Catholicism. One positive aspect of the 'No' campaign was the fact that individual bishops actually wrote pastoral letters in their own person to their own diocese in the final weeks of the campaign. (The anonymous statements by the Episcopal Conference had been ignored.) The individual pastoral letters were too little, too late. People had made up their mind, not least thanks to the five-year long, hugely funded, sophisticated publicity campaign on the 'Yes' side. It is significant that some 60 per cent of mass-goers in Dublin and 50 per cent in the rest of Ireland voted 'Yes'.

And yet, the potential of the Irish Church for renewal is enormous. Only lately has the Church began to tap into it. For almost three decades, I have had the privilege of teaching seminarians and young Catholic laymen and women of ability, genuine idealism and sincere commitment to their faith. The Irish Church has as yet little idea of how to use that talent, or indeed the talent and experience of older generations of laity and clergy and of how to channel and direct it to find ways and means of renewing the Christian life in the cities and in the countryside. In every area of life – literature, the arts, music, business, technology and politics – we have produced world leaders. The one exception is religion. And the reason is simple: we have lost our primary focus, the holiness (or true happiness) of all.

As in any area of life – medicine, agriculture, science and technology, economics – research is the source of new ideas. In Church terms, this means theological and philosophical research. Yet, although we had a number of impressive individual theologians of international repute, there is no serious tradition of theological research in Ireland, nor are there any centres of specialised scholarship, and what theology there is finds little resonance within the broader Church membership. Theology was (and still is) largely limited to training seminarians and catechists. Until this situation changes, the Irish Church will not be able to tap into its own potential.

The recent closure of All Hallows College (founded by the Vincentians in 1842 to provide diocesan priests for the missions) and the Jesuit Milltown Institute of Theology and Philosophy (whose faculty of theology has an unbroken history going back to 1889) marks the end of an era. Both had produced theologians of international standing. Their closure is a huge loss, not least in terms of fostering a keen theological edge among its students. The past fifty years saw the closure, one after the other, of all the diocesan seminaries: Carlow, Kilkenny, Thurles, Waterford, Wexford and Clonliffe (Dublin), which, since 1782, trained thousands of priests for service at home and abroad in the English-speaking world. In addition, the missionary seminaries training an equal number of priests specifically for the 'foreign missions' in Asia, Africa and Latin America closed their doors in the same period, not to mention the colleges run by the numerous religious orders (Franciscans, Vincentians, Redemptorists, Passionists, etc.) who went down the same route. The Dominicans are the exception in that they have reopened their *Studium Generale* in Dublin. The only full faculty of theology (with research resources) left standing is that of St Patrick's College, Maynooth, the national seminary. That is not a healthy situation.

Creative theology is not simply a scholarly discipline. It must be rooted in a living faith. Theology is faith-seeking understanding. And here the prospects are more encouraging. For years, prayer groups have sprung up in many parishes. Other signs of Church renewal, and they are many, include the many pastoral initiatives being undertaken by some dioceses, and by parish priests in cooperation with lay co-workers, some of whom are trained in theology. At present, a new movement has begun in various dioceses to provide a theological introduction to the Catechism of the Catholic Church at parish level, which means that adults are at last getting some systematic instruction in the truths of revelation. Other signs of hope for the future include the many young people who are beginning to encounter Christ through such movements as Youth 2000, the Legion of Mary, Focolare, Communion and Liberation, Neocatechumenal Way, the Fraternity of St Genesius. One must not overlook the potential of the Catholic Grandparents Association for the renewal of the Church in Ireland. It was the Russian grandparents (the *babushkas*) who kept alive the flame of faith in the long dark winter of the Soviet Union.

When the faith is again awakened in the younger generation, who are at present like sheep without a shepherd, then Irish theology will perhaps be reborn. But there is also a need for scholarly institutes that can provide the technical know-how to enable theology to find its true expression. A start has been made by the Priory Institute, Tallaght, run by the Irish Dominicans, and Maryvale Institute, Birmingham, which offer long-distant courses in theology; though their numbers are down somewhat, they are attracting an impressive number of students.

The recent withdrawal of state funds from Accord, the Catholic pre-marriage preparation provider, is to be welcomed. To the best of my knowledge, those courses were practically devoid of Catholic teaching on faith, morals or spirituality; they had become purely horizontal in their orientation. Accord would seem to be no longer fit for mission. The 2015 Synod of Bishops on the Family stressed that more attention should be given to authentic Christian preparation for marriage. In England, an impressive programme for serious pre-marriage courses and post-marriage accompaniment has been devised by experienced married couples, often grandparents, who have lived their marriage in harmony with the Catholic vision and who themselves give the courses.

The withdrawal of funds from Accord is to be welcomed for another reason. It might signal the beginning of what Pope Benedict XVI in Freiburg im Breisgau (25 September 2011) called the *Entweltlichung der Kirche*, a decisive end to the Church's cosy relationship with (indeed, dependence on) the State, in other words, the practical disestablishment of the Church. The effect of the State's initiative concerning Accord on the Church should be to learn to exist and minister as far as possible independently of state support, relying on its own spiritual and material resources. Since the majority of citizens are Catholic, and the State has obligations to provide certain services for all citizens (82 per cent Catholic!), such as education and health care, this can never be a total independence. Cooperation will be required, but without our losing that which is distinctively Catholic and Christian. For some years, there has been an intensive debate about the patronage of primary schools, the majority of which are under Catholic patronage.

If the report on the teaching of RE in primary schools mentioned above reflects the actual situation, then that alone should be sufficient reason for the Church as a whole to do what Archbishop Diarmuid Martin of Dublin has long advocated: namely to divest itself of as many schools as possible (presumably to whatever bodies the parents should form to educate their children). The Church's objective should be to support those schools that reflect a Catholic vision, namely schools that put Jesus Christ at the centre and where principals and schoolteachers witness to Christ in their lives; for those who cannot attend real Catholic schools, faith formation outside the school system (at home and in the parish) needs to be promoted. Divesting itself of nominally Catholic schools could be the occasion for constructive negotiations with the State for a new relationship between Church and State that should find its expression in a concordat between Ireland and the Holy See.

Divesting itself of schools that are Catholic only in name is only the first step. Other steps towards a real disestablishment should include the end of the role of clerics as solemnisers of marriages – not only because of the present legal redefinition of marriage but also as an end to last vestige of the established status of the Church (which we inherited from the Anglicans). Likewise, the faithful should be discouraged from contributing to the national church-gate collections for political parties. Similarly, there should be no special seats for the president or members of government at any church functions, such as episcopal ordinations. The list goes on. The purpose of this *Entweltlichung* is not for the Church to withdraw to the private sphere – that would be sectarian and would go against the mission of the Church – but rather to renew itself so that it can be more active in transforming political life through committed laity, who are inspired by their faith.

The mission of the lay faithful, as the Council taught, is primarily in their daily lives and in their chosen professions, including politics and economics. Václav Havel (1984) warned politicians not to leave their conscience in the bathroom when they are called to make decisions affecting the common good – and, we may add, the deepest human issues of life and death, of marriage and the family, of justice and peace. Catholics should take a lead here but are conspicuous by their absence *qua* Catholics among politicians. On the other hand, the Catholicism of Irish politicians (in particular in rural constituencies) seems largely to manifest itself primarily by attendance at funerals and by organising national church-door collections (despite adopting policies that contradict Church teaching). Even politicians are beginning to acknowledge that the party whip is far too stifling. It curbs real debate, the stuff of democracy.

Moral courage is notable by its absence, especially the courage to speak the truth when it is unpopular, to go against the party line on matters of genuine principle (rather than for political expediency). The result is a cynical attitude to politicians and lack of involvement in politics by the general populace. The recent defiance of the party whip by some TDs and senators in the Bill allowing for abortion and the policy of an alliance of some independent TDs and senators, which has resolved not to have a party whip, might betoken a change of attitude in the long term. For that to happen, it seems to me, broad agreement among all parties about what fundamental social issues should be given a free vote, even when proposed by the government of the day, without seeing a possible rejection as the equivalent of a no-confidence motion. Such issues should possibly include all constitutional amendments, since effectively the legislators are in such cases no different, constitutionally, from other citizens.

Corruption is a moral issue. No ethical guidelines or judicial tribunals will help eradicate it, though they may alert public consciousness for a while. In the long run, they will only make its practitioners more devious and more difficult to detect. All the wisdom traditions of humanity agree that the cultivation of virtue, otherwise referred to as personal integrity, is the only solution to corruption, wherever it is found. Trust is restored only if people are perceived to be trustworthy. Trustworthiness is based on personal integrity or virtue. The acquisition of virtue presupposes many things – not least a stable family life and the witness of upright parents and teachers, who provide the optimal conditions within which virtue can normally flourish, since virtue is primarily caught, not taught. Healthy families, in turn, need healthy local environments, where a genuine sense of community, including a sense of common identity, is experienced, and where people acquire a sense of their own dignity and irreplaceable role in life. Not only bad planning dictated by the avarice of property developers but also the absence of any genuine local political communities responsible for their own destinies must surely have also contributed to a sense of rootlessness and alienation – and so of broken homes and violence – that is on the increase.

It is rarely acknowledged that the separation of religion and politics, Church and State, is rooted in the New Testament, and forms the foundation of Catholic social teaching. Nevertheless, a secular state cannot be understood as an option for atheism. As Dostoevsky said, if God does not exist, then anything is possible in society. This was demonstrated dramatically in the twentieth century when expressly atheist states like Nazi Germany, Marxist Russia and Communist China wreaked havoc on their own citizens. Atheism is, in the long run, not an option for a healthy state or a healthy democracy – not even the Irish version, which is to act in public life as though God does not exist and, in the name of pluralism, to favour a vocal minority who call themselves secularist or even atheist.

As the German Supreme Court Justice Böckenförde once pointed out, the modern or pluralist democratic state lives off resources which it cannot provide of itself. These are the religious and moral resources of a people. Chief Rabbi

Jonathan Sacks made a similar comment in recent years, as indeed de Tocqueville confirmed in his observations on the significant role played by mostly Protestant communities in American democracy. In Ireland, it is the Catholic Church, which has traditionally supplied the greater part of those resources. In the past, there were good reasons for politicians to distance themselves from the Church – like the undue influence of the Catholic hierarchy on politicians in the years after Independence and, more recently, the fear of being seen to be 'ruled from Rome'. But the time has come to take a more mature look at the way the Church and State need each other, each not only respecting the due autonomy of the other but also recognising the need for the other. The trouble is, as a colleague once pointed out to me, that while most modern Irish people know they need the State, they are not so convinced they need any church, especially not the Church they have come to know over the past fifty years. The challenge facing the Church is precisely that: to convince people of its *bona fides* by responding to their deepest spiritual longings and intellectual searching.

But above all, the State needs a vibrant church, humbly self-confident in the truth that is entrusted to it, the truth that alone can set us free – and gives us hope to face the future with confidence. There are some signs of a renewal of that vibrancy. To begin with, I would point to the new generation of students, both lay and clerical, who are swimming against the tide and opting for the study of theology. Then there are the thousands of other young Catholics who have discovered the excitement of the adventure of faith and are beginning to form different movements. We have today a small but growing cohort of articulate Catholics in all walks of life, ready and able to enter into public debate – and they are increasingly gaining public respect. Up and down the country, older people are hungry for theological and intellectual nourishment, and some are turning to read theology late in life. The growing presence of immigrants, Catholics from other countries and cultures, is an enrichment, making the Church less parochial, more universal or Catholic. Already immigrant families are beginning to supply vocations. Finally, the majority of older people, clerical, religious and lay, are the main source of hope. They have remained faithful despite the recent turmoil and scandals. Their suffering and their endurance will in the future bear much fruit.

And yet, we have still to heed Pope Benedict XVI's call to repentance in his Letter of the Catholics of Ireland, which, on the whole, was received with some resentment. He pointed out that the Church needs to be purified through penance. That was a call to be humble, which is not easy to hear and is even harder to implement. The first step in the process of penance is a humble recognition of past misdeeds, and a frank examination of the ethos that nurtured them, as revealed, above all, in the Ryan Report on the industrial schools and reformatories. The phenomenon of the industrial schools/reformatories reflected most dramatically the negative aspects of the prevailing Catholic ethos at the time which, for good reason, is rejected today by so many of our contemporaries. Nevertheless, we also need to make long-term public amendment for past misdeeds, perhaps in the

form of a stipulated day of communal public penance (fasting and abstinence) during Lent each year. With regard to the industrial schools, reformatories and Magdalene laundries, a public museum (perhaps at a location such as Artane, where one of the most notorious industrial schools was located), documenting what actually went on would ensure that the future generations would not forget the victims. The most apt response would be the foundation of a contemplative community dedicated to making reparation in perpetuity for the sins of former generations of priests and religious – like the Carmelite convents set up just outside Dachau concentration camp.

Catholics must also contribute to forging a New Ireland. There is an urgent need for the benefit of both Church and State, for independent Catholic academies in the main cities along the line of those found in Germany – minus their massive buildings and bureaucracy – which would promote ongoing dialogue with politicians, civil society and the arts about every aspect of our life together, past and present. Neither Catholic theology nor philosophy pretends to have answers to the practical problems – that is precisely the remit of politicians – but theologians and philosophers do have access to a tradition of wisdom to help foster ongoing systematic reflection on the human questions that often underlie these practical problems. Catholic academies, it is to be hoped, could inspire the vision that Ireland needs, and that alone can help us solve what at present seem to be the insoluble problems of a society that, despite its new-found prosperity (or because of it), seems to be imploding spiritually and morally before our eyes today.

In the absence of such wide-ranging debate, Irish society will be at the mercy of well-intentioned attempts by centralised government to engage in social engineering, often following politically correct agendas advocated by various vocal minorities or lobbies that enjoy the active support of a sympathetic media. There appear to be few serious differences between the political parties, and so there is little serious, reasoned political debate. Academies might provide the occasion for that debate – and they should be Catholic in the most all-embracing way, i.e. not exclusive to the Catholic Church.

Hope is at the core of the Good News, the Gospel ('So your faith and love are based on what you hope for', Col 1:5). Hope is not optimism, which, like its contrary pessimism, is either an emotional state or a personality trait. Neither is usually justified by a sober appreciation of real life in all its ambiguity, fragility and transitory nature. Unfortunately, we in Ireland tend to oscillate between optimism and pessimism when we try to estimate the state of the nation. Hope is based on truth (the recognition of the world as it is), coupled with the God-given capacity to endure and be triumphant over all present ills, personal or social; it is marked by a deep joy and a capacity to smile in the midst of trials.

But, first of all, Catholics at every level must seek to catch the imagination of modern Ireland. At present, that imagination is dominated by images making fun of the Church, as in the TV series *Father Ted*, or, more widespread, images of the dark side of traditional Irish Catholicism, now being used subliminally in the present campaign to repeal the Eighth Amendment protecting the life of the unborn. The Irish Church once invested heavily in the world of the media, in the shape of the Catholic Communications Centre, Booterstown and Kairos Communications. Such investment is needed today more than ever to proclaim the Good News in contemporary Ireland. In the sphere of the media, there are also some hopeful signs, such as the ecumenical Spirit Radio (88.9 FM), Radio Maria Ireland (DAB licence) and Kildare and Leighlin's iCatholic (social-media outlet).

We also need to discover anew what it means to be Christian and so to recover a sense of gratitude about being Catholic in a way that finds expression in works of art, literature, music, drama and film. The Church needs also to celebrate the great achievements of the past and find inspiration in them. The failure of the Irish Church to promote the beatification of Irish men and women of heroic sanctity – like the Venerable Catherine McAuley, Nano Nagle, Mother Mary Martin or the Columban missionary martyrs in China and Korea – betokens an alarming disinterest in holiness, the Church's *raison d'être*. Moreover, we must rediscover the importance of public Church festivals (the old pattern days), pilgrimages on foot to local shrines and celebrations both liturgical and social in the heart of the local community, the diocese and the nation. Joy needs to be experienced communally, and this can only be when we have a reason to celebrate, to affirm the goodness of life and to give thanks to God for his great works in the lives of his people.

Above all, we need to engage in the huge task of re-evangelising the nation, starting with the cities. The Irish Church has been primarily rural-based; the cities as cities received little pastoral attention in the past. The cities, especially the university cities, are where the future of the nation is forged. The Early Church directed its missionary attention to the cities: Antioch, Alexandria, Rome, Corinth. Though we may be reluctant to admit it, secularised Ireland has become mission territory, and its main mission territory is to be found in the city. Europe provides many models of such re-evangelisation, such as the Court of the Gentiles in various cities, the Communities of Jerusalem in Paris, Strasbourg, Brussels, etc., and the manifold activities of the Academy of Evangelisation founded by a lay Catholic movement in Vienna. In this context, the Loyola Institute (a recently established department of Catholic theology in Trinity College, Dublin) is a sign of hope. According to its mission statement, it aims to 'to reflect academically on Christian faith, social justice and contemporary culture in the context of the Catholic tradition and our central concern is the creative intersection of theology, Church and society'.

Taking his cue from Dostoevsky, Alexander Solzhenitsyn affirmed in his Nobel Prize Lecture that, when truth and goodness are smothered in society, then beauty will save the world. For the Church, that means above all that the liturgy, especially the Sunday mass, must become a taste of Heaven on earth, of the transcendent in our midst, an experience of the 'other world' that enables us to take up our humdrum daily tasks and absorb the setbacks of this world with renewed interior energy.

The re-evangelising of Ireland also calls for the beauty of lived Christianity: everyday sanctity. Only in the personal encounter with Jesus Christ can hope enter into our world. The effective collapse of traditional Irish Catholicism has laid bare the ground for the renewal of the Church in Ireland, and with that renewal, the inner transformation of society.

It is a time of hope.

Notes

1 *Irish Times*, 16 October 2003, available at http://www.irishtimes.com/opinion/letters/compensation-scheme-for-abuse-1.384227 (accessed 22 September 2016).
2 *Irish Times*, 16 October 2003, available at http://www.irishtimes.com/opinion/letters/compensation-scheme-for-abuse-1.384227 (accessed 22 September 2016).

Works cited

Böckenförde, E.-W. (1982) *Staat-Gesellschaft-Kirche*, Freiburg: Herder Verlag.

European Values (2016) *European Values Survey 1981–present*, available at www.europeanvaluesstudy.eu (accessed 28 November 2015).

Havel, Václav (1986) 'Politics and Conscience', in Jan Vladislav (ed.), *Living in Truth: Twenty-Two Essays Published on the Occasion of the Award of the Erasmus Prize to Václav Havel*, London: Faber, pp. 136–63.

Houellebecq, Michel (2015) *Submission*, trans. Loren Stein, London: William Heinemann.

McGarry, Patsy (2015) 'Efforts to Divest Schools "Disappointing", Says Forum Chairman', *Irish Times*, 10 November.

Myers, Kevin (2015) 'The Bland Will Lead the Blind in Our Cultural Suicide', *Sunday Times*, 8 November.

National Council for Curriculum and Assessment (2015) *Education about Religions and Beliefs (ERB) and Ethics in the Primary School: Consultation Paper*, available online at http://www.ncca.ie/en/Curriculum_and_Assessment/Early_Childhood_and_Primary_Education/Primary-Education/Primary_Developments/ERB-and-E/Developments/Consultation/Consultation-ERBE.pdf (accessed 22 September 2016).

Sacks, Jonathan (1991) *The Persistence of Faith: Religion, Morality and Society in a Secular Age – The Reith Lectures*, London: Bloomsbury.

Solzhenitsyn, Alexander (1973) *Nobel Prize Lecture*, trans. Nicholas Bethell, London: Stenvalley Press.

Tocqueville, Alexis de (2000) *Democracy in America*, trans. George Lawrence, ed. J. P. Mayer, New York: Perennial Classics.

Twomey, D. Vincent (2003) *The End of Irish Catholicism?* Dublin: Veritas.

—— (2009) 'The Ryan Report', *The Irish Catholic*, 28 May, p. 10.

PART II
Going against the tide

6

The poetry of accumulation: Irish-American fables of resistance

Eamonn Wall

Writing on Eiléan Ni Chuilleanáin's poetry, Andrew J. Auge, in a devastating piece of reportage, describes the recent change that has taken place in the reputation and role of Irish Catholic Church: 'by the turn of the millennium, the once imposing edifice of Irish Catholicism appeared increasingly derelict' (Auge 2013: 145). Given all we have learned from reports into how the Church has dealt with abuses committed by its clergy and cover-ups initiated by its hierarchy, it seems quite fitting that a once proud edifice and standard-bearer would appear increasingly derelict. No longer is Sunday mass the centrepiece of the Irish week; instead, many Catholics flock to shopping centres and malls. In elegantly lined and nicely marbled halls, shop assistants pass credit-card receipts to consumers while in old cathedrals and cold churches priests look forlornly across the pews and know how easy nowadays it is to count the number of worshipers who will receive communion. Auge, like many Irish-American writers and scholars in recent decades, provides timely and nuanced explorations into the role and influence that the Catholic Church has played, and continues to play, in Irish life. Looking towards Ireland from the USA, Irish-American Catholic intellectuals, guided by their own traditional upbringings and by American notions of egalitarianism and individual freedom, help us see the past and imagine the future of Irish Catholicism more clearly.

Because of the Church's horrific acts and reluctance to admit wrongdoing, its insistence on moving priests from parish to parish to hide abuses, its refusal to listen to distraught parents, its arrogant disregard for the law, many Irish Catholics have turned their backs on the institution so that the Church has now become a ceremonial rather than a vital entity in Irish life. Nevertheless, the Catholic Church is still possessed of elegant rituals and structures, and these continue to give formal shape to baptisms, weddings and funerals – many of the key events in people's lives. Even if the Church has lost its place in the hearts of many Irish people, it has retained through its elaborate ceremonies much of its symbolic power. Perhaps more than symbols, these solemn rites continue to serve as the meeting places of body and soul, reality and imagination, our lives on earth and in the great beyond. Even at a moment in history when the Church has lost its appeal, its cultural legacy retains much that is potent and important even to its sharpest critics.

In a wonderful essay, 'Getting Here from There: A Writer's Reflections on a Religious Past', Mary Gordon, whose first novel *Final Payments* infuriated traditional American Catholics when it appeared in 1978, reflects on the many-sided role that her Catholic upbringing played in her formation as woman and writer:

> Those names come very easily to my mind – names learned in childhood, memorised in childhood. They form one of those lists, those catalogues that made the blood race with the buildup. So many catalogues there were in the church I grew up in, so many lists: seven capital sins, three theological virtues and four moral ones, seven sacraments, seven gifts of the Holy Ghost. A kind of poetry of accumulation, gaining power like an avalanche from its own momentum. (Gordon 1991: 160–1)

In addition to faith and integration into a community, the Church provided systems and a phenomenology that gave substance to Gordon's world, 'a poetry of accumulation' that would serve as a starting and testing point for her life as an adult. Two important aspects of her cultural upbringing that Gordon highlights are the global and the local, and their interplay:

> so to be a Catholic, or even to have been one, is to feel a certain access to a world wider than the vision allowed by the lens of one's own birth. You grew up believing that the parish is the world, and that anyone in the world could be a member of the parish. But of course, the parish was a fiercely limited terrain: the perfect size and conformation for the study of the future novelist. (Gordon 1991: 163–4)

Part of the Church's cultural legacy, locally and globally, is a doctrine of inclusiveness, although this has been tempered, as Gordon is quick to point out, by exclusion as a consequence of social class and gender, among other factors. The rooting of the Church in the small unit of the parish, and vice versa, indicates the degree to which the Church has remained true to Irish and Irish-American attachments to, and feelings for townland, village, town and city neighbourhood. In this scenario, the relationship between Church and worshipper is organic. Also, as Gordon believes, the Church's international aspect provides its faithful with contact to a wider world. At some level, the ideal version of the Church is a local and global one rather than a national one. It would hardly be an exaggeration to claim that part of the Church's legacy is the invention of community itself.

Ultimately, Gordon finds for herself everything that is attractive and honourable in the Church to be deposited in individuals and groups and these direct us to the deepest legacy of Catholicism: people who profess to be Catholics:

> I'm in a queer position: the Church of my childhood, which was so important for my formation as an artist, is now gone. As Gertrude Stein said of Oakland, 'There is no there there'. But there *is* something there, something that formed me and that touches me still: the example of the nuns killed in El Salvador, of liberation theologians standing up to the Pope, of the nuns – the 'Vatican 24' – who signed the statement asserting that it was possible for Catholics to have different positions on abortion and still be Catholics. These sisters, many of them in their sixties and seventies, faced the loss of everything – their sisterhood, their community, their lives, and things we wouldn't think of, like their medical insurance. They had no Social Security; they had no pension plans; they faced literally being thrown out on the street. They are extraordinary women. (Gordon 1991: 175)

There are at least two important elements in this discussion. First, that the Church through its theology and individual and collective action by its believers has long preached the importance of resistance to injustice. As Gordon points out, this injunction continues to be taken seriously by Catholics even when it entails resistance to the Church itself. Liam Ryan, an Irish priest and sociologist, noted that the hierarchy should pay close attention to such resistance from women, remarking that 'male geriatric dictatorship may well have been what finally toppled Communism in Eastern Europe' (O'Toole 1998: 73).

A second element is the role that women have played and continue to play in the Church and their embrace of the faith. Women serving as nuns, Mary Gordon and others have pointed out, have played the roles of carers, teachers, doctors and nurses, and they have often been fearless leaders. Gordon reminds us that a church that welcomes everyone does not treat everyone with equality. Implicit in her argument is the positive legacy of nuns that should be widely imitated so that the Church can retain something of its soul. As a woman, and an author, and an individual from an Irish-American background, Gordon has been quick to speak out, and her voice is an influential one. She writes that 'the Catholic Church in America is the Irish Church. And the Irish Church is a church that is obsessed and committed to the idea of keeping silence' and that while the Irish will love to talk to you they 'don't like to tell you anything' (Gordon 1991: 174). Today, many brave people who suffered terrible abuse have spoken out and bravely resisted silence. John McGahern took a similar route in 1965 when he published *The Dark* and was driven from his job as a teacher for being so honest. However, to speak out belongs, at least in part, to Catholicism's cultural legacy.

In Ireland, Catholic religious practices incorporate belief systems derived from two traditions – the pre-Christian and the Christian – so to dismiss them would be to invent a specious reality. Also, in both the USA and Ireland, the drift of worshippers away from the Church predates the reporting of abuse and had been a consequence of the Church's resistance to modernisation and the voices of its flock, as Maureen Dezell has noted of the USA:

> The impression from the outside is that a splendid and sanguine American Catholic Church started hemorrhaging in the 1960s and had yet to stanch its bleeding. Attendance at Mass has fallen off dramatically among practicing Catholics, including some nuns who are dissatisfied enough with the pastorate that they conduct their own Eucharistic services. Catholics live together before marriage and receive the Eucharist – a mortal sin compounded by a sacrilege, according to Baltimore Catechism standards. Nine of ten reject the Church's position on artificial birth control; Catholics' attitudes on abortion are indistinguishable from those of Protestants. A majority disagree with Vatican teachers on divorce, clerical celibacy, the ordination of women, homosexuality, and the role of the laity – and 80 percent of those see no conflict ignoring Church teaching and being good Catholics. (Dezell 2001: 163–75)

Interviewed by Dezell, Monsignor Kelley of Sacred Heart Parish in Roslindale, Mass., put it another way: 'men got back from the war, they went to college', and 'by the sixties and seventies, priests and nuns who'd once had a free hand were now preaching to people who were as educated as they were if not more so' (Dezell 2001: 175). In *The Irish Americans: The Rise to Money and Power*, Fr Andrew M. Greeley provides a cultural history of Irish America that is engaging and irreverent. On one level, he surmises that Irish Catholicism, as it has developed in both Ireland and the USA, lost much of its energy by separating itself from its Celtic past and agreeing to be subservient to Rome. Greeley points out that women once enjoyed a greater degree of sexual freedom in the early Church and that practices that are not allowed by the Church nowadays, such as the ability of clergy to be married, were available in earlier times. Slyly, Greeley reminds us that the cultural legacy is a long one and the further back one goes the more complex it becomes. Nowadays, we have been trained to think of the Church as being a post-Cardinal Cullen phenomenon whereas, in fact, a much different, and a looser, church existed for centuries before the nineteenth century. Greeley, too, pins his faith in the parish and notes that Fr Theodore M. Hesburgh, a former president of the University of Notre Dame, a man whom he much admired, was 'still a parish priest who also happen[ed] accidentally to be a university president' (Greeley 1981: 161). Like Gordon, Greeley places much hope in the lower clergy, in the brilliant but modest priest, in the ordinary Catholic, rather than in the hierarchy. It is among these classes where the Church's true legacy is more likely to be found.

Recent events make it necessary to examine Catholicism and its legacy critically and to revisit the work of Greeley and other authors who are able to understand the Church, its true history and the various social and historical movements with which it has interacted. One of the great contemporary American Catholic theologians was the Revd Richard McBrien, who passed away in 2015 and who advocated throughout his career for deep critical examinations of the Church. He spoke for 'the ordination of women as priests, the repeal of obligatory celibacy and the acceptance of birth control [and defied] the papal doctrine of infallibility' (Roberts 2015: 17). At the same time, McBrien, while pushing for change within the Church, remained steadfast and orthodox in his faith, 'there is only one Christian faith, but there have been literally thousands of beliefs held and transmitted at one time or another' – some have endured, while others 'have receded beyond the range of vision or even of collective memory' (Roberts 2015: 17). It must seem that this is the moment for the Irish Catholic Church to reinvent itself in a more egalitarian shape that responds to its own particular history in Ireland.

Many of Maureen Dezell's conclusions are in agreement with what Greeley and McBrien have found. Nevertheless, the American Catholic Church continues to thrive, as Timothy O'Meara, retired provost at the University of Notre Dame reminds her: 'there is no place on earth that Catholicism is more alive than on Catholic university campuses', with students enjoying mandatory classes in theology and involving themselves in 'Catholic social action' (Dezell 2001: 165). In the USA, where major Catholic universities enjoy a large degree of independence from their overseers, a kind of reinvention and détente is in place that allows young people to remain part of, and be welcome in, the Church while, at the same time, going their own way on social issues. Given how Irish universities have evolved, such opportunities are less available to Irish Catholics, so renewal is more difficult to achieve. For adults beyond universities and out in the world, Dezell provides an example of how the twenty-first-century Church might look. She focuses on Old St Pat's in Chicago:

> It is laity-centered, geared to young adults – who have a tendency to drift away from organised religion – and linked to Chicago's business, social action, and Irish communities. The church calendar lists regular meetings of a variety of groups – one for 'devotion to Our Lady', one offering divorce support, a Jewish-Catholic couples group, and a Bible study meeting, along with choir practice, community outreach, and liturgy meetings. Coming up the following month were a Valentine's Day Mass, a civic forum on art as an expression of the sacred, a reading group meeting (*Portrait of the Artist as a Young Man*), and a Celtic St Patrick's Day Mass followed by an Irish breakfast, a Mass featuring Irish musicians, and Siamsa na Gael: a celebration of the Celtic Arts at Chicago Symphony Center. (Dezell 2001: 186)

Though some of these events might seem like novelties, all are of substance and in keeping with, and made possible by, Catholicism's cultural legacy – a legacy built on faith, inclusiveness, forgiveness, the word as it is read, spoken and sung, discussion and community. At Old St Pat's in Chicago, the parish is built on the various interests that parishioners share rather than on narrow clerical dictates.

Last year, in a question–and–answer session after a reading of hers I attended in Iowa City, Marilynne Robinson said that she thought there was no better explanation available for the reality of our world and humankind than what is found in sacred Christian literature. Her remark reminds us that while we might dispense with the Catholic hierarchy, it would be rash to erase the tradition. Irish religious faith, as I have mentioned, is connected to place, to *dinnseanchas*, in the same manner as Native American faith is. In the Lakota tradition, the original people emerged from Wind Cave in South Dakota, and came into the world thereby establishing this wonderful connection between earth and person. In Ireland, too, land is sacred and has helped shape who we are and what we believe in. To a degree, we Irish take our faith from the land, a land/faith that is encoded in Catholicism. The land, the whole space of Ireland, is sacred in itself and also sanctified by the Catholic Church and by other faiths and beliefs, as Paula Meehan eloquently gives voice to in her interrogation of Marianism:

> Or the grace of a midsummer wedding
> when the earth herself calls out for coupling
> and I would break loose of my stone robes,
> pure blue, pure white, as if they had robbed
> a child's sky for their color. My being
> cries out to be incarnate, incarnate,
> maculate and tousled in a honeyed bed.
> (Meehan 1991: 41)

Culture is complex and develops in ways that make it difficult to dismantle. Whereas, as Auge correctly points out, 'the once imposing edifice of Irish Catholicism appear[s] increasingly derelict', much life is to be found beyond the great stone buildings (Auge 2013: 145), and many of the clergy inside such buildings are men and women of great honour. In language and thought, sign and dream, love and hate, man and woman, boy and girl, the Catholic legacy lingers to enrich and complicate life.

In *Irish Catholicism since 1950: The Undoing of a Culture*, Louise Fuller defines the role and influence played by the Church in Irish life:

> One of the most outstanding features of Irish Catholic culture in the post-independence era was the extent to which the state, by the actions, words and public appearances of its representatives, legitimated the Catholic ethos. An alliance was formed between the Catholic Church authorities and the Free State government during the Civil War years, and W. T. Cosgrave during his tenure of office looked to the Church to augment the authority of the government. The alliance was a mutually reinforcing one. This bishops were prepared to throw their weight behind the new state and endorse its political legitimacy, which was being contested by the anti-Treaty republicans, and the rulers of the new state were not disposed to question the authority of

the Church in matters having to do with education, health or sexual morality, traditionally seen by the Church as its area of competence. (Fuller 2002: 3)

The support of the hierarchy lent an additional layer of legitimacy to the new regime, and, in return, the Church was allowed to influence legislation and action. Though a great deal of the semiotics of this relationship was lost on me as child growing up in the 1950s and 1960s in Co. Wexford, one aspect of the relationship between Church and State was crystal clear – that the primary power resided in the Church. It was a familiar sight in Enniscorthy whenever Bishop Donal Herlihy appeared in public to witness our public figures kowtowing to him. As a child, I remember how easy and approachable our public figures were, how even a boy might accost Mr Seán Browne TD or Mr Andy Doyle, a local councillor and business leader, and demand a word or two. In contrast, Bishop Herlihy was regally unapproachable. Our public figures were of our world; the bishop was from another planet. In the Ferns report, Bishop Herlihy came in for fierce criticism:

the report's harshest judgments were against Donal Herlihy, the former bishop of Ferns, who has since died, and his successor, Brendan Comiskey, who resigned in 2002 after the BBC broadcast a documentary about Mr O'Gorman. The Ferns report also touched on the Vatican's demand for secrecy in sexual abuse cases – on pain of excommunication – and revealed how Bishops Herlihy and Comiskey repeatedly placed priests whom they knew to be paedophiles in positions that made it easy for them to abuse children. (Lavery 2005)

Looking back, my sense is that our bishop resided outside of our world. In our rural town, loyalties were to each other and to our own priests, about whom there was no end of discussion and speculation. The regal entrance of the bishop of Ferns for confirmations and other high liturgical occasions in St Aidan's Cathedral seemed disassociated from our lives of faith, aberration rather than affirmation. The old people I knew and loved referred to the cathedral as 'the chapel' so that it seemed less grand and more of us. It was not difficult for the hierarchy to abandon us because of the degree of separation they had established between their domain and ours. In hindsight, we depended on our bishop's oversight, his remoteness from the day-to-day should have allowed him to understand and quickly root out evil; however, he thought it more important to protect the image of the Church than to do what was right.

Richard P. McBrien begins his *Caesar's Coin: Religion and Politics in America* with an excerpt from Lincoln's 'Gettysburg's Address' rather than a church homily or quote from the Bible:

'Fourscore and seven years ago', President Abraham Lincoln began, 'our fathers brought forth on this continent a new nation, conceived in liberty, and dedicated to the proposition that all men are created equal'. This book is a book about the American Proposition as it applies to the issue of religion and politics. (McBrien 1987: vii)

An American theologian beginning a history of the relationship between religion and politics with a quotation from a political speech that emphasises liberty and equality makes complete sense in the American context where such tenets as freedom of speech, equality and the separation of church and state are the cornerstones of law and thought. Though God was and remains integral to American thought, no such 'mutually reinforcing' relationship that Fuller finds in Ireland has existed in the USA between church and state, notwithstanding the fact that America's founding fathers were descended from the Pilgrim Fathers (Fuller 2002: 3). In America, as McBrien points out, religions are connected to public life 'by what has come to be known as public and/or civil religion, by their common commitment to "civic republicanism" and to that "public virtue" which seeks to promote the political and social involvement of all citizens' (McBrien 1987: ix).

In Ireland, both the Church and the State, by ceding authority to the Church, placed the reputation of the Church above the welfare of Ireland's citizens. My sense is that the weakness here lies with the civil authorities who had been elected to provide oversight over the country and its people but who abdicated this responsibility. All organisations, great and small, civil and religious, require oversight. In America, it is, or should be, the 'public good, the real welfare of the great body of the people', James Madison insisted, which is the final measure of any form of government and to which 'the voice of every good citizen' must be reconciled (cited by McBrien 1987, ix). McBrien reminds us that the blending of ideals and ideologies from Church and State can be a positive one so long as some separation is maintained. In Ireland, therefore, we can say that the cultural legacy need not be erased from state matters but that it instead should be at play in a dynamic that McBrien labels as 'civic republicanism' (1987: ix). Writing in 1967, another Irish-American priest, Fr James Kavanagh, notes that 'Catholicism as a monolithic structure is disappearing. Once a man who differed with the party line stole quietly away … He refuses to accept irrelevant sermons, a sterile liturgy, a passé and speculative theology' (Kavanagh 1967: xi). Though the Cloyne and other reports have driven worshippers away from the Church, the need for reinvention predates these reports.

Frank McCourt provides an often quoted and provocative declaration at the beginning of *Angela's Ashes*, his best-selling memoir of his family's life in Ireland and America: 'When I look back on my childhood I wonder how I survived at all. It was, of course, a miserable childhood: the happy childhood is hardly worth your while. Worse than the ordinary miserable childhood is the miserable Irish childhood and worse yet is the miserable Irish Catholic childhood' (McCourt 1996: 11). Published in 1996, at a time when many shocking revelations about the role of the Catholic Church in child abuse were being revealed, McCourt's statement caught something of the *Zeitgeist*, albeit in an exaggerated tone. Given all that we have learned in recent decades, it is tempting to discard everything associated with Irish Catholicism, to throw out the baby with the bathwater as it were. Given McCourt's outburst, it is no surprise that the Catholic hierarchy in Ireland believed that 'the returned emigrants, on the other hand, also posed a challenge to traditional values and ways of thinking' (Fuller 2002: 43). The power of the returned emigrant to undermine traditional sexual practices is given eloquent voice in John McGahern's *Amongst Women* in the character of Nell Morahan, a young woman who is home on vacation from America. However, abuse and misery, though they are predominant images and realities of the present, do not negate all of the Catholic light. Part of the journey that McCourt chronicles is the throwing off of Catholicism in favour of freedom and hedonism, an effort that is facilitated by leaving Ireland for America and described with great comic effect near the close of *Angela's Ashes*:

> She takes my hand and leads me into a bedroom, puts down her glass, locks the door, pushes me down on the bed. She's fumbling at my fly. Damn buttons. Don't you have zippers in Ireland? She pulls out my excitement climbs up on me slides up and own and down Jesus I'm in heaven and there's a knock on the door the priest Frank are you in there Frieda putting her fingers to her lips and her eyes rolling to heaven Frank are you in there Father would you ever take a good running jump for yourself an oh God oh Thomas do you see what's happening to me at long last and I don't give a fiddler's fart if the Pope himself knocked on this door and the College of Cardinals gathered gawking at the windows. (McCourt 1996: 361)

For McCourt, the various miseries underlining an Irish Catholic upbringing are prerequisites for the independent artistic life.

We should understand though that McCourt does not throw off his upbringing completely; rather, like the relationship that Blake forges between innocence and experience in his work, McCourt's contrasting states – Ireland/America and Catholicism/hedonism – serve as two sides of a single coin rather than wildly separate opposites. In fact, this excerpt from *Angela's Ashes* pays homage to tradition in its pastiche imitation of the dramatic monologue that Joyce employs in the 'Penelope' episode that concludes *Ulysses*. Ironically, the priest participates in McCourt's sexual encounter, though from a safe distance, the door dividing him from Frank and Frieda acting as a kind of Atlantic separating America from Ireland. Until recently, the Irish hierarchy's obsession with sexual matters gave the impression that were always standing guard outside people's bedrooms, like the hapless priest in *Angela's Ashes*, who is not even given a name by McCourt. In the end, it was sex, in part, that brought down the Church. Irish men and women liked sex so much that they eventually felt confident enough to disregard the Church's wishes while the hierarchy somehow persuaded itself that sexual abuse of children was neither a serious nor a criminal matter.

Though an increasingly maligned and marginalised figure in Ireland, the Irish Catholic priest has received favourable coverage in two recent acclaimed novels by Irish writers: Colm Tóibín's *Brooklyn* (2009) and Colum McCann's *Let the Great*

World Spin (2009). Interestingly enough, the two clerical figures in these novels are ministering outside of Ireland – in Brooklyn and the Bronx, respectively. Both resist the image of the stereotypical Irish priest that McCourt favours while at the same time conforming to another image of the helpful and useful Irish clergy-man doing service overseas. Though their missions are outside of Ireland, both Fr Flood in *Brooklyn* and John Corrigan in *Let the Great World Spin* are involved in a long-standing process of the Irish Catholic Church intervening overseas for the improvement of the lives of individuals living in far-flung places. Both Flood and Corrigan offer assistance without proselytisation. In addition to making it possible for Eilis Lacey to emigrate to America, his primary role in the plot of *Brooklyn*, Fr Flood encourages Eilis in her pursuit of a third-level education that would been impossible for her to have access to in Ireland, and in his dealings with her is generally supportive and non-judgemental. He presides over his Brooklyn parish genially and paternally and is more interested in engaging with his parish-ioners and seeking to help them get what they need rather than in meddling in their private lives. From America, Fr Flood has learned a degree of tolerance and accommodation that is necessary to prosper and be useful in a quickly changing society, where Church and State exist in dialogue and not some form of seamless communion. In the 'Baby Boom' years following the Second World War, a time of upward mobility, educational opportunities resulting from the GI Bill, increased wealth and a lively and diverse culture, the American Catholic Church had a fight on its hands to retain the loyalty of its flock. To remain relevant, it could not adopt the heavy-handed tactics of its Irish counterpart that promulgated a Catholic cul-ture infected with what the Revd Liam Ryan, a prominent sociologist, called the 'four deadly sins of Irish Catholicism: an obsession with sexual morality, clerical authoritarianism, anti-intellectualism or at best non-intellectualism, and the crea-tion of a ghetto mentality' (O'Toole 1998: 75).

Ciaran Corrigan notes of his older brother John in *Let the Great World Spin* that 'he was at the origin of things and I now had a meaning for my brother – he was a crack of light under the door, and yet that door was shut to him' (McCann 2009: 67). Corrigan is, as Eóin Flannery has pointed out, a rogue priest who is ministering outside of the traditional Church, a man raised on a blend of libera-tion and traditional theology:

> But the insertion of an Irish character, John Corrigan, as one of the protagonists, arguably the central personality, permits the introduction of religious faith into the narrative. Corrigan's religious vocation, rooted in Catholicism, but gradually receding from its institutional forms, is key to the enactment of redemption in the story … The lived context of Corrigan's vocation is prostitution and drug addiction; he effec-tively dwells among a group of black prostitutes in the South Bronx. His dedica-tion to these harassed women is absolute and is tested by repeated physical assaults by pimps, as well as the proximity of the prostitutes' semi-clad, sexualised bodies. (Flannery 2011: 216–19)

In addition to working with a group of prostitutes, Corrigan also takes groups of senior citizens on day trips. Corrigan falls in love with Adelita in the novel, eventually after much soul-searching agreeing to consummate their relationship. One notices that little divides Corrigan's private and public lives both of which are defined by patience, kindness and deep generosity. He serves as link between the priest of the ancient Irish Catholic Church, who was often married and comfortable living among and serving under women, and a priest of the future guided by a mixture of traditional liturgy and the writings of Gustavo Gutiérrez and Ernesto Cardinal, two father-figures of liberation theology who not only resisted oppression by dictators in Central and South America by word and deed but who also pushed back against the Vatican's reprimands of their ways of thinking and leading. One should note, too, that an Irish cleric, albeit a most unconventional one, is at the centre of a great American novel, and a major force in healing after 9/11, and after his own martyrdom in a wreck on the East Side Highway. One senses in Corrigan a Christ-like resonance, a power and an influence that endures long after his death. McCann has noted that he 'wanted for a long time to write about faith and belonging, especially in a radical Catholic context. I wanted a man who would look at the world in all its filth and poverty and yet still believe that, one day, the meek might actually want it' (McCann 2009: 365). Corrigan also links Ireland and America, with the latter being the diverse place, as in *Angela's Ashes* and *Brooklyn*, where independent and mature experience is possible. Given the climate in Ireland in recent decades and the collapse of the influence and integrity of the Church, it would have seemed impossible to Tóibín and McCann, I would guess, to have imagined similar lives for Fr Flood and John Corrigan in Ireland. America, though clerical abuse and cover-ups occurred there with great frequency, offered both authors elements of diversity and reinvention that would have been impossible in Ireland. Both novels shine bright and positive lights on the cultural legacy of Irish Catholicism.

It is my sense of things that the cultural legacy of Irish Catholicism, and its American counterpart, will be tied to, and inseparable from, the abuses of young people committed by clergy, and subsequent cover-ups by its hierarchy, for a long time to come. In his controversial analysis of the role that ordinary Germans played in the Holocaust, Daniel Jonah Goldhagen notes that 'the Holocaust defines not only the history of Jews during the middle of the twentieth century but also the history of Germans' (1996: 8). Without trying to lessen the impact of the Holocaust by comparing it to a reality that is quite unlike it, one can apply the frame of Goldhagen's thesis to events that occurred in Ireland. Even though, as I have pointed out, many aspects of the cultural legacy of Catholicism are positive and enduring, the abiding reality is one of abuse and horror. Our celebration should be muted. What is most important is that the innocent victims of the Church remain in the forefront of our thoughts.

Works cited

Auge, Andrew J. (2013) *A Chastened Communion: Modern Irish Poetry and Catholicism*, Syracuse, NY: Syracuse University Press.

Dezell, Maureen (2001) *Irish America: Coming into Clover*, New York: Doubleday.

Flannery, Eóin (2011) *Colum McCann and the Aesthetics of Redemption*, Dublin: Irish Academic Press.

Fuller, Louise (2002) *Irish Catholicism since 1950: The Undoing of a Culture*, Dublin: Gill & Macmillan.

Goldhagen, Daniel Jonah (1996) *Hitler's Willing Executioners: Ordinary Germans and the Holocaust*, New York: Knopf.

Gordon, Mary (1978) *Final Payments*, New York: Anchor.

—— (1991) 'Getting Here from There: A Writer's Reflections on a Religious Past', *Good Boys and Dead Girls and Other Essays*, New York: Viking, pp. 160–75.

Greeley, Andrew M. (1981) *The Irish Americans: The Rise to Money and Power*, New York: Warner Books.

Kavanagh, James (1967) *A Modern Priest Looks at His Outdated Church*, New York: Trident Press.

Lavery, Brian (2005) 'Irish Report on Sexual Abuse Causes Outrage', *New York Times*, 13 November, available at www.nytimes.com/2005/11/13/world/europe/irish-report-on-sexual-abuse-by-priests-stokes-outrage.html?_r=0 (accessed 29 April 2015).

McBrien, Richard P. (1987) *Caesar's Coin: Religion and Politics in America*, New York: Macmillan.

McCann, Colum (2009) 'A Conversation with Colum McCann and Nathan Englander', *Let the Great World Spin*, New York: Random House, pp. 361–71.

—— (2009) *Let the Great World Spin*, New York: Random House.

McCourt, Frank (1996) *Angela's Ashes*, New York: Scribner.

McGahern, John (1965) *The Dark*, London: Faber and Faber.

—— (1990) *Amongst Women*, Faber and Faber.

Meehan, Paula (1991) 'The Statue of the Virgin at Granard Speaks', *The Man Who Was Marked by Winter*, Loughcrew: Gallery Press, pp. 40–2.

O'Toole, Fintan (1998) *Lie of the Land: Irish Identities*, London: Verso.

Roberts, Sam (2015) 'Rev. Richard McBrien, Catholic Firebrand, Dies at 78', *New York Times*, 29 January, p. 17.

Tóibín, Colm (2009) *Brooklyn*, New York: Scribner.

7

Prophetic voices or complicit functionaries? Irish priests and the unravelling of a culture

Eamon Maher

Priests in Ireland have suffered extreme reputational and existential damage in the wake of the clerical abuse scandals and the ever-increasing process of secularisation within Irish society. Ever since two of the most high-profile clerics of recent times, Bishop Eamon Casey and Fr Michael Cleary, were discovered to have fathered children with Annie Murphy and Phyllis Hamilton respectively, the formerly enviable position of Irish priests has gradually been transformed into a nightmare scenario which has resulted in their being often loath to appear in public wearing the Roman collar and where it is increasingly difficult for them to pronounce on issues of a moral nature with any degree of authority.

In France, secularism and a loss of faith in religious institutions took root far earlier, with the French Revolution initiating a total dismantling of the Church's prominent role in society, ultimately resulting in the official separation of church and state in 1905. Ever since that time, there has been an interdiction on the display of any religious symbols in state-subsidised schools, and religion is increasingly relegated to a largely private affair for those who still wish to practise it. Priests in France have therefore been dealing a lot longer with a secular state apparatus than their Irish counterparts and have developed various strategies for ministering to an ever-decreasing number of people attending mass and the sacraments. This chapter will analyse the extent to which some French and Irish priests have attempted to grapple in their writings with a changed religious landscape, and it will ask the question, 'Are they prophetic witnesses to gospel values or mere mouthpieces for the Catholic Church?'

The chapter will deal with just one French priest, Jean Sulivan, whose insights into what was happening in his native Brittany and beyond have more than a little relevance for the Irish context. His memoir, *Anticipate Every Goodbye*, and spiritual journal, *Morning Light*, speak to the changed role of the priest in French society. On the Irish side, we will consider Joseph Dunn's *No Lions in the Hierarchy*, Vincent Twomey's *The End of Irish Catholicism?*, Mark Patrick Hederman's *Kissing the Dark* and *Underground Cathedrals* and Brendan Hoban's *Change or Decay: Irish Catholicism in Crisis* and *Who Will Break Bread for Us?* Unlike Sulivan, the Irish priests did/do not write fiction, but in many ways Sulivan's novels were very close reflections of his personal experience and contain many characters that are barely fictionalised.

The chapter will argue, therefore, that when one is closely aligned to an institution like the Catholic Church, as priests inevitably are, it is difficult to become part of its dismantling. In other words, it is painful and professionally dangerous for a priest to point out fault lines and champion causes that could be viewed as unacceptable, or even heretical, by other priests and members of the hierarchy. A priest's training instils in him a respect for authority and for his superiors, which may explain the absence of too much open revolt among the Irish clergy in recent times. Silence should not be read as compliance, however. One of the priest-authors whom we will discuss, Brendan Hoban, is not afraid to speak out about the dilemma of people like himself who go against the tide: 'Saying the awkward word meant exclusion from the clerical club: the resentment of my colleagues; the unwanted attention of bishops, my own and others who sought to pressure them; the confusion of my parishioners; sometimes even the hurt of my family and friends' (Hoban 2005: 10).

Given that he was writing during the 1960s and 1970s, in a France that was still at a fair remove from what could be referred to as the post-Catholic Irish society of the twenty-first century, it has always struck me just how succinctly the priest-writer Jean Sulivan (1913–80) predicted the imminent crisis that would take hold of the Catholic Church decades before it fully manifested itself in the Western world. The only child of a Breton couple who were modest farmers, Joseph Lemarchand (Sulivan's real name) lost his father in the trenches of the First World War and then suffered the heartbreak of his mother's remarriage (born out of economic necessity), which her young son viewed as a betrayal.

Notwithstanding, there can be no doubt that the simple, pious faith of his mother played a major role in Sulivan's decision to go to junior seminary and to continue with his studies up until ordination in 1938. His first appointment was to the Catholic lycée Saint-Vincent in the Breton capital, Rennes, where Sulivan became a well-known figure as a result of the key role he played in setting up successful initiatives such as a cinéclub (La Chambre noire), a local newspaper (*Dialogues-Ouest*) and an important cultural centre (La Renaissance spirituelle). His involvement in these cultural activities probably fuelled his appreciation of the artistic and literary milieus, and his initial foray into writing was a series of articles published in *Dialogues-Ouest* under various pseudonyms. However, his first novel was not published until 1958, when he was forty-five years of age, but from that point until his death in 1980, he would publish ten novels, two short-story collections, several book-length essays and an important spiritual journal, *Morning Light*, the vast majority of which appeared under the prestigious Gallimard imprint.

A priest-writer is not as free to express himself as he might like to be. He has a responsibility not to be a source of scandal to the Church, and he must also be careful not to fall foul of his ecclesiastical superiors. Sulivan was very fortunate in having a supporter in Cardinal Roques, who took the exceptional step of allowing this priest devote himself full-time to literature during the 1960s. One wonders if the benevolent prelate ever regretted this decision, as Sulivan was not one to toe the party line and on numerous occasions criticised what he viewed as abuses within the Church. He was particularly dubious about ostentation and excessive formality, as can be seen in this declaration from *Morning Light*:

> Pompous words seem to go along with official dress, with ornaments and decorations, even when those who wear them in ceremonies are themselves poor. It is impossible not to grasp the contradiction between the speech of Jesus and the ecclesiastical phraseology, mitres, capes – the whole show. That's not a judgement, but an observation. It's jarring. (Sulivan 1988: 10)

Some of the Irish priests whom we will discuss later show a similar scepticism with regard to how the Church has wandered a long way from the simple example provided by its founder, Jesus Christ, because of its preoccupation with power and prestige. Later on in his spiritual journal, Sulivan has this to say:

> When the Church's prestige diminishes, when freedom shatters various forms of hypocrisy, when priests who for centuries have been under pressures that forced a large number to choose between a dishonest vocation and social disgrace are able to make their own decisions a little more freely, when churches begin to recognise that they can no longer use their political weight to influence moral decisions, there are clear signs of a Christian renaissance which, obviously, has nothing to do with social structures. (Sulivan 1988: 149)

When one considers that these words were written in 1976, it becomes apparent just how prophetic a figure Sulivan was. Many within the Church, and certainly at the upper echelons of the institution, might well counter his arguments by saying that such a massive organisation makes a certain form of centralised government inevitable, even desirable. They might also underline how doctrine has to be clearly stated and that people who are anxious to remain members of the Church should adhere to its governing principles. Similarly, they could argue that ecclesiastical robes and elaborate ceremonies are designed to honour God and to make people aware of his grandeur: in other words, they have a symbolic and spiritual value in and of themselves. If the Church were to allow its members to make up their own minds about moral issues, then what would result would be relativism and a lack of rigour in terms of what constitute the main tenets of Catholicism.

While such assertions are certainly valid and need to be voiced, they do not hide the glaring disparity that appears occasionally between the actual words and example of Christ and what the institutional Church has done with them. In his memoir, *Anticipate Every Goodbye*, Sulivan wondered at the extent to which the Church of his native Brittany sought to deprive people of their individuality:

> The priests at this time tended to preach about laws and obligations. In this way they had succeeded in transforming Christianity into something approaching a natural religion. In their eyes the rural order in which the Church still played a dominant role was an expression of the divine will. They had forgotten about freedom, without which there is no real faith. (Sulivan 2000: 52)

It seems opportune at this stage to leave Sulivan aside for a moment to concentrate on the Irish priests' testimony and the degree to which they may echo some of the French writer's concerns, especially with regard to the importance of freedom of conscience and freedom of choice.

Joseph Dunn's collection of essays *No Lions in the Hierarchy* made a considerable impact when it was first published in 1994. A priest in the Dublin archdiocese, Dunn had a successful career as a producer of the highly influential religious television programme *Radharc*, which in the period from 1962 to 1997 was responsible for recording over 400 documentaries filmed in seventy-five countries, and which covered a vast array of topics that were viewed as being pertinent to the Church of the twentieth century. Sometimes the independent approach adopted by the programme producers caused trouble with certain members of the Irish hierarchy, but in general its work was applauded and welcomed for giving voice to a broad range of opinion within the Church.[1] For example, there were items on patriarchy in the Church, women's ordination, liberation theology in South America and the poverty of life in missionary Africa. Matters of domestic concern were not neglected either, with documentaries dealing with fair days, seminary education, Matt Talbot (a former alcoholic who worked tirelessly for the Pioneer Total Abstinence Association in Dublin), British justice in Ireland, Irish holidays and such like. His career in broadcasting undoubtedly imbued in Dunn an awareness that the Church was a distinctly different entity depending on where one lived in the world. He also appreciated the extent to which the advent of television led to a significant change in how people perceived the Church and society in Ireland. Dunn regarded himself as being in the fortunate position of being able to express things plainly because of the nature of his work:

> I am probably freer than most priests to look at different sides of a problem – as well as to express my own views for whatever they are worth. Because while I am a priest in good standing, I am neither a professional theologian nor a practising parish priest. Nor indeed a writer who has to please editors or publishers to earn a living. (Dunn 1994: 10)

Unlike Dunn, a number of the other Irish priests dealt with in this chapter encounter difficulties in relation to speaking out about certain failings within the Church.

There are, in fact, several Irish priests who have paid a heavy price for their criticisms of redline issues such as celibacy, women priests, homosexuality and access to artificial contraception. Those who have been censured or silenced in recent times include the Passionist priest and journalist Brian D'Arcy; the Marist theologian Seán Fagan; a columnist with the Redemptorist publication *Reality*, Tony Flannery (the subject of Catherine Maignant's chapter in this book); and the outspoken Augustinian Iggy O'Donovan. Critics from the inside, it would appear, are quickly brought to heel. Contrary to expectation, the election of Pope Francis has not led to a reinstatement of these men, who must continue to endure the cold shoulder from a church they served with love and by which they are now being sanctioned. Joseph Dunn did not think that disagreements with the captain and officers of his ship (namely the Pope and his entourage) justified his abandoning it: 'So if I am sometimes critical of the captain and crew, it's my ship as well, and I'm sticking with it' (Dunn 1994: 11).

In his description of the formation he received in the seminary, Dunn found what was at best an unhealthy attitude to sex: marriage was more often referred to as 'a remedy for concupiscence', echoing St Paul's view that it was 'better to marry than to burn' (Dunn 1994: 20). Such a theology presented marriage as a far less noble calling than the celibate priesthood, which to all intents and purposes was viewed as the supreme vocation of human beings. Dunn admits that he had the same sexual drive as any normal male, and yet he managed to respect his vow of celibacy. However, he acknowledges that it is a huge sacrifice to make. In discussing the politics of episcopal appointments, Dunn argues that suitability and popularity among priests were qualities that were often viewed in a negative light by Rome and its representatives (apostolic nuncios) in various countries around the world when it came to appointing bishops, especially during the papacy of John Paul II. His chapter on the latter is scathing in its criticism of a man whom many regard as a saviour, as the one who rescued the Church from the excesses of Vatican II. Dunn sums up his reaction in these words: 'as a Catholic priest I hate to say it, but [...] pretty well everything I have seen and everybody I have met in the course of my work have led me towards a negative judgement on the pontificate of John Paul II' (Dunn 1994: 71). He resented the Pontiff's harsh stance on liberation theology, contraception and the silencing of certain well-known theologians, most notably Leonardo Boff, Hans Küng and Bernard Haring.

On the issue of contraception, Dunn is at a loss to comprehend the difference in principle 'between wearing a condom and confining intercourse to infertile periods, or indeed prolonging the infertile period, which is what the basic contraceptive pill is designed to do' (Dunn 1994: 111). The Vatican, with its obsolescent structures and inward-looking curia, and its fascination with power and prestige, will always, in Dunn's view, have difficulty deciphering what its true path should be. He quotes a Lutheran, Dr George Lindbeck, a delegate-observer at the Second Vatican Council, whom he interviewed for *Radharc*:

> One way of describing the changes that have taken place in the Roman curia is to say that the Roman Catholic Church still has not learned to deal with a loyal opposition. It has not learned how to make a distinction between a loyal opposition and a disloyal one. And no church can, it seems to me, have the kind of renewal that was projected by the second Vatican unless it learns to live with those who, out of love for the church, for God, for Jesus Christ, criticise the church. (cited by Dunn 1994: 175)

How strange it is that a member of a Protestant church should point out this inevitable stumbling block of Vatican II, namely an inability to accept criticism from within. 'Loyal' opponents were certainly not shown much tolerance during the pontificates of John Paul II and Benedict XVI. The Irish group of dissident priests already mentioned find themselves languishing in a type of 'bold boys' corner', obliged to obtain permission to speak at public functions, to publish their opinions or even to preach. They are left in no doubt as to how their 'loyal opposition' is viewed. Dunn's own stance on the issue of loyalty is clear: 'When the laws of the church, when the institutions of the church, become more important than people, so that these are used for the benefit of the people and crushes people, in fact, then no matter how holy that institution is, it's not following Jesus Christ' (Dunn 1994: 225). By its very title, *No Lions in the Hierarchy* challenges the received wisdom within the Catholic Church and calls for the rediscovery of the true message of Jesus Christ. Reading through Dunn's essays a few decades after they were first published, one senses a real tension between a priest's loyalty to the institution and his abhorrence of the actions of those who claim to be acting in its best interests when in fact they are merely serving their own. Like the other priests in this chapter, Dunn knew that his role was not to be the passive recipient of accepted knowledge but to question constantly certain 'givens', even when such a course of action would get one the reputation of being a troublemaker. Every institution needs its loyal opponents, its rebels, if it is to maintain its prophetic charge. Dunn was just one such figure.

A member of the Divine Word Missionaries, Vincent Twomey is probably the most 'orthodox' of the priests dealt with in this chapter. After his training in Germany (he did his doctoral studies in Regensburg under Joseph Ratzinger), he worked in Papua New Guinea and the Solomon Islands, before returning to Ireland and a position as lecturer in theology in St Patrick's College, Maynooth, during the 1980s. He would later accede to the chair of moral theology in the same university. A man with a sharp intellect, Twomey's most significant contribution to the topic of this chapter is *The End of Irish Catholicism?* In it, he seeks to promote an intellectual discussion of Irish Catholicism at the start of the third millennium. The study opens with the following observation:

It is a measure of the cultural sea change in Ireland that, whereas half a century ago to call oneself an 'Irish Catholic' was a badge of honour proudly worn for all the world to see and admire, today in the upwardly mobile, modern Ireland south of the border, it is more often than not an embarrassment to be reluctantly admitted. (Twomey 2003: 17)

Twomey is naturally not overjoyed at this development, but he points out that there has tended to be a hostile and one-sided coverage of the clerical abuse scandals and of the horrors visited on children and young women in Church-run institutions such as the industrial schools and the Magdalene laundries. On the other hand, the great work done by priests, religious sisters and Christian Brothers in the realms of health and education is rarely acknowledged by the media. While acknowledging the vital role played by journalists in unveiling the crimes perpetrated on innocent young children by certain priests and the attempted cover-up of same by people in authority, most particularly bishops, Twomey states that from the point of view of the Catholic Church the Irish media 'can be described as the most hostile media in the developed world' (Twomey 2003: 67). This may be the result of a backlash against centuries of deference shown towards men and women of the cloth, which led to unthinking and uncritical commentary on Church-related matters, but Twomey has the impression that there is a more sinister agenda at play: 'to be interviewed by an Irish journalist is more an interrogation by the thought-police, and any slip-up can be fatal' (Twomey 2003: 69). He contrasts this to his experience of being interviewed by foreign journalists, which he finds invariably positive, due in large part to his being treated with respect.

In my estimation, much depends on the journalist and the interviewee. There are journalists such as David Quinn (*Irish Independent*) and Breda O'Brien (*Irish Times*) who are definitely well disposed to the Catholic Church, and Patsy McGarry, religious affairs correspondent with the *Irish Times*, while never afraid to raise legitimate concerns and inconsistencies in the Church's stance on many subjects, could not be accused of lacking respect when interviewing a priest or a bishop. The problem is that certain Church figures (especially a number of bishops) resemble rabbits caught in the glare of car headlights when they are being interviewed on contentious issues. They look and sound uncomfortable when they are on radio or television, and it is difficult not to form the opinion that this is due to their having something to hide.

Archbishop Diarmuid Martin, on the other hand, is very comfortable when in the glare of the media, but he is an exception. Hence I would not concur with Twomey's statement that the general coverage of religious affairs in Irish newspapers is 'hostile', and I certainly do not agree that it is at times 'downright nasty' (Twomey 2003: 68). Editor of the *Irish Catholic*, Michael Kelly, quotes the views of Bishop Edward Daly of Derry, who worked with RTÉ as a religious adviser and who was tasked with establishing a press office. Interestingly, Daly noted, 'I have experienced both the frustrations of the media with the church and the frustration of the church with the media, first as Broadcasting Officer with RTÉ, and ... as a member of the Irish Episcopal Conference. I believe that both parties must accept a share of the guilt' (Kelly 2015: 148). Just like the vitriol they poured on politicians and bankers in the wake of the financial meltdown, Irish journalists did not spare the Catholic Church when revelations of 'groupthink', collusion and self-protection emerged over their handling of the abuse scandals. In both instances, the once benign and respectful coverage these institutions enjoyed at one stage from the same newspapers, radio and television broadcasters was replaced by a much tougher and less forgiving editorial approach. Kelly notes 'a near state of paralysis at the level of the Irish Bishops' Conference when it comes to communications' and goes on to say that constructive criticism is often met with bewilderment, with comments such as 'and I thought you were on our side' (Kelly 2015: 150, 152). The hostility of which Twomey speaks is not all one-sided, therefore: the bishops regularly reveal their displeasure at what they feel is unfair reporting and can be very defensive when dealing with journalists who are essentially only trying to do their job. Kelly defines the main source of the conflict thus: 'The scandals have exacerbated this situation, and the overall lack of a communications strategy has left church leaders constantly on the back foot – and Catholics bewildered when it comes to the church-media relationship' (2015: 144).

While not totally in agreement with his comments on the Church's relationship with the media, I would have to acknowledge that Twomey's presentation of Irish Catholicism is generally reasonable and well argued. He looks on modernity and the unbridled individualism it brought with it as having been responsible for much of the disillusionment with Irish Catholicism. The various referendums of the 1980s and 1990s revealed a growing divide between those wishing to hold on to the traditions of the past and the harbingers of change. The latter were successful, in Twomey's view, for three main reasons:

> In the first instance, there was a weak political class seemingly preoccupied with staying in power (now intimidated by the media as they were once intimidated by the hierarchy). Secondly, there was an insecure clergy unsettled by the revolution that was Vatican II, weakened by scandals, and unsure of their role in a modern secular state that emerged almost as an alternative to the 'sectarian violence' in the North. Finally, we have [...] a rather long tradition of social conformity in this country, for which the Catholic Church must accept some blame. (Twomey 2003: 115)

It is likely that if the Catholic Church in Ireland had more proponents of the calibre of Vincent Twomey its voice would receive a more positive response among the public. His stated regrets about the neglect of philosophy and theology in our schools and universities, the lack of a cutting-edge Catholic newspaper such as *The Tablet* or *La Croix*, the dearth of lay Catholic intellectuals in Ireland, are definitely valid. And while he is generally perceived as being a conservative, on closer examination many of Twomey's views are quite radical. He retains loyalty to the Church, but it is not a loyalty that blinds him to its many failures.

The Benedictine abbot from Glenstal Abbey in Co. Limerick, Mark Patrick Hederman, is an example of someone whose expertise spans a number of different disciplines such as ontology, theology and literature. He studied in Paris under Emmanuel Levinas in the 1960s, and co-edited *The Crane Bag* with the well-known philosopher Richard Kearney for many years. As an author, Hederman is closer to Sulivan than any of the other Irish priests dealt with here, a difference that could be a result of the time he spent in France or his wide knowledge of literature. In 1999, I remember reading *Kissing the Dark* for the first time and being struck by its prophetic and uncompromising tone, its determination not to dress things up but to state it as it is. Talking about the newly formed, independent state that emerged in Ireland in the early decades of the twentieth century, Hederman writes:

> Both the Church and the government were obsessed with warding off the constant threat to Catholic purity from foreign, most especially, English, influence. This was most explicit in the hectoring sermons and blatant propaganda of *The Catholic Bulletin* and *The Catholic Mind*, which were set up for the purpose of supervising the rigorous enforcement of Catholic morality. (Hederman 1999: 87)

In Hederman's view, the Censorship of Publications Act of 1929 represented a 'major victory' for those Irish people intent on restricting freedom of speech and protecting the population from the ever-present threat of sexual incontinence. The dance halls were thus closely supervised as all those attending were inevitably exposed to 'occasions of sin'. He quotes from a joint pastoral issued by the bishops in 1927 that encapsulates the dominant attitude of the Church at the time:

> The evil one is forever setting his snares for unwary feet. At the moment, his traps for the innocent are chiefly the dance hall, the bad book, the indecent paper, the motion picture, the immodest fashion in female dress – all of which tend to destroy the characteristic virtues of our race. (cited by Hederman 1999: 87–8)

Hederman's impatience with the prescriptive nature of Irish Catholicism is obvious. Rather than suppressing writers and artists, the Church would be better advised to nurture and cherish them. In both art and religion, there is a reverence for beauty, a seeking out of truth. The novel, according to Hederman, gives utterance to feelings deep within ourselves that we do not appreciate until we encounter them on the page before our eyes: 'but once we see it we recognise that this was something lurking at the back of our minds which we were never able to identify or articulate for ourselves' (Hederman 1999: 95). Art is a precious window to the soul, and in the third millennium it is often to artists that people turn in an attempt to find consolation and peace rather than to the Church and its priests. The lack of real vision among the Church leadership is a source of concern and disappointment to Hederman:

> [T]he role of the hierarchy in the Church might well be to discern rather than to dictate, to peruse rather than prescribe, to exercise their authority and responsibility in a more passive way, by examining the evidence produced and expressed by the scouts and the spies, before endorsing the strategy and confirming the direction that will lead us into the twenty-first century. (Hederman 1999: 105)

Sadly, in my view at least, the approach adopted by the Church hardened if anything in the first decade of the twenty-first century. 'Scouts and spies' were encouraged to give evidence against priests and religious who were deemed to be at variance with official Church teaching. The victims of these accusations did not even have the right to know who their accusers were or what they were saying about them. Being found guilty without even being accorded the right to defend oneself is not really how justice should operate in any organisation, but especially in one which is supposed to hold truth and ethics in high regard. Surely priests accused of wrongdoing deserve to be afforded the same type of rights as any person who appears in court. However, this is not how the Catholic Church conducts its business, and the result is a lot of pain and frustration for many who have given the institution loyal service over many years. The election of Pope Francis filled those within the Church desirous for change with hope, but their expectations remain largely unfulfilled. What Hederman sought to achieve with *Kissing the Dark* is well encapsulated by the subtitle of the book: *Connecting with the Unconscious*. He tried to force people out of their comfort zone and to put them in contact with parts of themselves that remained largely unexplored, particularly that scary place that is the unconscious.

Underground Cathedrals (2010) develops a similar theme, but this time Hederman makes the argument that the Holy Spirit is unearthing an underground cathedral to replace the pretentious, over-elaborate architecture of the twentieth century. 'Underground cathedral' is a metaphor to describe an alternative place and time of worship. Artists are once more described by the author as 'secret agents' of the Holy Spirit:

> Art has the imagination to sketch out the possible. When this happens something entirely new comes into the world. Often it is not recognised for what it is and is rejected or vilified by those who are comfortable with what is already there and afraid of whatever might unsettle the *status quo*. (Hederman 2010: 13)

This is actually very close to what Sulivan said in relation to his own art, which he viewed as continuing the work of the Gospel in its desire to provoke readers out of their apathy and to incite them to change the course of their lives. In *Morning Light*, he explains his motivation for becoming a writer:

> I don't believe I write because of the need to share secrets. I prefer to tell stories, to give emphasis to a narrator and some characters while I watch from the backstage. My personal journey is mixed up with my books. My preference would be to speak neither about faith nor about myself, but of men and women who set out against the night, [...] of the rejects of society, of love, its wounds and cures, in the secret hope that the absolute would offer a sign in spite of me. (Sulivan 1988: 9)

Sulivan's writing is rooted in the everyday, in the joys and afflictions of ordinary people. He did not see his role as one of preacher but rather aspired to be a mediator between this world and the next. Like prophets, artists tend to suffer at the hands of the ruling elites: they are often banned, condemned, excommunicated, sanctioned by the organs of church and state, because of the threat they pose to established values. Hederman quotes many Irish writers – Friel, McGahern and Heaney in particular – to underline how these sensitive souls, although alienated by the oppressive nature of the authoritarian Catholicism with which they were raised, see beyond the Church's harsh exterior and glimpse the beauty in its rituals and stories. The playwright Tom Murphy, growing up in Tuam, Co. Galway, admitted that he 'believed totally and implicitly in the fairytale of religion' (cited by Hederman 2010: 158). The singing, the incense, the music, the elaborate vestments worn by the priests, the stories they told of martyrs, of salvation and damnation, of good and evil, there was in all this a huge appeal for someone with a literary sensibility. In an interview with Richard Pine, Brian Friel declared in 1972 (when he was forty-three years of age), 'I hope that between now and my death I will have acquired a religion, a philosophy, a sense of life, that will make the end less frightening than it appears to me at this moment' (cited by Hederman 2010: 176). Only Friel himself, or his family members and close friends, would know if he acquired what he was looking for before his death in 2015.

Underground Cathedrals calls for a 'deep listening to the voice of the artist in our midst, and also to the supreme artist who tries to lead us to completion, the Holy Spirit of God' (Hederman 2010: 14). Hederman is someone who is attuned to many of the cultural signs and spiritual manifestations that assail us every day but that most of us fail to notice. Sometimes we need prophetic witnesses to show us what is happening, to trace the route that might well lead to a rich inner life. This Benedictine monk is a most persuasive advocate of a new way of teaching and living out Catholic ideals, and he recommends that we listen to our artists when we are in doubt as to how to exit the labyrinth in which we find ourselves.

Brendan Hoban works as a parish priest in Co. Mayo and is a founding member of the Association of Catholic Priests, a group that raises many issues that are common to priests in Ireland and that do not always receive a fair hearing when they are brought to attention of bishops and senior members of the hierarchy.

Change or Decay: Irish Catholicism in Crisis was an early attempt by Hoban to draw attention to the betrayal of the spirit and energy that Vatican II unleashed in the Catholic Church and the abject incompetence of its clerical members to deal with child abuse and other scandals in a telling manner. He underlines the struggle that is going on 'between those who want an open, accountable, participatory Church that finds its rationale in the Vatican II documents and in the compulsions of our people, and those who have turned the wagons into a Tridentine circle' (Hoban 2005: 26). Hoban would unashamedly identify with the former group, being a fan of Vatican II, which shaped his priesthood in a positive way. Hoban maintains that the apparatus of Vatican II was slowly dismantled by an influential group within the Church that felt nostalgic about the deference shown to the clerical function in the past. Clericalism, the mentality that views God's anointed as being superior to its lay equivalents, and which is prone to be less enamoured of consultation with the laity, has been a major stumbling block for the Church, according to Hoban, and has resulted in elitism and arrogance: 'The Church, despite the public relations spin we seem to need to put on things, will continue to be controlled by a secretive, exclusive, male, celibate, hierarchical and authoritarian elite. Around that exclusive club is a way of life that has to do with status, deference and privilege' (Hoban 2005: 58).

This type of plain talking, no nonsense approach is a feature of the various writers with whom we have dealt. They all share a certain frustration with what they view as regressive practices (they would not all agree as to the nature of these practices) and a failure of governance on matters of major concern to priests. It is they who often have to deal with decisions that are mostly foisted on them without consultation. It is they who deal on a daily basis with parishioners suffering the loss of a loved one, with couples in second relationships who still want to be involved with the life of the Church, with practising homosexuals who are marginalised – often by clerics who, ironically, share their sexual orientation – and sometimes even vilified by their church. They see the reality on the ground: a stark decrease in numbers attending mass, a general dissatisfaction with the quality of the rituals by people who do attend them, a failure in general to communicate the tenets of the faith in a manner that might appeal to young people. As is customary in his presentation of the crisis in the Church, Hoban puts a lot of it down to ambitious men anxious to climb the corporate ladder at any cost:

> We have to accept the triumph of incompetent careerists who have successfully played the clerical game – wearing their black clothes, deferring to those who can influence appointments, addressing everyone by their formal ecclesiastical titles, sycophantly [*sic*] praising every utterance of their superiors, saying all the right things, cultivating all the right people and professing their utter orthodoxy on litmus-test issues of loyalty like celibacy, the ordination of women, *Humanae Vitae* and Marian devotion. (Hoban 2005: 60)

Being a committed priest for over forty years gives people like Brendan Hoban the right to state explicitly what he sees as the faults at the heart of an institution to which he has devoted his life. His frustration with 'the sense of disconnectedness between what comes from the sanctuary and what is experienced in the pew' (Hoban 2005: 119) is one of the things that forces Hoban to conclude that there is no plan in place as to what will happen when the present cohort of priests (with an average age of sixty-five among the diocesan clergy) retire or die.

This is the theme of *Who Will Break the Bread for Us?*, which opens with an interesting anecdote that occurred during a meeting of the Association of Catholic Priests in 2012 when Denis Crosby, the parish priest of Liscannor, 'unpeeled the layers of pretension and presumption that seek to minimise and sometimes deny the prevailing crisis in the Irish Catholic Church' by asking who will actually say mass for the people in another decade or two:

> Suddenly there it was, like a pearl glistening in a clearance, demanding our attention. It isn't, of course, the only question that needs to be asked as our Church faces a difficult future, but it is of immediate and critical concern. For, at most, we have a window of a decade or so to come to terms with this imminent crisis. And unless we do a Eucharist famine will prevail in Ireland as parishes without Mass will lose their focus and their resilience. Without priests we have no Mass and without Mass we have no Church. It's as simple as that. (Hoban 2013: 11–12)

It is indeed a stark scenario that is evoked here, especially when one considers how hard-pressed the elderly priests who are currently working in parishes are. If there are no priests, or far fewer priests, it stands to reason that the Eucharist, the cornerstone of Catholic practice, will dissipate in certain parishes and disappear altogether in others. Hoban wonders why certain men ordained into the priesthood but subsequently laicised could not be called upon again to celebrate the sacraments, if they were prepared to do so. It seems somewhat confusing and inconsistent that former Anglican priests with wives and a family are accepted into ministry by the Catholic Church, whereas a Catholic priest in the same situation is not. Hoban, quoting Margaret Heffernan, says that the Church is suffering from 'Wilful Blindness', a term that is explained thus:

> If you commit your thinking and your practice to a certain truth for some years, it takes a long time to see what eventually appears as a blindingly obvious reality. And even when a doubt is created in the mind, we tend to search out data that confirms our previously-held convictions – talking to those who agree with us and reading books and articles that support our own opinions. The last opinion we tend to consider is anything that might challenge our world-view. (Hoban 2013: 154)

These lines supply an excellent summary of the sort of mindset that can so easily take hold of priests, whose lifestyle tends to encourage a sort of 'groupthink' that is endemic in many major organisations. Conditioned from an early age to look at the world in a certain way, mixing with people of similar views, or with others who do not challenge the views they propound, deprived of a wife and family who would probably educate them to the ways of the world, priests generally live quite self-contained and restricted lives. Only a few become full-time academics and have the time to devote to writing.

None of those included in this chapter could be described as a 'complicit functionary', and all, it seems to me, have the courage to share their vision of the Church with a wider audience, often in the knowledge that what they write may well earn for them the disdain of their confreres, and even sanction from the Vatican. Jean Sulivan observed that prophetic witness comes at a price: 'there is no spiritual life which does not encounter deception and disillusionment, suffering and confusion' (1988: 103). One has the impression that priests who commit themselves to writing are in a sense continuing the Word, a form of expression that does not seek universal acceptance but that chooses the few who are capable of interior conversion and who are prepared to struggle with truths that are often unpalatable. Sulivan accepted that the trajectory was not meant to be easy: 'Instead of satisfying our desires, Jesus sends us back to ourselves at a deeper level. Morality, politics, economics, the intellectual harmony I keep looking for – none of these are his concern. He points in another direction, he drives me toward nothingness' (Sulivan 1988: 40).

The Irish Church has a greater need of prophetic witnesses now than at any time in its history. In the four priests dealt with in this chapter, we have examples of men who are prepared to make sacrifices, to endure scorn, to persevere in the face of unbelievable opposition, in the unflinching belief that Catholicism, for all its faults, is worth fighting for. I will conclude with the words of Mark Patrick Hederman:

> There are those who no longer believe in any God or any religion because of disappointment with the Churches or because of disillusionment caused by the scandalous and criminal behaviour being daily reported among so-called professional representatives of the clergy and the religious orders. Nothing of the sort should allow us to be deflected from our own particular journey, our own personal connection with the living God. Indeed, such revelations are a healthy clearing of the Augean staples. And the manure being spread by such puncturing of the cess-pool, which is long-overdue, can only contribute to more healthy and abundant growth when the springtime comes. (Hederman 1999: 160)

We await the 'abundant growth' of springtime more in hope than expectation. But who can ever say what the future might hold when there are still priests of the prophetic quality such as we have encountered in this chapter.

Note

1 It was actually set up under the stewardship of Archbishop John Charles McQuaid, who was anxious that the new television station should have a good list of religious programming.

Works cited

Dunn, Joseph (1994) *No Lions in the Hierarchy: An Anthology of Sorts*, Dublin: Columba.

Hederman, Mark Patrick (1999) *Kissing the Dark: Connecting with the Unconscious*, Dublin: Veritas.

—— (2010) *Underground Cathedrals*, Dublin: Columba.

Hoban, Brendan (2005) *Change or Decay: Irish Catholicism in Crisis*, Ballina: Banley House.

—— (2013) *Who Will Break Bread for Us? Disappearing Priests*, Ballina: Banley House.

Kelly, Michael (2015) 'Media and Church in Ireland since the Council', in Niall Coll (ed.), *Ireland and Vatican II: Essays Theological, Pastoral and Educational*, Dublin: Columba, pp. 144–53.

Sulivan, Jean (1988) *Morning Light: The Spiritual Journal of Jean Sulivan*, trans. Joseph Cunneen and Patrick Gormally, New York: Paulist Press.

—— (2000) *Anticipate Every Goodbye*, trans. Eamon Maher, Dublin: Veritas.

Twomey, Vincent (2003) *The End of Irish Catholicism?* Dublin: Veritas.

8

Tony Flannery: A witness in an age of witnesses

Catherine Maignant

Introduction

Tony Flannery is an emblematic priest. He grew up in John Charles McQuaid's Ireland, was ordained in the aftermath of the Second Vatican Council and witnessed the Catholic Church's drift away from its ideals. An enthusiastic supporter of the Council's progressive policy, he became an early critic of what he perceived as Rome's renewed conservatism and authoritarianism, defending as he did what he viewed to be the Church of Christ against the clerical Church imposed from above by the Vatican. In the forty years of his mission as a Redemptorist preacher, he sought to breathe new life into the Christian message and to be alert to the signs of the times. Tony Flannery is no theologian, but the books and articles of this prolific religious writer have articulated the frustrations and views of a whole generation of reformists who are appalled at the dwindling number of faithful, the vocations crisis and the marginalisation of the Church in Irish society. In 2010, he co-founded the Association of Catholic Priests (ACP) with a view to promoting the spirit of Vatican II and protecting priests from the scapegoating that he says resulted from the revelation of sexual abuse cases involving religious in Ireland.

Even though Flannery's liberal views have been vented in his publications for thirty years, they only attracted the attention of the Congregation for the Doctrine of the Faith shortly after the launch of the ACP. In 2012, he was threatened with excommunication, silenced and removed from ministry on suspicion of heresy. In the spring of 2013 he decided to challenge the Vatican's orders and go public about the way he had been treated. In spite of appeals made to Pope Francis, he is still out of ministry today, but he has become a key promoter of dissent at national and international level. Yet, like his fellow reformists, he wants to remain at the heart of a church that he loves and tries to save from decay. In his eyes, the institution is in dire need of an injection of reality to stop its terminal decline. The governance of the Church is clearly the central issue at stake in this perspective, but disagreements in that area have wide-ranging implications, especially in relation to the understanding of truth. Tony Flannery, a first-hand witness of recent developments in the history of the Church, seeks to give witness to the truth of Christ as best he can, but he has tended to do so in ways that clash with the Vatican's teaching.

As one who listens and speaks out, it may be argued that he has become a prophetic voice in contemporary Ireland, where those who have not yet left the Church desperately cling to the hope that their call will be heard. Flannery and the supporters of the ACP embody a generation of Catholics who value human rights and reject the message of the traditional Irish Church based on self-denial, guilt, fear and ready-made answers dictated by an all-powerful institution. This chapter will suggest that such people can be considered agents of what Hervieu-Léger describes as an attempt to invert the traditional from-the-top-down Catholic pattern of authority (Hervieu-Léger 2003: 90), in the hope of building a future where what they see as the true word of Christ will recover its life-giving quality. Then, Tony Flannery says, 'the word of God will set us free, because it is a word of love, a word of life' (2004: 12).

The making of a liberal

Tony Flannery is an unlikely rebel priest and an unexpected victim of Rome's heresy-hunting zeal. He should more adequately be described as the typical product of his age. Now in his late sixties, he was born and bred in the West of Ireland where social pressure rather than God's call made him a priest. In the stifling atmosphere of the 1950s he grew up to become a guilt-ridden God-fearing young adult, uncomfortable with emotions and body contact. Like so many of his generation, he was sexually abused as a young child – not by a religious in this instance – but what he remembers of this event has more to do with guilt and the fear of being found out than the actual trauma of the abuse. At a time when confessors brandished the threat of Hell's eternal flames as a reasonable retribution for the slightest 'impure' thoughts, victims simply did not talk. Silence and manic secrecy protected aggressors and turned Ireland into 'a paedophile's paradise' (Flannery 1999: 61).

At the age of twelve, Flannery was sent to a Redemptorist junior seminary. This did not leave him much of a career option, especially as he was the youngest of four, all of whom initially went on for religious life. Just like his two older brothers, he was eventually to join the senior seminary with a view to becoming a Redemptorist. In his first book, published in 1997, *The Death of Religious Life*, he retrospectively wonders that nobody, including his parents, 'seemed to see anything unusual in three brothers from a sheltered background joining the order and wanting to become priests' (Flannery 1997: 38). In Catholic Ireland, the status of being a member of a religious community was indeed desirable: it made one superior to a married person, and closer to God. It ensured a comfortable social position in this life and gave a better chance of salvation in the next. In his personal account of his dealings with the Catholic Church, *From the Inside*, Flannery notes how deferential people suddenly became once he had been ordained: 'a mixture of faith and superstition told them that I had power to do many wonderful things, to bring healing, to impose and to lift curses, to choose whom to bless, even, on occasions, to tell the future' (Flannery 1999: 12).

This can easily be understood as one reflects on the highly negative spirituality of the time, based on an understanding of God as terrifying, judgemental and vengeful. The faithful were intimidated into obeying the dictates of an all-powerful church, whose 'special position' in the Irish Constitution guaranteed it had political as well as moral authority over society. As a result, the institution effectively controlled all aspects of people's lives, including the most intimate. Flannery, who has never been comfortable with this unquestioned authority, is very critical about the perception of Christianity it implied, namely one that suppressed the human person and prevented them from developing their full potential. Christianity, he writes, 'is not first and foremost a religion of dogmas; neither is it a collection of commandments and moral guidelines. It is belief in one person, Jesus Christ. Everything else comes secondary' (Flannery 2004: 39). For all his unhappiness about many aspects of religious life, he decided to stay, maybe less because of the authorities' threat that the founder of his order, St Alphonsus, might accuse him on the Day of Judgment, than on account of social pressure. Around the same time, tediousness and dissatisfaction with mind control were also slowly yielding to the intellectual and emotional quivering brought about by a new context.

When his career started in 1974, the changes introduced by the Second Vatican Council were beginning to breathe new life into Irish Catholicism. As a young Redemptorist priest living in a community, he was able to perceive the effects of the generation gap between the older religious, who were unable to adapt, and the younger ones, who enthusiastically seized the occasion. His description of the disarray and confusion of those whose world was collapsing is extremely moving. But a world of new opportunities opened to his generation as the loving and compassionate face of Christ came to replace the stern awesome features of his frightening predecessor. The definition of the concept of church also evolved from being focused on the clergy to encompassing the whole community of Catholics. Tolerance towards other Christians and ecumenism were recommended. Humanity in all its facets came to the forefront of a new understanding of the Christian heritage. A new respect for private conscience granted each individual the right to think and make decisions for himself or herself. The damaging duality inherited from the early times of Christianity, and spectacularly revived by Pius IX in the nineteenth century, gave way to an image of man that reconciled body and soul. Original Sin did not irremediably condemn ordinary human beings to labour against their own nature in order to reach the unreachable goal of becoming angels. Love, in both its emotional and physical expressions, was good so long as it remained within the boundaries of Catholic moral teaching. Sex and mortal sin were no longer synonymous, which, from the start, clearly raised the question of the legitimacy of clerical celibacy and of the distrust towards women.

In the initial stages of the process, Archbishop McQuaid ignored the rulings of Vatican II. In Rome, he appeared as one of the most reactionary contributors to the council debates. A defender of Latin masses and a staunch opponent of ecumenism, his vigorous stand on sexuality, women and the rights of the Church within the State made the requested changes naturally hateful to him. The new generation of higher clergy was more liberal, but it remained conservative by international standards. The notion that religious life was not special enough in the eyes of God to justify a privileged access to salvation was difficult to accept, especially as the new status of lay people imposed deep modifications in the culture of control and led to a reconsideration of authority. However, the tide could not be stopped. The traditional understanding of obedience was shattered and dialogue acquired an unprecedented importance.

Given the spirit of the age, the package of reforms introduced by the Vatican Council in the 1960s appeared very moderate to anti-Church radicals across the world. Yet it seemed revolutionary in the Irish context, and it became a source of division. In the eyes of Flannery, the key contribution of the council to the renovation of Catholicism was 'that it set loose a wave of freedom of thought in the Church. And like the genie escaping from the bottle, once it was set loose, it was almost impossible to stop it' (Flannery 1997: 509). Nevertheless, the Irish Church's traditional submission to Rome ensured that the decrees of Vatican II were eventually enforced to the letter of the law, including all the prescribed liturgical changes. In spite of its tradition of hellfire preaching, the Redemptorist order was at the forefront of innovation, especially in respect of the transformation of confession from a personal ordeal possibly leading to public humiliation to a form of respectful and helpful counselling. Flannery remembers those years as exhilarating, as the young generation of religious and priests tried their best to unshackle fetters and reinvent Catholicism along new lines. Christian humanism was brought to the fore. Experimentation was exciting, as was the feeling that the true message of Christ was now being delivered in the spirit of compassion and open-mindedness that stands at the heart of the Christian ethos.

The context made Flannery a committed liberal, but his faith made him wish 'to re-introduce Christianity into Christendom' (Flannery 2005: 31), a provocative project already formulated by Kierkegaard in the 1850s. In the eyes of the latter, Christendom had left New Testament ideals so far behind that a radical transformation rather than piecemeal reforms was badly needed. A dedicated Christian, he hoped to make the Church evolve from within. Following the model of Christ, he also believed that, 'What matters is to find a purpose, to see what it really is that God wills that I shall do; the crucial thing is to find a truth which is truth for me and to find the idea for which I am willing to live and die' (Kierkegaard 1829–48: 34). Although Flannery is no philosopher, his writings often mirror this approach to life and meaning.

A witness

In his capacity as an enthusiastic preacher who spent decades travelling across Ireland from parish missions to novenas, Tony Flannery has an insider's knowledge of all aspects of religious life in Ireland, from the changing atmosphere in monasteries to the spiritual aspirations of the communities of faithful. His testimony is all the more precious for its being so frank and outspoken. His is a first-hand witness's approach to the reality on the ground and not the forensic and supposedly objective work of a journalist. Throughout his writings, he expresses his suspicion that the Irish media have an anti-Church agenda, but he also suggests that individual experience is the only accurate mediator of reality. Commenting on his latest book, *A Question of Conscience*, a commentator writes that it is not a book about himself but about the Vatican (Association of Catholic Priests 2013). In the same way, all his books, which have an undeniably personal dimension, may be said to mediate the truth about different aspects of Catholicism in general and the Catholic Church in particular. It may be argued that this echoes not only the growth of individualism but also the privatisation of attitudes towards the sacred and the divine, a product of late modern developments. Flannery is a human being of flesh and blood, not the faceless agent of a dehumanised institution. He is also a free man endowed with a legitimate freedom of thought who stretches the liberal message of the Second Vatican Council to the limit of its revolutionary potential.

In the 1960s, the Church was extremely divided over the issues brought forward by the organisers of the council. Unsurprisingly, consensus was obtained at the expense of coherence, and some conclusions were ambivalent. If freedom of thought was granted, the religious had to remain subservient to their superiors, which promulgated a type of ambiguity that was bound to lead to conflicting interpretations. Flannery chose to favour and embrace the call for renewal and downplay the conservative undertones. He was eager to embrace the return to the sources of Christianity while contributing to the recommended adaptation to the needs of his day and age. His priority was to preach the word of Christ for the benefit of his enlightened contemporaries not to impose on submissive crowds the outmoded rules of the institution.

The following anecdote is significant in that respect. Much to the surprise of many, Flannery did not like wearing the traditional black suit that was the norm for priests at the time:

People have sometimes argued with me that I should wear it for the witness value of it, to proclaim the presence and meaning of the priest. But it is precisely because of the witness factor, that the black suit is for me too much of a witness to the negative sides of clericalism and the Church, that I do not wear it. (Flannery 1999: 33)

In the biblical sense of the term, the witness follows the model of Jesus, who was the primary witness to the Good News proclaimed in the Scriptures. Bearing witness was also the mission entrusted by Christ to his followers: 'you will be my witnesses in Jerusalem, and in all Judea and Samaria, and to the ends of the earth' (Acts 1:8). All Christians are now called to this task as Pope Francis recently reminded Catholics: 'we can say that the road for a Christian follows in the footsteps of Jesus' witness, in order to bear witness to him' (Francis 2014).

This is precisely what Tony Flannery has tried to do as best he could throughout his career. The witness's perspective, however, is based on an individual's subjectivity; it implies the will to share personal experiences and interpretations and to articulate them with the Christian legacy. However, it may make it difficult to submit to a supposedly objective truth imposed from above. In Flannery's estimation, this is justified by the very nature of Jesus's witness. Jesus rejected the orthodoxy of his day, and he was a revolutionary in many ways. According to Flannery, bearing witness therefore means picking up a 'substantial challenge'. Indeed, 'the Christian, the person who is trying to follow Christ, needs, like Jesus, to have an alternative voice that is different from the accepted voices in society and live by alternative values, the values of the kingdom' (Flannery 2004: 33). In the same way as Jesus rebelled against the religious leaders of his day and 'condemned as the most blind of all', 'the righteous ones who were living good lives and observing the laws' (Flannery 2004: 38), Flannery has little time for the institution's authoritarianism. He thinks the Vatican's pomp, splendour, insistence on orthodoxy and pretensions to truth would not have appealed to Jesus, and he doesn't hesitate to wonder, 'Would we crucify him?' (Flannery 2008: 79–89). The growth of conservatism and fundamentalism he perceives within the institutional Church, and also among lay Catholics, is abhorrent to him because he finds it contrary to the message of the Gospel and the spirit of the Second Vatican Council.

In the same way, he is extremely critical of the place held by church tradition in the Catholic doctrine. He repeatedly demonstrates that the Vatican's eternal truth is in large part a historical construct and that many of its aspects have no sound foundation in the Scriptures. He exposes the age-old misogyny of the Church, the well-attested medieval origin of mandatory clerical celibacy, the nineteenth-century roots of papal infallibility, the unjustified position of the Virgin Mary in the Catholic pantheon and the dubious creation by Jesus of the Church as we know it. Rehistoricising solidly held traditional beliefs also leads him to go so far as to question the literal interpretation of Mary's virginity.

In so doing, he is merely being true to the recommendations of *Dignitatis humanae*, Vatican II's Declaration on Religious Freedom: 'on their part, all men are bound to seek the truth, especially in what concerns God and His Church, and to embrace the truth they come to know, and to hold fast to it' (Paul VI 1965: 1). Flannery himself used this argument in his defence against the Congregation for the Doctrine of the Faith's accusations in recent years; but we may add that he obeyed the council's orders further by leading his inquiry 'freely', 'with the aid of teaching or instruction, communication and dialogue' and by ordering his whole life in accord with the demands of that truth (Paul VI 1965: 3 and 2). Yet *Dignitatis humanae* is an ambiguous document that 'leaves untouched traditional Catholic doctrine on the moral duty of men and societies toward the true religion and toward the one Church of Christ' (Paul VI 1965: 1). It also places the respect for 'the truth that is unchanging' at the heart of men's duties (Paul VI 1965: 3). If we admit that the debate over the issue of authority and governance in the Catholic Church ultimately revolves around the meaning of truth, the ambiguities of Vatican II documents leave much ground for interpretation.

In *Fides et Ratio*, John Paul II reminded bishops of 'the Second Vatican Council's insistence that (they) are "witnesses of divine and Catholic truth"' and that 'to bear witness to the truth is therefore a task entrusted to (them)' (John Paul II 1998: 6). By contrast, Tony Flannery's witness seeks truth in the Gospel and in history. Following Pius XII, John Paul II denounced such an approach as a symptom of 'biblicism' and 'historicism' which, he believed, resulted in the denial of 'the unity which the Spirit has created between Sacred Tradition, Sacred Scripture and the Magisterium of the Church in a reciprocity which means that none of the three can survive without the others' (John Paul II 1998: V-55). Unlike contemporary reformists, Rome interprets the decrees of Vatican II only in the light of earlier traditions, in particular the proceeds of the First Vatican Council, which, among other things, proclaimed papal infallibility in 1870. In 1998, the Pope lamented that 'a legitimate plurality' of religious positions had 'yielded to an undifferentiated pluralism' (John Paul II 1998: 6). Recent developments actually testify to the deep polarisation of opinions within the Catholic Church.

It is interesting in that respect to note that Flannery's witness has attracted widely diverging comments that reflect the diversity of opinions within the Catholic Church. To his supporters, it 'would count as what used to be called "white martyrdom"' (Association of Catholic Priests 2012), the total, often heroic, offering of one's life to God. This parallel is all the more significant from our perspective as the word 'witness' is etymologically a literal translation of the Greek for martyr. At the other end of the spectrum, traditionalists call him an apostate and a heretic. For his part, Cardinal Levada, the prefect of the Congregation for the Doctrine of the Faith who initially condemned Flannery, commented that some of his positions were reminiscent of Martin Luther and other Protestant reformers' views (Levada 2013). Beyond the Catholic teaching on priesthood and the Eucharist to which Cardinal Levada referred, it could be argued that

Flannery's understanding of the place, role and duties of the witness echoes that of reformed churches. In the eyes of Protestants, the individual testimony of witnesses is in effect a crucial element in terms of the transmission of the faith. In an age marked by a transmission crisis, Flannery supports this approach, which may arguably make him an emblem of what some call the Anglicanisation of the Catholic Church. However, this attitude more accurately bears the mark of a desire to go back to the sources of Christianity openly advocated by the Second Vatican Council.

The situation in which Flannery finds himself today is in fact a sign of the blatant failure of reformists to convince the majority in the institution of the merits of modernisation. In his eyes, the 1960s were a period of 'missed opportunities' as 'the Church turned away from the spirit that imbued the Vatican Council' (Flannery 1999: 165). His attachment to the principles of his youth and the desire to make the Church evolve from the inside led him to a position he had not anticipated and is not prepared to acknowledge, that of 'a radical fringe priest' (*Irish Times*, 3 May 1999), accused of holding heretical views (Levada 2013).[1]

A liberal, a radical or a prophetic voice?

Tony Flannery firmly denies all accusations of heresy and does not even consider himself a radical. Yet, in 2012, the Congregation for the Doctrine of the Faith expressed concern about a few sentences included in some of his articles published in *Reality* in 2010 and 2011. The following passage, published in the summer of 2010, seems to have appeared particularly objectionable and justified vigorous condemnation and penalties:

> I no longer believe that the priesthood, as we currently have it in the Church, originated with Jesus. He did not designate a special group of his followers as priests. To say that at the Last Supper Jesus instituted the priesthood as we have it is stretching the reality of what happened. More likely that sometime after Jesus, a select and privileged group within the community who had arrogated power and authority to themselves, interpreted the occasion of the Last Supper in a manner that suited their own agenda. (Flannery 2013: 535)

Flannery responded to criticism by a statement in which he denied the heretical nature of the controversial sentences, notably on grounds that they had been removed from their context and that their contents did no more than reflect current theological debates. However, he admits in *A Question of Conscience* that the Vatican's action against him should not have come as a surprise in a context of renewed conservatism following John Paul II and Benedict XVI's choice to return to nineteenth-century fundamentals.

Pope John Paul never appealed to Flannery. He recalls his unease during the Pope's visit to Ireland in 1979 when he realised that 'the hardness, tightness in the pope's face [...] foreshadowed authoritarianism' (Flannery 2013: 249). Increased centralisation led to bishops being appointed for their orthodoxy rather than for their talent or their leadership qualities. This, he says, has been especially true in Ireland, where lay involvement has consequently been hindered more than any-where else in the Western world. Flannery also regrets the divisive effects of John Paul II's traditionalist approach: 'For a leader to identify too much with a position that is on the extreme of the Church is not good leadership', he commented. Besides, the mistaken elevation of popes to 'a semi-divine status' (Flannery 1999: 170) ensured absolute obedience to John Paul's outdated moral and social teachings on the part of the many who 'tended to put their head down, unaware that they were becoming anachronisms in their own time' (Flannery 1999: 166).

The perception of time is indeed another central issue at stake as it regulates the understanding of reality. Flannery lives in the present and tries to be close to people's lives. The official Church has chosen a radically different course. Its will to place itself in the timeless vacuum of eternity is reminiscent of the utopian space-time continuum that proceeds from a form of nostalgia of origins which, as Raoul Vaneigem suggests, hovers between past and future and never materialises in the present (Vaneigem 2000: 43). The Church is disconnected from reality, Tony Flannery says; it is now completely out of touch with real people.

For many years he respected the Papal Nuncio's recommendation that a priest ought to work 'without publicity or fanfare' (Flannery 2013: 231). In his latest book he explains that experience taught him that 'the nuncio's ideal priest was not adequate for the time we lived in, that there was too much that was dysfunctional about the Church and Vatican that needed to be voiced' (Flannery 2013: 250). He is a witness, but not a passive one. For that reason Flannery undoubtedly features among the 'whistle-blowers', identified by Diarmaid McCulloch in his *Silence: A Christian History*, who in the past 150 years have exposed the weak-nesses and discreditable behaviour of an all-too-human institution (McCulloch 2013: 225). From that perspective, *A Question of Conscience* can be seen as a blatant indictment of the inquisitorial methods of the Congregation for the Doctrine of the Faith, and of its secrecy, which aims to hide from the public eye its denial of human rights and its unfairness.

The publication of *The Death of Religious Life* was the first significant trans-gression of the rule of silence. Noting what he held to be the terminal decline of apostolic religious congregations, Flannery suggested that young people be dis-couraged from joining them, a move which would ultimately lead to the demise of these anachronistic institutions. Unsurprisingly, the book was not well received. He went further in his later works, notably *Keeping the Faith*, where he expounded his analysis of the current problems of the Church and advocated solutions based on the crucial importance of reconnecting with the world. Referring to Hans Küng on the question of the suppression of ideas in the Catholic Church, he indirectly expressed his support for this major theologian who was silenced by the Vatican in the late 1970s. He was later repeatedly to complain of the Vatican's estrangement from the contemporary theological debate. Such was not the ambition of the book, however. *Keeping the Faith* sought to identify problems connected to the structures of government and current forms of ministry. He already denied their divine origin and suggested reforms, including a return to the Gospel understanding of ministry as service – particularly to the poor and the marginalised – and the abolition of compulsory clerical celibacy. Moreover, he insisted that the Church did not have the monopoly of truth and that it had been 'a big mistake to ever declare the pope infallible' (Flannery 2005: 57). Finally, he believed that the place of women in the Church ought to be re-examined if only as a gesture to the example given by Jesus and the Early Church. From this time onwards, and to the present day, Flannery has been an active supporter of the ordination of women.

If Levada's accusations had exclusively concerned priesthood and the Eucharist, his successor Gerhard Müller added that Flannery should acknowledge that Jesus chose men as his apostles, a gesture that forms the basis of the Church's interdiction on the ordination of women. Although he eventually agreed to make a statement of faith regarding the first two points – apparently to the satisfaction of Levada – he was not prepared to go any further. Referring both to the legacy of the Gospel and the Early Church, Paul VI's *Dignitatis humanae*, the work of the Pontifical Biblical Commission (1976) and his experience of women's alienation and feelings of injustice, he refused to retract. In the same way, he said he 'could not have looked at himself in the mirror' (Barry 2013) if he had submitted to the last request of the Congregation for the Doctrine of the Faith and conformed to the teaching of the Magisterium on moral issues.

Tony Flannery has always been an outspoken critic of *Humanae vitae*, Paul VI's encyclical that reiterated the Vatican's ban on contraception in 1968. He also has a liberal stance on homosexuality, especially in view of the large number of homosexuals within the ranks of the Church, an undisputable fact even within the Vatican, as evidenced by John Thavis in his *Vatican Diaries* (2013). In May 2015, he supported same-sex marriage in defiance of the official Church's position, just as he had previously supported the Protection of Life during Pregnancy Bill (2013), much to the horror of traditionalist groups who, in this as in other circumstances, could not find words harsh enough to condemn him.

The Vatican, Hervieu-Léger notes, is caught between two types of activism – radicalism and fundamentalism – that she sees as the expression of a new more communitarian form of socialisation in Catholic circles. Pressure comes from individuals in search of a collective validation of their positions. The success of the individual witness perspective makes this inevitable. In Hervieu-Léger's eyes, the emergence and growth of active lay and religious groups is the sign of a break in the history of Catholicism since it is leading towards a radically new, from-the-bottom-up approach to authority (Hervieu-Léger 2003: 285–6). When the views of such communities reflect their obedience to the Vatican's orders and contribute to the legitimation of its authoritarianism and conservatism, then it is fine. When they openly defy its authority and teachings and go public about it, they are silenced.

As Flannery suggests, it most certainly is no accident if the Congregation for the Doctrine of the Faith took action against him shortly after the launch of the ACP. When Flannery refused to make the requested statement, he told the *New York Times* that 'it would be betrayal not only of myself but of my fellow priests and lay Catholics who want to change' (Dalby 2013). He is aware that he has become a prominent mouthpiece of a loose but significant movement seeking renewal in the Church on the basis of the decrees of Vatican II. The ACP is thus widely supported by liberal lay Catholic associations such as the Association of Catholics in Ireland, founded in 2012, which actively defends the ordination of married men, a fight reminiscent of Flannery's battle for a greater involvement of lay people in the Church. It is no accident either that one of the penalties imposed on him was to leave the leadership of the ACP. The priests of the Pfarrer initiative in Austria have similarly been disciplined as they, just like the ACP, are considered a threat to the Vatican, whose authority they undermine.

Conclusion

Flannery is not so much a thinker as a voice, not so much the holder of unorthodox views as a leader. In the same way as a prophet, he expresses the preoccupations of his day and states clearly what many people think in private but do not express publicly. He looks on change as a necessary step towards the Church taking a serious look at itself. In his classic study of postmodernity, Jean-François Lyotard noted that our contemporaries favoured individual tales and disparaged mega-narratives (Lyotard 1979: 7). Catholic reformists exemplify this analysis, on the one hand by re-reading the Gospel in the light of individual experience and, on the other hand, by taking into account their own life stories in order to bear witness to the love of Jesus. Ours is an age of witnesses who try to reconcile the Christian message with their experience of life. In modern democratic societies, legitimate power comes from the grass roots. As Frédéric Lenoir convincingly argues, the developments of individualism and humanism have resulted in a dramatic evolution of people's attitudes towards structures of authority. Men are now at the centre of preoccupations, and any analysis of contemporary religious phenomena must take into account this all-pervading context (Lenoir 2003: 55–6).

According to Sheila Cassidy, prophets 'must listen to God, to the signs of the time, and to the cries of the oppressed, and when they have understood the message, speak out, whatever the personal cost' (1997: 159). It may be argued that Flannery has become a prophetic voice, not only in Ireland but in the Western world, as he leads progressive Catholics towards a reinvented church, closer in spirit to Christianity as he understands it, founded on the belief in 'Jesus the life-giver, [...] the light of the world, [...] the one who has come to set us free' (Flannery 2002: 60).

Epilogue

In December 2013, the Veritas Catholic bookshop in Dublin announced that it would not stock Flannery's *Question of Conscience*. More recently, in August 2015, the Bishop of Cloyne prohibited a talk the sanctioned priest had been invited to give at the community centre in Killeagh. Such moves bring to mind McCulloch's comment that 'efforts to silence dissidents armed with historical evidence have the temporary success and long-term failure of the child defending a sandcastle against the tide' (McCulloch 2013: 228). Indeed, Flannery has toured America, England and Ireland to give lectures on Church reform; he gives interviews in Ireland and abroad; and the Internet is an effective medium to convey his message worldwide. It seems in fact that the difficulties he had with the Congregation for the Doctrine of the Faith have increased rather than reduced his aura and influence. Today, even though sanctions against him have not been lifted, it is his hope that Pope Francis's efforts to liberalise the Church will bear fruit. His comments on the prelate's addresses during his 2015 US trip were extremely laudatory, except in relation to his conservative stand on women's ordination. Yet the extreme fragmentation of opinions within the institution, and the strength of conservativeness that was evidenced during the Synod on the Family, may well indicate that the road to the restoration of what Flannery sees as the true church of Christ will be long and steep.

Note

1 'Speaking for the Ordinary Catholic', *Irish Times*, 3 May 1999, available at www.irishtimes.com/culture/speaking-for-the-ordinary-catholic-1.184225 (accessed 20 October 2015).

Works cited

Association of Catholic Priests (2012) 'Tony Flannery Can Wear the Holy Office-Imposed Silentium Badge with Pride', available at www.associationofcatholicpriests.ie/2012/04/tony-flannery-can-wear-the-holy-office-imposed-silentium-badge-with-pride (accessed 22 October 2015).
—— (2013) 'A Question of Conscience Is Not About Tony Flannery but About the Vatican', available at www.associationofcatholicpriests.ie/2013/09/talk-by-bill-oherlihy-at-launch-of-tony-flannerys-book (accessed 25 October 2015).
Barry, Aoife (2013) 'Fr Flannery "Couldn't Look in the Mirror If He Signed Church Statement"', 21 January, available at http://www.thejournal.ie/fr-tony-flannery-762835-Jan2013/ (accessed 6 September 2016).
Cassidy, Sheila (1997). 'Hospice, a Prophetic Movement', in Stanislaus Kennedy (ed.), *Spiritual Journeys*, Dublin: Veritas, pp. 159–64.

Dalby, Douglas (2013) 'Priest Is Planning to Defy the Vatican's Orders to Stay Quiet', *New York Times*, 19 January, available at www.nytimes.com/2013/01/20/world/europe/priest-is-planning-to-defy-vaticans-orders-to-stay-quiet.html?_r=0 (accessed 24 October 2015).

Flannery, Tony (1997) *The Death of Religious Life*, Dublin: Columba.

—— (1999) *From the Inside*, Cork: Mercier.

—— (2003) *Waiting in Hope: Reflections on Advent*, Dublin: Veritas.

—— (2004) *Come Back to Me with All Your Heart: Reflections on Lent*, Dublin: Veritas.

—— (2005) *Keeping the Faith*, Dublin: Mercier.

—— (2008) *Fragments of Reality: Collected Writings*, Dublin: Columba.

—— (2013) *A Question of Conscience*, Dublin: Londubh Books.

Francis (2014) 'Bearing Witness to Christ, Morning Meditation in the Chapel of the Domus Sanctae Marthae', available at https://w2.vatican.va/content/francesco/en/cotidie/2014/documents/papa-francesco-cotidie_20140506_bearing-witness.html (accessed 20 October 2015).

Hervieu-Léger, Danièle (2003) *Catholicisme: la fin d'un monde*, Paris: Bayard.

John Paul II (1998) *Fides et ratio*, available at http://w2.vatican.va/content/john-paul-ii/en/encyclicals/documents/hf_jp-ii_enc_14091998_fides-et-ratio.html (accessed 16 October 2015).

Kelly, Michael (2013) 'Levada Breaks Silence on Flannery Case', 7 November, available at www.irishcatholic.ie/article/lavada-breaks-silence-flannery-case (accessed 23 October 2015).

Kierkegaard, Søren (1978) *Søren Kierkegaard's Journals and Papers*, vol. V: *Autobiographical. Pt. 1, 1829–1848*, ed. Howard V. Hong and Edna H Hong, Bloomington, Ind.: Indiana University Press.

Lenoir, Frédéric (2003) *Les Métamorphoses de Dieu: la nouvelle spiritualité occidentale*, Paris: Plon.

Lyotard, Jean-François (1979) *La Condition postmoderne*, Paris: Éditions de Minuit.

McCulloch, Diarmaid (2013) *Silence: A Christian History*, London: Allen Lane, Penguin.

Paul VI (1965) *Dignitatis humanae*, available at www.vatican.va/archive/hist_councils/ii_vatican_council/documents/vat-ii_decl_19651207_dignitatis-humanae_en.html (accessed 22 October 2015).

—— (1968) *Humanae vitae*, available at http://w2.vatican.va/content/paul-vi/fr/encyclicals/documents/hf_p-vi_enc_25071968_humanae-vitae.html (accessed 22 October 2015).

Thavis, John (2013) *The Vatican Diaries*, London: Penguin.

Vaneigem, Raoul (2000) *De l'inhumanité de la religion*, Paris: Denoël.

9

'Belief shifts': Ireland's referendum and the journey from *Gemeinschaft* to *Gesellschaft*

Eugene O'Brien

I would begin this chapter with two pieces of narrative: one from fantasy literature and one from recent political discourse. The fantasy writer Terry Pratchett
wrote a book in his Discworld series about religion, gods and belief, entitled *Small
Gods*. In the Discworld, he created a country called Omnia, a theocracy within
which everyone and everything revolved around the worship of the Great God
Om. Omnianism was the hegemonic ideological position in this country, and the
capital city was made in the image of the Great God Om:

> It extended for miles, its temples, churches, schools, dormitories, gardens, and towers
> growing into and around one another in a way that suggested a million termites all
> trying to build their mounds at the same time. When the sun rose the reflection of
> the doors of the central Temple blazed like fire. They were bronze, and a hundred feet
> tall. On them, in letters of gold set in lead, were the Commandments. There were five
> hundred and twelve so far, and doubtless the next Prophet would add his share. The
> sun's reflected glow shone down and across the tens of thousands of the strong-in-
> faith who laboured below for the greater glory of the Great God Om. Probably no
> one did know how many of them there were. Some things have a way of going criti-
> cal. Certainly there was only one Cenobiarch, the Superior Iam. That was certain. And
> six Archpriests. And thirty lesser Iams. And hundreds of bishops, deacons, subdeacons,
> and priests. And novices like rats in a grain store. And craftsmen, and bull breeders, and
> torturers, and Vestigial Virgins … No matter what your skills, there was a Place for you
> in the Citadel. (Pratchett 1992: 10)

Those who believed and carried out the rituals prospered; those who did not
were subject to the 'quisition' (a parody of the inquisition). The premise of the
book is that of a reciprocal relationship between gods and belief. In this universe,
gods grow according to the amount and strength of belief in them. The process

is described as beginning organically as a shepherd, seeking a lost lamb, 'finds it among the briars and takes a minute or two to build a small cairn of stones in general thanks to whatever spirits might be around the place':

> Often it stops there. But sometimes it goes further. More rocks are added, more stones are raised, a temple is built on the site where the tree once stood. The god grows in strength, the belief of its worshipers raising it upwards like a thousand tons of rocket fuel. For a very few, the sky's the limit. (Pratchett 1992: 7)

It is an interesting idea, though in fact it is one that can be seen throughout the world: in real terms, the strength of Islam is on the rise, due largely to the fervent belief of its adherents, though regrettably this is resulting in destructive as much as in creative acts, as evidenced by the increase in terrorism throughout the world that claims to be based on the notion of jihad in the Qur'an. Similarly, the strength of Christianity, in all its forms, can be seen to be on the wane, certainly in the Western, developed world, as evidenced by the increasingly secularist and pluralist cultures within which it must preach its faith.

However, Pratchett's book has a twist: as in the manner of many religions, there is a second coming, and the Great God Om returns to earth. Given that there is a whole country that is dedicated to his cause, and seeing that this country is a theocracy where the highest priests are *de facto* the political and cultural leaders of the society, one would surmise that his strength would be truly awesome: this assumption would be wrong. Revealing himself to a simple novice monk called Brutha, Om is surprised that he has been incarnated as a tortoise, as his more traditional incarnations have been those of a bull or a lion or an eagle. He appears to Brutha because he senses his true belief, but, as the novel progresses, it becomes very clear to Om that 'the thing about Brutha's flame of belief was this: in all the Citadel, in all the day, it was the only one the God had found' (Pratchett 1992: 83). So, despite the structural centrality of Omniamism in the country of Omnia, the actual real belief in Om has been attenuated to one rather simple-minded novice. Later in the book, Om explains the process as he sees it:

> 'Right', said Om. 'Now … listen. Do you know how gods get power?' 'By people believing in them', said Brutha. 'Millions of people believe in you'. Om hesitated. All right, all right. We are here and it is now. Sooner or later he'll find out for himself …
> 'They don't believe', said Om.
>   'But – '
>   'It's happened before', said the tortoise. 'Dozens of times. D'you know Abraxas found the lost city of Ee? Very strange carvings, he says. Belief, he says. Belief *shifts*. People start out believing in the god and end up believing in the structure'. (Pratchett 1992: 166; italics in original)

The second narrative is rooted not in fantasy but in contemporary politics. On 22 May 2015, the Irish people participated in a constitutional referendum on two issues: the thirty-fourth amendment to the Constitution was about permitting same-sex marriage, while the thirty-fifth amendment suggested reducing the age of candidacy for the post of president of Ireland from thirty-five to twenty-one. Ireland had long been seen as a de-facto theocracy in which the Catholic Church held a hegemonic position. Issues of law, health and education have all been subject to strong levels of control, both implicit and explicit, by the Catholic hierarchy, and this is especially true in terms of matters pertaining to sexual morality. In the 1980s and 1990s, rancorous debates were held around issues of contraception, abortion and divorce as a gradual process of secularisation challenged the older dispensation's view on these matters. As the Irish people became more educated (ironically often due to the good work of religious teaching orders of nuns and brothers), and as the access to a broader range of media outlets through satellite channels, broadband and the Internet became more prevalent, a plurality of viewpoints became available to the Irish people, and these meant that opinions were now being formed that were outside of the control of the Catholic Church. This picture is similar to what has happened in other developed countries, albeit at a much slower pace, and has been described in the work of Jean-François Lyotard, who speaks of the 'postmodern condition', which he defined as being an 'incredulity toward metanarratives. This incredulity is undoubtedly a product of progress in the sciences: but that progress in turn presupposes it' (Lyotard 1984: xxiv). These metanarratives are now broken down into a series of competing 'little narratives (*petits récits*)' (Lyotard 1984: 60), which must compete in the public sphere to gain any semblance of belief, commitment or value. Increasingly, this public sphere is operative online.

The thirty-fifth amendment was defeated, as people felt that twenty-one was too young to be a candidate for the largely symbolic office of president; also, it was very much overshadowed by the other issue, namely the legalisation of same-sex marriages. The wording was straightforward and as unambiguous as such a legalistic discourse can be: 'marriage may be contracted in accordance with law by two persons without distinction as to their sex'. The result came as something of a surprise, especially in terms of how decisive it was. A total of 1,201,607 people (62.1 per cent) voted 'Yes', and 734,300 (37.9 per cent) voted 'No'. The total valid poll was just under 2 million, which was the highest number of people to vote in any Irish referendum since the foundation of the State. All of the major political parties were officially in favour of the amendment, even if a significant number of the parliamentary party members of a more conservative bent were notable by their absence in campaigning for the measure. The Church, and its supporters, were significantly against the amendment but were defeated by a factor of some 24 per cent of those who voted.

One might well ask what a fantasy novel about religion and the thirty-fourth amendment to the Irish Constitution have in common, or even why Pratchett's novel is being mentioned in the first place. The reason is that fiction is often one of the clearest ways in which the real of any situation can be uncovered, and I will argue that the generic juxtaposition with which this chapter began will allow for a new and different understanding of the nature of the referendum result and for some kind of explanation as to the current state of religion in Ireland. Fiction regularly provides access to truths about reality that otherwise remain unspoken. Jacques Lacan speaks of how language is always prone to leaving a gap in meaning – he stresses that what he calls the symbolic order, while necessary for communication, is nevertheless incapable of what might be termed full communication, or of accessing the real of a situation or emotion. Through its imbrication of syntax, linguistic structure, associative structure of the signifier through rhyme, and image-clustering, fiction allows 'a glimmer of signification [to] spring forth at the surface of the real, and then causes the real to become illuminated with a flash projected from below' (Lacan 2006: 468). For Lacan, the real is that which is always there but which is impossible to express fully in language, and he says that it 'carries its place stuck to the sole of its shoe, there being nothing that can exile it from it' (Lacan 2006: 17).

The language of fiction, which can focus on imagined details and singular incidents, has the capacity to provide access to aspects of the unconscious and the real, both of which are barred from normal language: as he puts it, what does not 'come to light in the symbolic *appears in the real*' (Lacan 2006: 324; italics in original). In this sense, Lacan sees that 'truth shows itself [*s'avère*] in a fictional structure' (Lacan 2006: 625), and this is possibly because when the reader knows that the genre is fictional, then there is a habit of connecting this fiction with different real-life situations and structures. Giorgio Agamben puts it very well when he notes that prose, 'takes place in such a way that its advent always already escapes both toward the future and toward the past' (1991: 76); in other words, fictional prose always has an effect beyond itself. In the case of Pratchett's comments on the way that the structure created around a religion becomes the object of belief, as opposed to the religion itself, there is a palpable correlation with the situation in Ireland in the current socio-cultural context.

Theodor Adorno's conception of 'truth content' (*Wahrheitsgehalt*) 'indicates the crux of artistic knowledge and of philosophical interpretation in *Aesthetic Theory*' (Zuidervaart 1991: xxii). Adorno sees the aesthetic as a form of thinking: 'the truth content of artworks is fused with their critical content' (1997: 35). He also sees the aesthetic as composed of a dialectic between form and content, between fiction and reality and between language and the real. Adorno notes that aesthetic truth content and history are 'deeply meshed' (1997: 41), and he is distrustful of pan-generic appeals to concepts of 'spirit', as his is a particularist perspective, which foregrounds the necessity of 'critique' if the truth content of the aesthetic is to be revealed, and it is in this sense of critique 'that art and philosophy converge' (Adorno 1997: 88). Thus, in the present context, I would argue that Pratchett is making a deeply philosophical point about the relationship between religion as a structure and religion as a belief system, or as a mode of access to, and explanation of, the transcendent. In Ireland, as in *Omnia*, the religious and political were structurally imbricated across all levels of society. The influence of the Church on education, health, legal issues and social policy has been traced in academic discourse, and indeed in this book, and hence this chapter will focus on one such social system in particular: that of marriage.

In Ireland, the result of the referendum was seen as a significant signifier of a new form of modernity, as all the political parties and many social groups were in favour of the legalisation of gay marriage. The Catholic hierarchy, and other pro-Catholic groups, were very much against this proposal, and in arguing their case, they had little enough to offer by way of reason apart from the argument that, traditionally, marriage was between a man and a woman and also that it was the societal structure wherein children were reared and looked after. Their campaign was quite negative in this sense, as indicated by the poster slogans that bedecked the country during the campaign:

> Surrogacy? She needs her mother for life, not just for 9 months – Vote No.[1]
> We already have civil partnership. Don't redefine marriage – Vote No.[2]
> Children deserve a mother and a father – Vote No.[3]
> A mother's love is irreplaceable – Vote No.[4]
> Two men can't replace a mother's love – Vote No.[5]

Those in favour of the change in the legislation had a more positive range of words to use:

> Yes – Let's treat everyone equally.[6]
> Children deserve equality – Vote yes.[7]
> Vote yes because marriage matters.[8]
> Vote yes – equality for everybody.[9]

The fact that three of these slogans use the word 'equality' is telling: morally, it would be hard to argue against treating people equally, so by seeming to argue against this, the 'No' side were arguing that people should not be treated equally, which was a difficult position from which to mount a campaign. The demographics and the general mood towards secularisation would suggest that the referendum was likely to be carried, and in more recent social debates, the hierarchy and the Catholic Church have been less inclined to take a strong position. However, in this case, the Church and Catholic bodies such as the Iona Institute were deeply involved in the campaign and argued on quite essentialist philosophical principles regarding natural law and the traditional definition of marriage as between a man and a woman. In a pastoral letter on marriage, the Irish bishops set out their conceptual stall in the first paragraph:

> Married love is a unique form of love between a man and woman which has a special benefit for the whole of society. The Catholic Church, with other Christians and

those of no particular religious view, regard the family based on marriage between a woman and a man as the single most important institution in any society. To seek to re-define the nature of marriage would be to undermine it as the fundamental building block of our society. (Irish Catholic Bishops' Conference 2014: 1)

David Quinn, of the Iona Institute, writing in the *Irish Independent* on 21 May 2010, asked why is marriage 'treated uniquely' and went on to answer his own question: 'because it is unique. Out of all the myriad forms of relationships that people can form, only it can provide a child with a mother and a father who have made a formal, public commitment to one another' (Quinn 2010). While aware of the general drift towards secularisation and a concomitant pluralisation of social and legal structures, nevertheless the Church was trenchant in what it must have known was a lost cause. The reason for this is clear, I think, if we look at marriage in terms of its place in the very specific historical relationship between the Catholic Church and the Irish State, but not just from a historical perspective. It is widely agreed that Church and State were hand in glove, to quote James Joyce, from the beginning of Independence. This point has been made, and various examples – de Valera looking for church approval for the social aspects of the Irish Constitution in 1937; John A. Costello's comment that he was a Catholic first and an Irishman second in 1949; the furore over the Mother and Child Bill in 1951 – have been discussed at length. My aim is to take a step backwards from the particular instances and to situate the Irish case in terms of some work done by the sociologist Ferdinand Tönnies as a way of understanding how and why belief shifts.

Tönnies, an early German sociologist and a contemporary of Durkheim and Weber, used the German words *Gemeinschaft* and *Gesellschaft* to distinguish between two fundamentally different structural paradigms for social relations. For Tönnies, social relationships were grounded either in sentiment, friendship, kinship and neighbourliness (*Gemeinschaft*) or in contractual interests, rational calculation, monetary ties and legal codes (*Gesellschaft*): 'The relationship itself, and the social bond that stems from it, may be conceived either as having real organic life, and that is the essence of *Community* [*Gemeinschaft*]; or else as a purely mechanical construction, existing in the mind, and that is what we think of as *Society* [*Gesellschaft*]' (Tönnies et al. 2001: 17). *Gemeinschaft* and *Gesellschaft* are not mutually exclusive categories but, rather, abstract representations of social arrangements that may be found existing side by side in a given social context. For Tönnies, the sense of community is more attractive than that of society. As he puts it:

All kinds of social co-existence that are familiar, comfortable and exclusive are to be understood as belonging to *Gemeinschaft*. *Gesellschaft* means life in the public sphere, in the outside world. In *Gemeinschaft* we are united from the moment of our birth with our own folk for better or for worse. We go out into *Gesellschaft* as if into a foreign land. A young man is warned about mixing with bad society: but 'bad community' makes no sense in our language. (Tönnies et al. 2001: 18)

In general, Tönnies argued, elements of *Gesellschaft* increased as societies modernised (Witte and Mannon 2010: 153), and he has been accused of a cultural preference for the more organic communal *Gemeinschaft* which seems to hark back to a time when societies were, in fact, small communities, connected by kinship, friendship and the common bond of shared working and family experiences. I would suggest that in this analysis of a structured society, and of the way in which, as modernisation and postmodernisation begin to take root, the sense of *Gemeinschaft* begins to become one of *Gesellschaft* is most revealing. The gradual processes of industrialisation, and the movement from rural to urban life, which took several hundred years in Europe, happened belatedly in an Irish context, where the slow embourgeoisement of European culture was truncated into a few decades. As has been argued coherently by John Littleton and Eamon Maher, the visit of Pope John Paul II to Ireland in 1979, while seen as an endorsement of the hegemonic position of the Catholic Church in Ireland, in fact was more a grammatical conclusion to that narrative of church–state symphysis: 'The papal visit in 1979 saw massive crowds assemble at venues such as the Phoenix Park, Drogheda, Galway and Limerick. While allegedly providing a concrete sign of the good health of Irish Catholicism, in essence this visit marked the end of an era' (Littleton and Maher 2010: 7).

Vocations had already begun to decline in the 1970s, and the gradual permeation of the BBC and ITV channels across the country, as opposed to just the eastern seaboard, meant that orthodox opinion was no longer the only voice heard in the media. By the 1980s and 1990s, these channels were now becoming more widespread across Ireland. People now had an element of choice in terms of forming their attitudes, and where heretofore the voices they heard were almost univocal – being Irish, Catholic, conservative and republican – now there were pluralist voices on the radio and television, which often disagreed with the views that came from the traditional Irish perspective.

As well as the television and the airwaves, travel also broadened the mind. In 1985, Ryanair instituted a £99 return flight to the UK, which was less than half the price of the British Airways and Aer Lingus lowest return fare of £209. The advent of cheap air flights to and from Britain also meant that emigration was no longer a one-way journey; now it was becoming the norm for people to come back to Ireland more often, and in so doing they brought with them attitudes, commercial goods and opinions that were alien to what had traditionally been an Irish, Catholic, republican mindset. As Kearney points out, there can be little doubt about the 'impact of social changes such as immigration or urbanisation upon religion, education, and the family' (2007: 29). In the mid-1990s, the Internet became more readily available in Ireland, and now a broader and non-controlled world view, or to use Lyotard's terms, world views, were available on a computer screen (albeit at a very slow refresh rate) in houses across the country. In the 1980s, the first mobile phone calls were being made and by the 1990s phones and texts were becoming common. In contemporary Ireland, the Internet, chat rooms, news feeds, Facebook, Instagram and Twitter mean that the information from a multi-perspectival media world is available in one's pocket or one's handbag, and, similarly, one can post messages, thoughts and images that can be seen worldwide almost instantaneously. This is very different from the more traditional modes of communication that were available in the more community-oriented Ireland of the past.

So, in a country with fixed social, political and religious structures, governed autocratically and unquestioningly by the twin centres of power, the Catholic Church and the political elite, the restriction and strict control of information, allied to an educational system that perpetuated middle-class hegemony, meant that change was anathema to the elite in whose charge the governance of the country lay. In an undereducated, largely rural community, such power structures had little difficulty perpetuating themselves: they created narrow horizons of expectation, which limited any development or influence from outside. Information came from the pulpit on a Sunday, from Irish newspapers, which operated under censorship and under legal frameworks that were intrinsically conservative, and under a constitution that recognised the 'special position of the Catholic Church'. Clearly, this closed type of society bore all the hallmarks of a *Gemeinschaft*. Martin Heidegger spoke of the notion of *Gemeinschaft* in terms of the comradeship experienced by soldiers in war. Genuine community was formed only 'when each individual bound himself to what is higher than either individual or community' (Zimmerman 1990: 74), and the Irish State, as it was in its early years, placed the Catholic Church in this position.

Much of this is commonplace knowledge; most cultural critics are aware of these changes. What has not really been discussed, however, are the structural effects of these changes on both Church and State in Ireland. Referring to our notion of fiction as a form of truth, this is probably best illustrated by taking a fictive Irish person in the 1960s. This person would have been white, mass- and confession-going, socially and attitudinally conservative, republican to some degree and politically conservative, as the two main political parties, Fianna Fáil and Fine Gael were ideologically similar but historically differentiated by their attitudes to the Treaty signed in 1921, which gave the twenty-six counties a restricted form of independence, with Partition as the price to be paid. This meant that politically there was no connection between Ireland and the broader right-wing/left-wing ideological and political outlooks of Europe and the UK. Instead, there was a strong desire to attain national unity, while at the same time there was an implicit desire to shape the twenty-six counties as a separate identity – as an Irish Catholic organic community, valorising the classical qualities of the traditional family and community-oriented structure of the *Gemeinschaft*. Indeed, the use of the word *gemein* implies a strong sense of community, of something that is put in common: 'the *Gemeinschaft* is opposed to the *Gesellschaft* a spontaneous community of feelings, of practices, of mores that belong to a formally organised society, to an association by contract provided with rules and goals' (Lyotard 1994: 84).

I would argue that the somewhat ad-hoc nature of our independence, which was a slow process, was a factor here. The Easter Rebellion took place in 1916, but it was three years later, in January 1919, that the declaration of independence was made, and a further three years later, in 1922, that the Free State came into being. The Irish Constitution was published in 1937, and it would be another sixteen years before the Irish Republic was declared in 1948. This was a very gradual process, and one that took place, I would suggest, without any overarching ideological imperative. As has so often been the case in colonial societies, the main unifying focus was the desire to achieve independence from the colonial power. It was only in the advent of this independence that people started to look at the type of postcolonial society that they would like to set up. Often fractures occurred in the independence movement, and, in the pattern in many Third World nations, a war of independence was followed by a civil war and partition. To heal these divisions, certain signifiers of belonging were prioritised by the ruling elites, signifiers that stressed unity, togetherness and a sense of belonging – in other words, of sameness. To avoid reinforcing the divisions that already existed, there was a focus on looking into ourselves and into what made us similar, a point tellingly made by Seamus Heaney who noted that 'our pioneers keep striking / inwards and downwards' (Heaney 1969: 56), and the family is perhaps the ultimate source of such sameness. The *Gemeinschaft* has this sense of sameness at its core: it is created through the 'ties of kinship, fellowship, custom, history and communal ownership of primary goods' (Tönnies et al. 2001: xvii–xviii). Kinship is key, and marriage is very much the primary unit of such organic communities, as it is the core unit around which a community of sameness and relationship is built. Tönnies makes this very clear:

> The most important of these is *marriage*, which on the one hand provides the basis for a new family and on the other is formed by a free agreement between man and wife, although this can only be understood in terms of the idea and ethos of the family. Marriage in its moral sense, i.e. monogamy, can be defined as perfect *neighbourhood* – living together in constant physical proximity. Its whole nature consists in community of place by day and night, and the sharing of bed and board; the spouses' spheres of activity and influence are not just adjacent but identical, like the communal fields of fellow villagers. And likewise their *joint ownership of goods* can be seen most clearly in their possession of the same farmland. [italics in original] (Tönnies et al. 2001: 205)

Ireland, I would argue, was a *Gemeinschaft*, an organic community where the verities of sameness, or of what Heidegger would term gathering (*Versammlung*), were the core imperatives. Marriage, in the traditional sense of a relationship between man and woman, that produced children, and as a means of interpellating new people into the values and mores of the *Gemeinschaft*, is a core ideological state apparatus, to use the terminology of Louis Althusser. He differentiated between the repressive state apparatus (the army, the law, the police) and the ideological state apparatus (religion, education, the family, the legal and political establishments, the communications media and the arts) (Althusser 2001: 143). This is a way of replicating a culture through each generation, through education, culture and religion, because, as Althusser notes, culture 'is the ordinary name for the Marxist concept of the *ideological*' (2001: 242). He views education as the apparatus that has 'replaced in its functions the previously dominant ideological State apparatus, the Church' (Althusser 2001: 154).

By making marriage central to the *Gemeinschaft* of Ireland, such ideological conformity was ensured from the beginning of the State. Marriage in Ireland was largely sacramental, as already noted, but it was also generative of other sacraments for the children of such marriages. Therefore, marriage engendered the baptism of the child, the sacrament of penance, followed by that of first communion and then later confirmation. Ideally, the children would then progress to marriage, and the cycle would be repeated. The end of life was signified by the sacrament of last rites, where one's family surrounded the dying person as the priest ushered them into the next life. Thus, from the cradle to the grave, the Church provided the ideological signposts that guided the Irish person through their lives, and, as family was the central vehicle for the embodiment of this process, so marriage was the transcendental signifier of what was its ultimate and logical goal. By making marriage religious and quasi-transcendental through its sacramental nature, the Irish Catholic Church was creating what Julia Kristeva sees as a national community which is 'not a political one but organic, evolutionary, at the same time vital and metaphysical – the expression of a nearly irrational and indiscernible spirit that is summed up by the word *Gemeinsinn*' (1991: 176–7).

Thus, marriage, from this perspective of maintaining the seminal significance and organic nature of the Irish *Gemeinschaft*, came to be of central importance, and over the years, the Church, with the compliance of the State, made sure that marriage was ideologically constructed to ensure the survival and strengthening of the Catholic world view. This was especially true in the case of a marriage between a Catholic and a Protestant. In 1908, Pope Pius X, in his *Ne temere* decree, deemed any marriage performed by a Protestant minister to be 'invalid' and mandated that if a mixed couple wished to be married by a Roman Catholic priest 'they must sign a written promise that their children would be baptised, educated, and confirmed as Catholics' (Tobin 2012: 172). This decree was enforced rigidly in Ireland, and the net result was that if a Catholic married a Protestant, and they had four children, all of these would be Catholic. So of the six people involved, initially there were five Catholics and one Protestant; by the time the parents die, all that would be left was four Catholics. It could be seen as a non-violent and insidious way of ensuring that the *Gemeinschaft* replicated itself and also of stating unambiguously that any forms of difference were gently, but permanently, attenuated. Although there were Protestant TDs, and indeed a Protestant president, 'until the 1960s Irish legislation was almost unquestioningly infused with Catholic morality' (Edwards et al. 2005), and those who were not of the *Gemeinschaft* were made feel isolated and marginal to the concerns of the nation.

Hence, as well as being a central pillar of the generation of a sacramental interpellation of subjects into the Catholic religion, marriage as a sacrament was also a central pillar in the gradual decreasing of the other religious group. Thus, ideologically as well as religiously, marriage was a core instrument of social control and was constitutive of the *Gemeinschaft* that was Ireland, as it controlled the future by ensuring that children were interpellated as Catholics and were inducted into the ideological position of Irish Catholicism before being able to have any choice in the matter.

I think it now becomes clearer as to the huge importance placed by the Church on civil partnership, but more especially on the essentialist definition of marriage as being between a man and a woman and also as being the fulcrum around which a family was created and sustained. The notion of same-sex couples being accorded equal status would deal a death knell to this hegemonic mode of control as such marriages would either be childless or else would use what the Catholic Church would see as 'unnatural' methods of child production, such as in-vitro fertilisation, or surrogacy or donors in order to have children – children who, almost by definition, would not be Catholics. Thus, the redefinition of marriage means a substantial and qualitative change in the whole nature of the society as civil marriages between heterosexual or same-sex couples mean a significant loss of control over the institution by the Catholic Church in the present and also a significant loss of control over the ideology of the Irish people of the future. Without a Catholic marriage, there would be no sacraments of baptism, penance, communion, confirmation and last rites, which means that there is now a movement away from the organic *Gemeinschaft* and towards a more pluralist and democratically motivated notion of choice. The gradual process of secularisation and globalisation of which we spoke earlier had gradually weakened this organic community, and the plurality of views was also gradually introducing the more disparate notion of the *Gesellschaft* and of the shifting of belief.

The change in the definition and ideological function of marriage was a further and, I would suggest, irrevocable step in that direction. More choice, created by the pluralisation of opinion-forming agencies and a more educated population becoming active in the public sphere, meant that there has been a gradual loosening of the bonds of the organic community, and the redefinition of marriage has been a classic example of the difference between *Gemeinschaft* and *Gesellschaft*, 'between the older organic societies and those fragmented and atomistic social agglomerations with which we are familiar in the modern world, with their profound subjectivisation and their monadisation of individual experience' (Jameson 1988: 140). In the *Gesellschaft*, the individual appears to be more the focus of attention than the structural community, and this is very much the type of society in which we are now living. Each individual, with their personal computer in the form of a phone or tablet, is both connected to, and at the same time cut off from, society, and by a swipe of the finger, the communities within which they participate can change a number of times in a short period. This is at variance with the notions of sameness and connection that categorise the *Gemeinschaft*, as the individual now has a choice of communities as opposed to the older system wherein the community had its choice of individuals and interpellated them accordingly, and the core agent of this process was marriage.

In the Irish *Gemeinschaft*, Church and State were at one in marriage – the sacramental and the societal were fused in the same ceremony, and the couple were enculturated into the process of replicating the organic community of Irish Catholicism, even if one of them was not an Irish Catholic themselves. To refer back to Kristeva's point, such a ceremony is both organic and evolutionary but at the same time 'vital and metaphysical', and, as such, marriage was the *fons et origo* of the Irish Catholic organic community. Now, however, civil marriage is part of the range of options available to couples, and the necessity of couples being heterosexual has also been removed. Hence, over a period of time, the younger generations will increasingly be members of a *Gesellschaft*, where there are individual options and choices available to them. The broader consequences for church control over society are wide-ranging, as if a growing number of children are not members of the Catholic community in Ireland, then there will be an increasing demand for more choice in the provision of health and, crucially, education, and the process of pluralisation will increase exponentially, as the Church retreats from its position of societal and cultural dominance to one of ever-increasing marginality in a society 'as a conglomerate of alienated individuals' (Žižek 1991: 163–4). In such a secularising and globalising society, the question will be 'whether people have the feeling of belonging together (*Gemeinschaft*) or whether they see their ties with others more as a contractual link, something more exterior' (Ricœur and Taylor 1986: 189).

The consequences for society are very much what we are seeing in the Ireland of today: a forward-looking place which is open to many cultural, political and religious influences. Not all of these are positive, and there are many people experiencing feelings of alienation and a longing for the older sense of belonging and community that can express itself in a 'generally negative attitude in relation to modernity and their nostalgia for an original community of the *Gemeinschaft* type' (Mouffe 1993: 32). However, as the newer generations replace the old, the Irish Catholic *Gemeinschaft* will become a fading memory, and the individualised, consumer-capitalist-driven society that is in the process of development will be the norm. The connections between Catholicism and Irish nationalism have already been noted, and here one might agree with Benedict Anderson when he talks about the consequences of this connection: 'If the nationalist imagining is so concerned, this suggests a strong affinity with religious imaginings. As this affinity is by no means fortuitous, it may be useful to begin a consideration of the cultural roots of nationalism with death, as the last of a whole gamut of fatalities' (Anderson 1991: 10).

It is under the rubric of Anderson's notion of death that this chapter concludes, as we look at the consequences of the move from *Gemeinschaft* to *Gesellschaft* for the Irish Catholic Church. The Church in Ireland was focused on becoming part of an Irish organic community, and it was entrenched in the structures and the mechanisms of the state from the beginning of Irish Independence. Catholic priests and bishops have had ex-officio positions on boards of management of schools and educational institutions at all levels in Irish society and have had de-facto control over hospitals and health policy until relatively recently. Structurally, the Church was a partner with the State in the creation and perpetration of an organic community. In recent years, issues such as the ones discussed, as well as the infamous clerical child abuse scandals and institutional cover-up of many such instances have left the Church bereft of moral authority which meant that in recent campaigns they have been unable to mount as vigorous a statement of their own position, and the hierarchy have been quite restrained, using groups like the Iona Institute as proxies to voice their position. It is one of the core ironies of the Irish situation that it was the moral majoritarian position of the Catholic Church on sex outside marriage that resulted in so many pregnant young women being forced to put their children into Church-run institutions, orphanages and Magdalene laundries, as it was these very places wherein church abuse of children and teenagers took place and led, in many ways, to the downfall of the structural hegemonic position of the Church in Irish society.

Having been so involved in the structural trappings of societal control and ideological formation, it could be said that the central Christian message, which is, after all, the core reason for the Church's existence, has become rather lost in the paperwork, and now, in a society which it no longer controls, and wherein it no longer has a strong moral or ethical authority, the Church is searching for a new sense of vocation. Whether or not it can find this, with falling mass attendances, diminishing sacramental participation and a decline in the quantity, and probably the quality, of vocations, is a moot point. Only prophets can predict what the future may hold, and they are thin on the ground in Ireland at present. However, just as we began with a fiction that spoke, in an oblique way, the truth about reality, so we will conclude with the same book. In *Small Gods*, there is a discussion between Om, the god turned into a tortoise due to lack of belief, and Brutha about an old scroll by Abraxas, a philosopher who had written on religion. In this discussion, there is an account of what happens to the core belief of a religion, or 'the worship of a godde', when it becomes part of the structural matrix of a society with lots of power and authority. It is a message that, while fictive, holds within it a strong grain of truth:

> Abraxas says here: 'Around the Godde there forms a Shelle of prayers and Ceremonies and Buildings and Priestes and Authority, until at Last the Godde Dies. Ande this maye notte be noticed.'
> 'That can't be true!'
> 'I think it is. Abraxas says there's a kind of shellfish that lives in the same way. It makes a bigger and bigger shell until it can't move around any more, and so it dies.'
> 'But … but … that means … the whole Church …'
> 'Yes.'
>
> (Pratchett 1992: 177)

The second last sentence, ending on an ellipse, is an example of the rhetorical trope of *aposiopesis*. This term is derived from is derived from a Greek words *apo* ('away from') and *siope* (silent), so it means 'becoming silent', which signifies an unfinished thought. The *aposiopesis* here is telling as Brutha is unwilling to follow the comparison to its logical conclusion: just as the shellfish dies because it is gradually suffocated by the external aspects of its shell, so too the Church will die as it is gradually suffocated by the external trappings of its own structure. The living, breathing shellfish dies because it can no longer move; the living breathing message of the Church, 'Love your neighbour', and 'Do unto others as you would have them so unto you', is similarly in danger of being lost in the welter of legalistic and conservative attempts to retain control of a *Gemeinschaft* that is no longer a reality. In essence, the Catholic Church's campaign did not love its neighbour nor did it look to grant rights to others that they would like to have themselves: empathy and justice, both at the core of the Christian message, were sadly lacking. Irish society is now a *Gesellschaft*, and the Church must come to terms with this and reimagine itself if it is to be a living participant of this new social and cultural structure. In future referendums and cultural conversations, the Catholic Church must be on the side of equality, fairness and a sense of justice, and if this means changing its rules, then so be it. Otherwise, the Church, like Abraxas's shellfish, will wither and die, and we know this because it is a process that has happened before, and we are possibly in the middle of watching it happen again in an Ireland where belief has most definitely shifted.

Notes

1 See http://www.irishexaminer.com/viewpoints/analysis/marriage-equality-referendum-no-campaign-does-not-value-each-child-327323.html (accessed 16 January 2016).
2 See https://www.reddit.com/r/ireland/comments/33ewgy/3_posters_for_the_no_campaign_2_have_nothing_to/ (accessed 14 January 2016).
3 See http://www.thejournal.ie/no-vote-campaign-poster-couple-disagree-2086365-May2015/ (accessed 16 January 2016).

4 See http://www.familylaw.co.uk/news_and_comment/ireland-introduces-same-sex-marriage-by-popular-vote#.V9_WgYgrKHs (accessed 15 January 2016).

5 See http://utv.ie/News/2015/05/13/New-campaign-posters-for-Mothers-and-Fathers-Matter-37177 (accessed 17 January 2016).

6 See https://irishelectionliterature.com/2015/04/19/vote-yes-lets-treat-everyone-equally-marriage-equality-referendum-leaflet-from-labour/ (accessed 16 January 2016).

7 See http://www.thejournal.ie/vote-yes-2088609-May2015/ (accessed 15 January 2016).

8 See http://www.irishcentral.com/opinion/cahirodoherty/why-i-need-ireland-to-vote-yes-in-the-marriage-equality-referendum (accessed 14 January 2016).

9 See http://www.irishexaminer.com/referendums2015/referendums2015-analysis/time-to-decide-10-reasons-to-vote-yes-and-10-reasons-to-vote-no-332080.html (accessed 16 January 2016).

Works cited

Adorno, Theodor W. (1997) *Aesthetic Theory*, trans. Gretel Adorno, Rolf Tiedemann and Robert Hullot-Kentor, London: Athlone Press.

Agamben, Giorgio (1991) *Language and Death: The Place of Negativity*, Minneapolis, Minn.: University of Minnesota Press.

Althusser, Louis (2001) *Lenin and Philosophy, and Other Essays*, New York: Monthly Review Press.

Anderson, Benedict (1991) *Imagined Communities: Reflections on the Origin and Spread of Nationalism*, rev. edn, London: Verso.

Edwards, Ruth Dudley and Bridget Hourican (2005) *An Atlas of Irish History*, 3rd edn, London and New York: Routledge.

Heaney, Seamus (1969) *Door into the Dark*, London: Faber.

Irish Catholic Bishops' Conference (2014) *The Meaning of Marriage: A Pastoral Statement of the Irish Catholic Bishops' Conference*, available at http://meaningofmarriage.ie/the-meaning-of-marriage-pastoral-statement/ (accessed 15 January 2016).

Jameson, Fredric (1988) *The Ideologies of Theory: Essays, 1971–1986*, Minneapolis, Minn.: University of Minnesota Press.

Kearney, Hugh F. (2007) *Ireland: Contested Ideas of Nationalism and History*, Cork: Cork University Press.

Kristeva, Julia (1991) *Strangers to Ourselves*, trans. Leon S. Roudiez, London: Harvester Wheatsheaf.

Lacan, Jacques (2006) *Écrits: The First Complete Edition in English*, trans. Bruce Fink in collaboration with Héloïse Fink and Russell Grigg, London: W.W. Norton.

Littleton, John and Eamon Maher (eds.) (2010) *The Dublin/Murphy Report: A Watershed for Irish Catholicism?* Dublin: Columba.

Lyotard, Jean-François (1984) *The Postmodern Condition: A Report on Knowledge*, trans. Geoff Bennington and Brian Massumi, Manchester: Manchester University Press.

—— (1994) *Lessons on the Analytic of the Sublime: Kant's Critique of Judgment*, trans. Elizabeth Rottenberg, Stanford, Calif.: Stanford University Press.

Mouffe, Chantal (1993) *The Return of the Political*, London: Verso.

Pratchett, Terry (1992) *Small Gods: A Novel of Discworld*, New York: Harper Collins.

Quinn, David (2010) 'Christians Have the Right to Debate Civil Partnership Bill', *Irish Independent*, 21 May.

—— (2014) 'Can We Have a Respectful Debate on Same Sex Marriage? I Don't Think So', *Irish Independent*, 31 October.

Ricœur, Paul and George H. Taylor (1986) *Lectures on Ideology and Utopia*, New York: Columbia University Press.

Tobin, Robert Benjamin (2012) *The Minority Voice: Hubert Butler and Southern Irish Protestantism, 1900–1991*, Oxford: Oxford University Press.

Tönnies, Ferdinand, Josâe Harris and Margaret Hollis (2001) *Community and Civil Society*, Cambridge: Cambridge University Press.

Witte, James C. and Susan E. Mannon (2010) *The Internet and Social Inequalities*, London and New York: Routledge.

Zimmerman, Michael E. (1990) *Heidegger's Confrontation with Modernity: Technology, Politics, and Art*, Bloomington, Ind.: Indiana University Press.

Žižek, Slavoj (1991) *Looking Awry: An Introduction to Jacques Lacan through Popular Culture*, Cambridge, Mass.: MIT Press.

Zuidervaart, Lambert (1991) *Adorno's Aesthetic Theory: The Redemption of Illusion*, Cambridge, Mass.: MIT Press.

PART III

Challenges in the here and now

10

Faith, hope and clarity? A new church for the unhoused

Michael Cronin

If you happened to find yourself in Prague on St Patrick's Day 1977, and you went looking for flowers, you might eventually ask yourself the following question, 'Why were all the florists closed?' The answer was that one man, the philosopher, Jan Patočka, alone was responsible for this sudden dearth of flowers in the Czech capital. A founding signatory of Charter 77, he was repeatedly harassed by the state secret police. At the end of one particularly harrowing interrogation session, he died of apoplexy, aged sixty-nine. Determined that there should be no public display of support for the deceased thinker and activist, the authorities decreed that all flower shops remain closed on the day of his funeral. When the funeral orations began, the police started revving up their motorcycle engines, and a helicopter hovered low over the open grave. Five days before the interrogation session that cost him his life, Patočka wrote the following words in what was to be his last text: 'Let's be honest, in the past, conformism has never led to an improvement but a worsening of the situation [...] What is necessary is to behave at all times with dignity, not to be intimidated or frightened. What is necessary is to speak the truth' (Patočka 1977: 45). In speaking the truth, many dissidents from Central and Eastern Europe were lauded by intellectuals in the West. On the other hand, after the fall of communism in 1989, the writings of dissidents were increasingly regarded as historical documents of interest rather than political interventions of note. Dissidence was part of the ideological battleground of the Cold War, and, once the war was over, all was deemed to be 'Quiet on the Eastern Front'. Václav Havel, Patočka's co-signatory of Charter 77, pointed out, however, that what Western Europe had failed to understand about dissidence in Eastern Europe would come back to haunt it. Havel's main contention was that the totalitarian regimes that had wreaked so much havoc in Central and Eastern Europe were the manifestation of the darker sides of modernity and that any attempt to

think through modernity had to accept the unpalatable realities of coercion, terror and mass murder (Havel 1989: 234).

Havel, in a sense, was aligning himself with a long tradition of Central and
Eastern European writers and thinkers from Robert Musil and Elias Canetti to
Czesław Miłosz and Jan Patočka, who, alerted by historical experience to the
nightmares of reason, sought out new forms of transcendence that would drive
emancipation for human beings (Laignel-Lavastine 2005: 15–34). The drive for
emancipation was articulated in a context of extreme crisis where peoples in the
Soviet bloc were enslaved in the name of an ideology of emancipation. As Ireland
comes out of the most severe politico-economic crisis in its post-Independence
history, it is worth asking what kind of emancipation we might strive for and what
the role of religion and critical thinking might be in a new project of human
flourishing.

Political rationality

In July 2010, a detention order for a young girl in a County Cork industrial
school was placed for auction on eBay. There was considerable adverse reaction
from the victims of abuse in Ireland's industrial schools, and comparisons were
drawn with an earlier controversial auction of letters detailing the horrors of the
Irish Famine. Davoc Rynne, the owner of the company, Irish Celt, that put the
letter up for auction, said in his defence, 'I can understand that [negative reaction]
but we live in a capitalist society, so what can we do? I had to buy it' (McGarry
2010). The MD of Irish Celt simply articulated what has become a fatalistic commonplace in late modernity. The writer and theorist Mark Fisher has dubbed this
commonplace 'capitalist realism', which he defines as 'the widespread sense that
not only is capitalism the only viable political and economic system, but also that
it is now impossible even to *imagine* a coherent alternative to it' (Fisher 2009: 2;
italics in original).

To understand how even imagining alternatives has become impossible, it
is necessary to begin by asking why one system has become both 'political and
economic' in its expression? When neo-liberal thought first emerged from universities and conservative think tanks, it was presented as primarily to do with
economic arrangements. What neo-liberal economists sought was a radically free
market, maximum competition, free trade, business-friendly tax policies and a
light-touch regulatory environment. When neo-liberal thought became hegemonic in the economic arena, it began to shift from being a rationale for economic
policy to becoming a fully blown form of political rationality where all dimensions of human life were to be subject to market discipline (Brown 2005: 38–40).
Education, health, the prison system, social welfare, the security forces, all become
subject to neo-liberal political rationality. As neo-liberal political rationality sub-
sumes the state to its own ends, immigration policy is no longer a matter of

humane response to human suffering but a cold calculation of the economic cost of keeping people together in the one place, and the CEO of one company, Intel, commands more ministerial attention than all the faculty of the schools of education in the Republic of Ireland put together. The native expression of this form of rationality might be termed McCarthyism after the type of instrumental cost–benefit analysis that underlay Colm McCarthy's 2009 report on the full range of the State's activities and the logic for the extensive cuts proposed in the report. The sole criterion for judging the success of a state under the new regime is its ability to sustain and foster the development and extension of the Market (see Bobbitt 2002). Health, education and law enforcement, which previously served different, autonomously defined ends (physical and mental well-being, knowledge and wisdom, freedom and security) are now all subordinated to the one end: market sustainability. As societies such as Ireland in the late modern period repudiate transcendental beliefs such as Catholicism, the void is filled with new forms of instrumentalised transcendentalism in the form of the Market itself. In 2013, Pope Francis pointed to the vulnerabilities such blind belief engenders, 'whatever is fragile, like the environment, is defenceless before the interests of a deified market, which becomes the only rule' (Francis 2013: 56).

One of the crueller paradoxes of the crisis that beset Ireland from 2008 onwards was that the crisis that directly resulted from the excesses of extreme neo-liberalism led not to the delegitimising of neo-liberal rationality but, on the contrary, to an unprecedented intensification of the deployment of neo-liberal political rationality. As the Market proved itself to be the God that Failed, the response was not to dismantle a system or question a logic that had generated hitherto unseen levels of inequality, greed and environmental destructiveness but to use public monies to subsidise private losses and to introduce a series of austerity measures that primarily targeted public goods. Pope Francis, in his 2015 encyclical letter, *Laudato si: On Care for Our Common Home*, noted: '[s]aving banks at any cost, making the public pay the price, foregoing [*sic*] a firm commitment to reviewing and reforming the entire system, only reaffirms the absolute power of a financial system' (Francis 2015: 96). In a sense, the Market has come to function as a dark version of transcendence, operating across geographical space and historical time and informing every aspect of the lives of human beings. Further confirmation of this phenomenon was provided in July 2010 where EU leaders met around the clock to discuss an aid package for member-states, the stated aim being to finish the discussions at all costs before the markets opened on the following Monday. The markets were treated as if they were a parody of a pagan deity: irascible, touchy and only to be appeased with pledges, sacrifices and the burnt offerings of public services.

It is in this context that it is possible to argue that the greatest single threat to the sustainability and creative contribution of religious belief in Ireland is not some fantasmatic corruption of personal morality by hetero-normative sexual practices but the relentless instrumentalisation of human beings implicit in neo-liberal political rationality. For when all is subordinated to the logic of the Market, humans' only value lies in their market value, understood in exclusively monetary terms. The inhuman reductiveness of the Market also points up the falseness of the opposition in Ireland between religious believers and secular, progressive thinkers. A constant theme of public comment and mass-media presentation is the pitching of secularisng 'pinko' liberals against 'hardline' believers of the nation's different faith traditions (more particularly, the dominant faith traditions). In this Punch and Judy show of the Ancients and the Moderns, the enemy is alternatively the godless or the God-fearing Other. The effect of this false dichotomy is to conceal the very considerable overlap in concerns and values between believers and progressive secularists; notably, the mortal danger posed to both by what might be termed market totalitarianism.

To contend that there is no alternative to the Market is to argue, in effect, that democracy is meaningless. Democracy, if it is to mean anything, implies a set of choices between alternatives. Free will, as understood by mainstream Christianity, becomes null and void as one is no longer free to will anything other than the Market. In a paradoxical way, the Market totalitarianism which is the outcome of neo-liberal political rationality presents the ultimate triumph of the vulgar materialism that underpinned totalitarian regimes in the Communist bloc. All of human life and practices (superstructure) were reducible to the operations of the economic (base structure). The suppression of religious belief then was but one facet of this conviction in the supremacy of the material, which is enjoying renewed vigour as an ideology in the fetishisation of the Market. What I wish to argue for is the necessity of a new culture of dissent in Ireland that will bring together critical believers and non-believers. In response to the shock-and-awe tactics of market Stalinism, I want to consider how a number of key concepts, central to both many forms of religious belief and to progressive politics, can enable a new coalition of the willing dedicated to the construction of a free, humane, meaningful and spiritually transformed polity and educational system.

Empathy

One of the most celebrated poems by the Polish poet, noted dissident and Nobel laureate Czesław Miłosz (1911–2004) is entitled 'Campo dei Fiori':

> At times wind from the burning
> Would drift dark kites along
> And riders on the carousel
> Caught petals in midair.
> That same hot wind
> Blew open the skirts of the girls
> And the crowds were laughing
> On that beautiful Warsaw Sunday.
> (Miłosz 1988: 47)

The title refers to the square in Rome where the philosopher Giordano Bruno was burnt on charges of heresy. However, the square described in the poem is Krasinski Square in Warsaw, the site of a funfair in wartime Poland. Adjacent to the square was the Jewish ghetto, and it was here on 19 April 1943 that the Wehrmacht began to burn down the ghetto and kill its inhabitants. The poem juxtaposes the carefree joy of the city-dwellers making the most of the amusements on a sunny Sunday afternoon with the unmentionable horrors ('dark kites') of the slaughter taking place only yards away on the other side of the ghetto wall. At one level, Miłosz's poem, written in the year of the destruction of the ghetto, 1943, is a telling indictment of the almost casual anti-Semitism that condemns thousands of Polish Jews to atrocious deaths. But at another level, the poem is a more general snapshot of the terrifying consequences of indifference to the plight of one's neighbour. It is, above all else, a dark vision of the collapse of empathy.

A fundamental feature of a successful democratic society is the requirement for empathy. One of the duties of a citizen in a democracy is to learn what it is to be someone not like oneself and to be aware of the impact of choices that one makes on the lives of others. This can involve everything from the way we design entrances to our public buildings to the way we strive to avoid racial profiling in the policing of our streets. In a world of global interdependence, where our needs are catered for by people we will most probably never meet (the cotton shirt from India or the iPhone from China), forms of empathy need to be global as well as local. The capacity to imagine and understand the lives, feelings and historical experiences of others is crucial to the creation of sustainable human communities where citizens can remain equal in their difference. When we conceive of progress, it is typically in these terms. A particular group – the disabled, a sexual, ethnic or religious minority – is accorded rights of equal citizenship as a result of more inclusive forms of empathy. Conversely, bigotry, persecution, discrimination, exploitation are seen as undermining democratic promise because they fatally restrict empathy to privileged groups in a society. A singular contribution of the humanities and social sciences, from the disciplines of sociology, psychology, philosophy and anthropology to the teaching of history and literature is the potential to develop and strengthen the empathetic imagination. Without such imagination, the very cohesiveness of our societies is put in peril and the ability for a country to function in a globalised world becomes highly problematic. The rise of gated communities in urban centres all over the island of Ireland or the challenge, domestically and internationally, of coming up with humane responses to migration show that there is no room for complacency.

What we witness under conditions of market totalitarianism, however, is not simply the relentless celebration of individual gain but the popularisation of deeply anti-empathetic forms of social Darwinism. What is striking about programmes featured prominently on Irish television over the past two decades, from *Big Brother* and *The Weakest Link* to *The Dragon's Den* and *The Apprentice*, is that the supreme value is the survival of the fittest (the notion of 'fitness' being variously defined).

Rituals of expulsion, public humiliation and vituperative forms of denunciation are standard fare in the Circus slaughter of media innocents. Empathy for the feelings of others becomes a positive obstacle to the onwards and upwards strivings of individuals wholly devoted to a credo of ruthless self-advancement. It is precisely this credo that is repudiated by the teachings of the major faith traditions in Ireland. What Christianity, for example, has tirelessly argued for has been the absolute centrality of empathy – of doing unto others what you would have done to you – to its message (MacCulloch 2010: 88). This explains, in part, the immense hurt experienced by many believers on learning of the nature and extent of clerical abuse scandals, as they demonstrated, above all else, a catastrophic and systematic failure of the faculty for empathy. The brutal, anti-empathetic thrust of neo-liberal political rationality mediated by representations in popular culture is thus deeply inimical to what remains, despite the depredations of authoritarian clericalism over the years, a core value of religious belief in Ireland.

The philosopher Martha Nussbaum in her *Not for Profit: Why Democracy Needs the Humanities* (2010) speaks of the type of education presupposed by democratic self-governance. The type of citizen required is 'an active, critical, reflective and empathetic member of a community of equals, capable of exchanging ideas on the basis of respect and understanding with people from many different backgrounds' (Nussbaum 2010: 141). For a society to function as a democratic entity locally, and to flourish as a community of equals globally, it must incorporate the empathetic imagination into every aspect of its educational practice. Empathy, in effect, is a value that offers a crucial commonality to believers and progressive non-believers alike as they collectively resist the destruction of their capacity to care for and cherish the lives of others.

Responsibility

The President of Ireland, Michael D. Higgins, has argued that in Ireland, 'an enormous price has been paid for anti-intellectualism, which has closed out political theory, the best scholarship and celebration of the imagination' (cited in Dillon 2011: 44). Part of the price was the collapse of the Irish economy and the need for an IMF/EU bailout in 2010. What was readily apparent in the boom years was the serious absence of critical thinking, more especially long-term, structural thinking, from the private and public sector. The recourse to ill-conceived short-term solutions and active hostility to any serious questioning of an unconditional belief in the wisdom of markets led to the spectacular and costly failure of the banking sector and an unprecedented attack on the living standards of the least well-off members of society. However, what the crisis revealed more generally was a paradox endemic in everything from systemic failures in the health service to governance problems in major financial institutions. On the one hand, for example, the credit crisis was blamed on particular individuals – named bankers or property developers – who were said to have abused the system. The system itself was not to blame, only the proverbial bad apples. There was nothing inherently corrupt about present banking practices, only isolated instances of corrupt bankers. On the other hand, when any attempt is made to go after individuals, the causes of abuse are said to be so systemic and so diffuse that no one individual can be held to account. The bankers were only following orders; it is not they but the system which is to blame. This dual structure of disavowal runs as a common theme through the blood-transfusion scandal, the catastrophic failure of foster-care policies in the Health Service Executive and the controversy surrounding the bank bailout. The ultimate result, of course, is consequences without causes. Nobody is to blame, but almost everyone has to pay the cost.

This systematic evasion of moral responsibility has corrupted the language of public life. Public figures who have been shown to have done something that is patently wrong will only admit to an 'error of judgement' as if morality was a form of cost–benefit analysis and they had somehow got the figures wrong. When women die from contaminated blood products, children's lives are destroyed by criminally incompetent fosterage arrangements, and ordinary citizens face real hardship as they bear the collective costs of private losses, the sense of injustice is compounded by the abject failure to hold anyone to account. This, in turn, leads to an understandable and widespread discrediting of authority, whether it be vested in banks, institutional churches or the legal and medical professions.

The crisis in authority can, of course, be addressed in two ways. One way is to render authority more authoritarian by making the State and its agents more coercive in their response to forms of criticism and dissent (for examples of this response in the Irish case see Cronin 2009: 109–22). Another approach is through the development of what one might term a sense of structural responsibility, that is to say, a recognition of how personal, moral responsibility is determined, though not nullified, by structural constraints. The development of this sense of structural responsibility is dependent upon the introduction of critical, Socratic thinking at all levels in Irish education. Underlying such an approach to thinking are three assumptions. First, people who fail to examine themselves deeply and critically are more likely to be easily influenced by others, as was so apparent in the widespread consumerist materialism of Tiger Ireland. Second, a lack of clarity about values, goals, aims or objectives resulting from deep thinking leads to the temptation to defer unquestioningly to authority figures, whether they be political bosses or senior bankers. Third, when ideas are left unexamined, the temptation is to treat politics as a purely agonistic exercise, as all about Them and Us, where personalities are everything and policies count for naught. Crucially, when ideas are arrived at rather than simply given, there is a much greater sense of ownership. It is easier to feel responsible for values that are freely and deliberately chosen than for those that are imposed or that are vaguely sensed to be part of a prevailing *Zeitgeist*. The implication is that the sense of personal responsibility for deeds resulting from these values is all the greater in that there is a thoughtful engagement in the elaboration of the values themselves.

Central to the development of critical thinking must be an awareness of the structures that govern our lives. This is why I use the term 'structural' responsibility. If we are not aware of how larger politico-economic arrangements inform our lives, then our notion of responsibility diminishes to a form of therapeutic individualism where the person becomes the alpha and omega of the self-help industry. Nothing exists outside the mediated torments of the flattered self as exemplified by the relentless confessionalism on our airwaves. It is clear from the teachings of the dominant faith traditions in Ireland that believers are held to be accountable for their acts and that the teaching of religious morality is about, among other things, defining the nature and extent of a believer's responsibility with respect to thoughts and deeds. Faith traditions, however, not only counsel against narcissistic individualism, they also offer their own version of structural responsibility.

Diarmaid MacCulloch, in his discussion of Greek influences on Judaism and Christianity, argues that Plato's 'view of reality and authenticity propelled one basic impulse in Christianity, to look beyond the immediate and everyday to the universal and ultimate' (MacCulloch 2010: 31). Plato's view was articulated in his parable of the Cave where the particular phenomena humans observe are shadows of their ideal Forms which represent a truer and higher form of reality than the ones we habitually know. This would influence the development of the allegorical method of interpreting scripture among the sizeable Jewish diaspora in Greek-speaking Alexandria, and the method would be later practised by converts to Christianity (MacCulloch 2010: 69). Thus, a fundamental tenet of scriptural practice in Christianity is to look beyond circumstance and contingency to larger structures of significance. The notion of responsibility only makes sense in terms of these larger structures of significance that are the articles of Christian faith and belief.

If believers and progressive non-believers alike are committed to a strong sense of responsibility, this must inevitably bring them into conflict with vested interests which, as recent history has shown in Ireland, are extremely reluctant to be held accountable or responsible for their actions. Implicit in a renewed commitment to responsibility is the recognition of the ontological necessity of conflict in society, a notion that might on first reading appear somewhat objectionable.

Conflict

A substantial section of bookshops in many richer countries is given over to self-help manuals. Implicit in these manuals is the notion that there is an ideal self which is somewhat out of kilter because it lacks confidence, Vitamin B, the X Factor or has failed to dejunk its life. 'I am not myself today' implies that there is a unitary, consensual self which is the desirable default value for the good life. That is to say, reading the right book, taking the right therapy, buying the right product, will lead to the finding of a 'true self' beyond disharmony or conflict. This psychologised consensualism finds its correlative at a political level in the notion that representative democracy consists of a collection of points of view which are all equally valid. The point of view of the workers' representative where 2,000 jobs have been delocalised is as valid as that of the corporate vice-president who has engineered the 'rationalisation'. So, everybody gets to have their say. However, what they are saying is that real conflict is no longer acceptable. In other words, in reality, points of view are irreducible, as speakers are situated very differently, both materially and structurally. The false symmetrisation of the mediasphere, however, conceals the very genuine conflict of interests through the irenic fiction of the representative soundbite.

In another version of the tyranny of compliance, when social movements oppose government measures, such as penalising public-sector workers for the financial irresponsibility of the private sector, government spokespersons and stockbroker economists talk about a 'communications deficit'. If only the people understood what they were doing, they would realise it was ultimately for their own good. Opposition can only be conceived of as cussedness or stupidity. No allowance is made for the fact that there are grounded material interests and structural conditions that make opposition not only inevitable but vital.

As even the most rudimentary exercise in the study of others soon reveals, understanding is, above all, an initiation into unsuspected complexity. The simplest of situations involving other humans turns out to be not as straightforward as we thought. What this schooling in complexity reveals is the radical insufficiency of cultural shorthand. That is to say, the cultural categorisation of society as made of recognisable types designated by labels such as 'dyslexic', 'epileptic', 'Paddy', 'Gay', 'Muslim', reduces the multidimensional complexity of humans to one defining trait. Once a person is described using one of these labels, it is suggested that is all you need to know about them. They become transparent. Thus, if someone is 'Muslim' or 'Catholic', they must be, by definition, bigoted, anti-modern, misogynist and obscurantist. But what gay-rights activists and the women's movement, for example, in various parts of the globe and at different times have attempted to do is to restore multidimensionality and complexity to the lives of human beings who were deemed to be instantly intelligible as 'gay' or 'woman', gender or sexual orientation revealing all that was necessary to know about a person.

A multidimensional perspective on humans means opening up the infinite, internally conflicted, shifting desires, ideals and interests of complex human beings in the lifeworld. It means resisting the quantitative policing of one-dimensional clinical labels ('autistic') or social typing ('deviant'), to restore the infinitely rich constellation of human experience and possibility. It is in this respect that the current vogue for 'transparency' is a form of blindness that is more to with the coercive narratives of macro-modernity (name and shame) than with any desire to account for the exquisite detail of human fullness. Putting a figure on a number of articles published or on the amount of minutes spent in consultation may make the education or health service transparent to auditors, but it makes them and the society that pays their inflated fees blind to the open-ended multidimensionality of genuine education and health care.

Implicit in the understanding of humans advanced here is the inevitability, indeed, the necessity, of conflict. As Angélique del Rey and Miguel Benasayag have pointed out, part of the work of mourning for humanity is the acknowledgement that there will never be perpetual peace. Each time, they note, that there is a 'war to end all wars' which aims at bringing about the reign of ever-lasting peace, the scale of destruction and human suffering is greater than ever before (Benasayag and del Rey 2007: 56). This observation is crucial as an attention to the local, the micro, 'small' places, 'small' nations can lead to a kind of consensual smugness in the present or a censorious nostalgia with respect to the past when no false note was to be heard and everyone lived happily before in the greenhouses on the prairie. Local community does not entail an end to dissent. Much of the disappointed reaction of post-1968 activists was partly to do with an overly benign notion of community. Having excessively idealised the small community, they could not tolerate the inevitable and indeed desirable persistence of difference and conflict. The notion that having found the larger group difficult it is possible to retreat to the haven of your 'own' – peer group, buddies, family – and expect the comforts of uncomplicated, consensual intimacy, is to invite the counter-movement of disappointment. However, it is important to move the notion of conflict beyond the binary logic of specular confrontation where entities with putatively fixed identities, Catholics versus non-Catholics, face up to each other in a zero sum of binary opposition. Conflict from the viewpoint of richly differentiated human subjects is not confrontation; it is conflict as engagement with the multidimensionality of human beings, their texts, beliefs, languages and cultures. It resists the culturalist versions of contemporary biopower which, in the name of avoiding a 'clash of civilisations', presents all conflict as confrontation through the binary stereotyping of Us and Them. The ultimate triumph of dictatorships, as Benasayag and del Rey have pointed out, is to present their opponents as pure adversaries (Benasayag and del Rey 2007: 109). Confrontation in this scenario leads inevitably to elimination.

An agonistic conception of human community that runs directly counter to the beatific visions of universal understanding underlying many public pronouncements on the topic of globalisation takes as a basic premise the incomprehensibility of the other. That is to say, human interaction is not simply the revelation of what is already there. In the movement to engage with the complex being of others, in the creation of some form of shared sense, some degree of commonality, the operation is not one of uncovering a universal substrate, waiting to be revealed in its pre-formed state, but the contingent construction of bottom-up commonality.

The recent history of Northern Ireland has, understandably, given conflict a bad name. Indeed, the whole period of suffering and violence has often been summed in that one word: the 'Conflict' in Northern Ireland. Churchmen from all sides worked to bring an end to the misery that resulted from inter-communal hatred. However, the natural ally of conflict is not hatred but dissent. Believers, by acknowledging the infinite mystery of the divine made incarnate, acknowledge the multidimensionality of humans mentioned earlier. Accepting the necessity of conflict is recognising the need for both believers and non-believers alike to protect the multidimensionality of the human and challenge the murderous shorthand of labels. As Stanley Milgram showed in his famous torture experiments, and Solomon Asch demonstrated in his work on the reception of visual information, it often only takes one dissenting voice to prevent a group of people from erroneously misinterpreting as true clearly false information or, more worryingly, participating in acts of extreme violence against other human beings (Zimbardo 2007). The participation by believers and progressive non-believers in an active culture of dissent is vital in an era of market totalitarianism where bearing witness to core values of empathy and responsibility and the non-instrumentalisation of human beings becomes more difficult by the day. It is striking in this respect that one notion that occurred repeatedly in the lexicon of dissident writers and thinkers in Central and Eastern Europe was one that is central to Catholic moral teaching; namely, conscience. Ivan Klima, Czesław Miłosz, Karel Kosik, Arthur Koestler and Zygmunt Baumann all stressed the importance of recourse to conscience as a way of unmasking the public lie and establishing one's personal duty or responsibility to bear witness against what is manifestly untrue and dehumanising (Laignel-Lavastine 2005: 112).

Fear

Fear is predictably a great enemy of thought. It is difficult to think or believe freely if we fear for our life or our health or our well-being. Yet, fear is the predominant note of our age. Climate change, calamitous forest fires, catastrophic floods, extreme market volatility, pandemics (AIDS, SARS, swine flu), chronic youth unemployment, the list of contemporary terrors is endless. Each evening on the news, we are provided with updates on the state of fear. Each age, in addition, has its particular genre of fear. In Ireland, the religion of fear (1920s–1960s) has given way to the economics of fear (1960s–present), the fear of the priest superseded by the fear of the P45. One could argue that the changing genre of fear corresponds to a fundamental shift at another level, which is the shift from the figure of discipline to the figure of control. The figure of discipline is typically that of the worker as captured in Charlie Chaplin's *Modern Times* or that of the prisoner as depicted in Oscar Wilde's *The Ballad of Reading Gaol*. The figure of control, on the other hand, is the debtor or the addict. Debtors are controlled by their debts, addicts by their addictions. Characteristic of Ireland during the boom period was the prevalence of the figure of control as evidenced by the historically high levels of personal indebtedness and widespread instances of alcohol and drug abuse (Ging et al. 2009: 1–17). Indeed, the French philosopher Gilles Deleuze has argued that in contemporary control societies debt is the final form of enclosure, the ultimate form of imprisonment, 'A man is no longer a man confined, but a man in debt' (1995: 181). It was the similarity of states of fear in the East and the West that led Czesław Miłosz to ask the question, 'Why should we love societies based on fear, whether it is the fear of misery or the fear of the political police?' (Miłosz 2004: 41).

In Ireland, particularly in the post-Famine period, the Church was often associated with a regime of fear and punishment that has been well documented on the printed page and on the screen. This, of course, is all the more paradoxical or poignant in that the founding message of Christianity was one of hope, of the banishment of and resistance to fear. However, progressive politics in Ireland has promoted its own states of fear notably through an overwhelming emphasis on negativity. The problem with perpetual opposition is that the most popular word is no. Like Ulster in the past, the mind becomes captive to a monosyllable. In a society where the punitive superego has variously taken the form of the coloniser, an unforgiving church or the sententious stockbroker economist, the tendency is for critique to transform itself into the self-hatred of powerlessness. A more radical move is embrace a politics of hope that involves saying not 'No', but 'Yes'. 'Yes' to a better, fairer, more sustainable society. It is obvious that Irish society, like many other societies in the age of the Anthropocene – human-induced climate change – is at a decisive moment. The decisions taken now will affect not just the next few years but the fate of the island in this century and beyond. The ecological 'crisis' is not a passing moment but a permanent condition that involves a profound mutation of our relations to the world(s) we inhabit. Part of the challenge is the challenge to a notion of modernity itself as a hegemonic form of instrumental reason that finds its economic expression in the ideology of extractivism (Klein 2014: 169).

For progressive thinkers and market cheerleaders alike in Ireland, 'modernisation' has become the watchword of transformation. No longer preventing the future but embracing it, the Irish moderns see modernisation as the touchstone of legitimacy. The 'anti-modern' is variously the Church, the Irish language, state-owned monopolies or restrictions on the size of retail outlets. Bruno Latour, in an address to the American Association of Anthropologists pointed out, however, that there 'is a huge difference between being "modern" and being "contemporary"' (Latour 2014: 13). He goes on to claim that '"Modernise" is a *mot d'ordre*. Not a concept. Not a thing. It destroys your ability to be the contemporary of what happens around you' (Latour 2014: 13). In other words, the notion of an abstract, universalised, dichotomous (nature/culture) reason is *a* way, not *the* way, of approaching the situation in which we find ourselves, and it is precisely the task of other forms of enquiry such as anthropology and religion to show that there are other ontologies, other ways of being in the world. We need these other ontologies, these other perspectives, these other ways of dwelling in the world that have been banished beyond the pale of the 'modern' in Ireland if we are construct a viable habitus for an island in a period of profound environmental change. A profound and urgent engagement with the contemporary moment in Ireland demands the construction of a coalition of hope between those believers and unbelievers who are not 'intimidated or frightened' by the reductive dismissal of labels or by the foreclosure of the future by the deadly conformism of exploitative extractivism.

Works cited

Benasayag, Miguel and Angélique del Rey (2007) *L'Éloge du conflit*, Paris, La Découverte.

Bobbitt, Philip (2002) *The Shield of Achilles: War, Peace and the Course of History*, London: Penguin.

Brown, Wendy (2005) *Edgework: Critical Essays on Knowledge and Politics*, Princeton, NJ: Princeton University Press.

Cronin, Michael (2009) 'Rebel Spirits? From Reaction to Regulation', in Debbie Ging, Michael Cronin and Peadar Kirby (eds.), *Transforming Ireland: Challenges, Critiques, Resources*, Manchester: Manchester University Press, pp. 109–22.

Deleuze Gilles (1995) *Negotiations*, New York, Columbia University Press.

Dillon, Paul (2011) 'Interview: Michael D Higgins – Ireland's "Political" Intellectual', *Village*, December–January, pp. 42–4.

Fisher, Mark (2009) *Capitalist Realism: Is There No Alternative?* Winchester: Zero Books.

Francis (2013) *Evangeli gaudium*, Dublin: Veritas.

—— (2015) *Laudato si: Care for Our Common Home*, Dublin: Veritas.

Ging, Debbie, Michael Cronin and Peadar Kirby (2009) 'Transforming Ireland: Challenges', in Debbie Ging, Michael Cronin and Peadar Kirby (eds.), *Transforming Ireland: Challenges, Critiques, Resources*, Manchester: Manchester University Press, pp. 1–17.

Havel, Václav (1989) *Essais politiques*, trans. Jacques Rupnik, Paris: Calmann-Lévy.

Klein, Naomi (2014) *This Changes Everything: Capitalism vs. the Climate*, London: Allen Lane.

Laignel-Lavastine, Alexandra (2005) *Esprits d'Europe: autour de Czesław Miłosz, Jan Patočka, István Bibó*, Paris: Gallimard.

Latour, Bruno (2014) 'Anthropology at the Time of the Anthropocene: A Personal View of What Is to Be Studied', available at http://www.bruno-latour.fr/sites/default/files/139-AAA-Washington.pdf (accessed 6 September 2016).

MacCulloch, Diarmaid (2010) *A History of Christianity*, London: Penguin.

McGarry, Patsy (2010) 'Industrial School Order Placed on eBay', *Irish Times*, 17 August.

Miłosz, Czesław (1988) 'Campo dei Fiori', in *The Collected Poems: 1931–1987*, trans. Louis Iribarne and David Brooks, New York: Ecco, pp. 46–9.

—— (2004) *Abécédaire*, trans. Laurence Dyèvre, Paris: Fayard.

Nussbaum, Martha C. (2010) *Not for Profit: Why Democracy Needs the Humanities*, Princeton, NJ: Princeton University Press.

Patočka, Jan (1977) 'Testament', *Politique aujourd'hui*, pp. 3–4 and pp. 43–5.

Zimbardo, Philip (2007) *The Lucifer Effect: How Good People Turn Evil*, London: Rider.

11

The people in the pews:
Silent and betrayed

Patricia Casey

There was a sense among Irish Catholics in the 1950s, 1960s and 1970s that our faith and allegiance to the Catholic Church was greater and more pure that that of other so-called Catholic countries. We believed we were secure in our faith, and we even prayed for the conversion of Russia! The entwinement between church and state began probably with the founding of the Irish Free State, although the seeds were sown long before that. People had been persecuted for being both Catholic and Irish. When the Irish State was founded we needed to define what it was to be Irish, and we chose faith rather than language as our defining characteristic, because by then English was the spoken language of the majority of our citizens.

When we were being persecuted, in the past, our priests had not stood idly by: they acted as our spokespersons and defended us against the powerful English throne and parliament. Rural and uneducated, we had the priests marching shoulder to shoulder with us. This is celebrated in song and verse such as 'The Ballad of Father Gilligan' (W. B. Yeats), 'The Croppy Boy' (Carroll Malone) and 'Boolavogue' (P. J. McCall).

With the foundation of the State, the Catholics in the pews did not need to defend or explain their place in society or to speak up for their faith. Priests and bishops did so, as did some politicians. The faith of the ordinary person on the street was, with pride, referred to as 'simple', and a process began that gradually led to them ceding their voice, to the clergy, who were educated in seminaries from Maynooth to Rome. Clericalism was born.

This contrasted with British Catholicism in the late nineteenth and early twentieth century where some of the gentry, writers and poets were either cradle Catholics or converts and were in a position to bring their intellectual rigour to the understanding of Catholicism there. Included here were John Henry Newman, Gerard Manley Hopkins, Hilaire Belloc, G. K. Chesterton and Evelyn

Waugh, along with even current members of the royal family such as the Duchess of Kent and Lord Nicholas Windsor. Indeed, for centuries the dukes of Norfolk have been Catholic. Even in the media there have been some high-profile converts also such as Charles Moore, former editor of the *Daily* and *Sunday Telegraph* and of *The Spectator* magazine. For this reason, Catholicism has won greater respect from the media and would-be critics of Catholicism than that accorded it in Ireland. This disparity is still evident.

Throughout most of the twentieth century in Ireland, Catholicism was not questioned except in media and literary circles. It lay embedded in a comfort zone that led to conformity between the institutional Church and the State, and this contributed to passiveness among its members with respect to the emerging debate about faith in the public square. The inaction has persisted to the present, which, some will argue, has created a vacuum in religious thought and development among the population of believers and into which has stepped another world view that many are unable to challenge. This world view is militant secularism.

Against this backdrop, a number of events occurred that changed the dynamic between the institutional Church and the State on the one hand, and between the Church and the public on the other. Some of these were international and beyond local control, others were particular to Ireland and self-made.

A coalescence of events and ideas: international events

The first major international idea to challenge the Church's power in the past seven decades was the sexual revolution. By the time this happened, a number of avowedly atheistic states were in existence in the Communist regimes of the Union of Soviet Socialist Republics, and the Cultural Revolution was engulfing China. The sexual revolution reached its apogee during the summer of 1967 ('the summer of love'). This movement challenged traditional codes of behaviour related to sexuality and relationships throughout the Western world. Deference to authority figures such as parents, priests, God or politicians disappeared.

This period witnessed the search for direction and ethical guidance but not from religion, which by now was in serious decline. The New Age movement, beginning in England, stepped in and quickly became international. Adherents were encouraged to adopt whichever set of beliefs and practices they felt most comfortable with, including meditation, divination (foretelling the future) and channelling, and the more formal religious rituals were absent. Their search was located in the individual, and they identified their own gods. One of the defining books of the time was *Spiritual Marketplace: Baby Boomers and the Remaking of American Religion* by W. C. Roof (2001) which argued that for the first time 'spirituality' was no longer the preserve of the religious but could be appropriated by everybody, even non-believers.

Just before the summer of love was creating a melting pot of ideas in the secular world on a massive scale, Pope John XXIII convened the Second Vatican Council (1962–65). The aim was to modernise the Church so that its role in the rapidly changing world of technology, economics, politics and social thought could be advanced.

Apart from liturgical changes, such as the celebration of the mass in the vernacular facing the congregation, the role of the laity was reframed and enhanced. Yet the person in the pew in an Irish church had little experience of major involvement or responsibility at local level, since clericalism had dominated the Irish scene for such a long time. This was a period of great uncertainty for many, as members of religious congregations shed their habits and many practices that had been compulsory were abandoned, such as the obligatory Friday fast, women covering the head in church and so on. Indeed, to lament these practices was regarded as confirmation of excessive religiosity. I recall a nun chiding me in religion class when I asked why it was that fasting for three hours before communion was a requirement (under pain of venial sin) until recently and now was no longer regarded as such. She retorted that I resembled an old woman clutching her rosary beads because I feared change! I then reminded her that until recently she had worn her rosary beads visibly round her waist outside her habit and did she now think that was wrong? Some adopted the changes unthinkingly without question, as did my religion teacher, while others felt uncertain and even abandoned.

The local scene

The sexual scandals are by far the greatest contributors to the change in Church–State and Church–public relations in Ireland. This has been replicated internationally, especially in the USA and Canada, where similar abuse was reported, leading to episcopal resignations. There scandals are of two varieties. The first concerned clergymen extolling the virtues of chastity and ostensibly espousing celibacy only to be revealed as hypocrites for having sexual relations with women themselves. They were also decried for concealing their relationships even after they had children rather than leaving the priesthood to look after their family. The second and most significant of these was the sexual abuse of children that emerged in the 1990s and, in particular, the manner in which it was handled. This rocked the Church to its core. The cover-up of moving priests and other religious from parish to parish, rather than reporting their crimes to the relevant authorities, was horrifying. It is true that in many sectors the public in the 1970s and 1980s had little awareness or experience of dealing with sexual abuse. However, it is also true that the Church was in thrall to the opinions of mental-health professionals that abusers could be treated. Many were referred to mental-health professionals in Ireland and to specialist units in England and in the USA. Some were returned to 'limited ministry', working with adults only or in administrative positions under supervision. Some reoffended, and the victims paid a huge emotional price. Even in the 2000s, when there were clear guidelines in place, the language of some senior clerics indicating that they had been economical with the truth in reporting these abuses – the phrase 'mental reservation' was one such euphemism – shocked the public, and, not surprisingly, their confidence in the institutional Church was further damaged.

Studies from the USA concerning trust in the institution of the Church have documented the impact on those abused (Rosetti 1995) and at parish level (Kline et al. 2008). The consequences include a deep hurt at the perceived betrayal by Church leaders, a reawakening of pain connected to past injuries by clergy, an effort to cope by separating one's relationship with God from that with the Church and a concern for the spiritual well-being of other family members. This has contributed to what is referred to as 'cultural Catholicism'. The abuse scandals have also fanned the flames of hostility to institutional religion.

Facing such a breakdown in trust between the public and the institutional Church, the person in the pew would need knowledge and courage to withstand the onslaught that the Church in Ireland inevitably faced. The question is did we or do we now have these necessary skills?

The Sunday homily should be the vehicle for communicating the Word of God and the teaching of the Church to its followers. Yet for most, it is a disappointment. Contrary to what the non-mass-attending public might believe, there has been no exegesis on Catholic teaching from the pulpit for decades. Often inadequately prepared, and focused on being nice to each other, the ten-minute sermon has become a time to shut down cognitively or, at worst, an opportunity to plan the coming week. Of course there are some exceptional preachers, but these are regrettably rare. I experienced an example of deeply suspect preaching when a priest delivered a homily in a church which I attended recently by informing the congregation with sage-like certainty that the idea of 'telling your sins in a dark room to an elderly man was not where the Catholic Church was at any more'. This comment exemplifies the challenge that the Catholic Church in Ireland faces and especially the person in the pew, when the lacuna in theological knowledge is so enormous that priests such as this are ignorant of even the basics of the Catholic tradition. Reducing the nature and purpose of the sacrament of reconciliation to an elderly man in a dark room is entirely secular, superficial and dismissive while masquerading as *faux* progressiveness, on a par with the utterances of our worst politicians.

Incidents such as this raise questions about the training that our priests receive. This came to prominence because of the apostolic visit of Archbishop Timothy Dolan in 2011 to the Irish seminaries. He spoke of the divergence between Church teaching and what was being taught in the seminary. In a similar vein, the Jesuit historian Oliver Rafferty opined 'even the most important centre of clerical training in this county, St Patrick's College Maynooth, tends to concentrate on producing capable ecclesiastical functionaries … there is no rigorous pursuit of theology by the majority of seminarians' (2015). The writing of Mark Dooley (2011) also raised concerns when he elaborated on what had been disclosed to him by seminarians concerning the attitude of those charged with their training to traditional religious practices and teachings. More recently, reports have surfaced that seminarians were asked to desist from their training in Maynooth (Barry and Daly 2015) because of their Catholic traditionalism. On the other hand, the claims in Dolan's report have been criticised by the archbishops, and the allegations that 'conservative' students were being asked to leave the seminary are denied by its president, Revd Hugh Connolly.

Therefore, while the people in the pews are committed, they do not have the knowledge, the language or the arguments to promote their faith to a secular audience. The clergy are ill equipped as educators in this regard due to their own poor understanding of theology, their terror of the media and the desire of some to appear 'progressive'. The consequence is silence on matters of faith that could and should be discussed in the public square.

'Cultural Catholicism' and 'the spiral of silence' in Ireland

While 84 per cent of people in the Census report that they are Catholic, this very impressive figure belies the reality that the numbers engaging in weekly mass attendance are far lower and stand at around 33 per cent, while about 50 per cent attend once per month. This represents a massive drop from the figure in the 1960s when over 90 per cent of the population were weekly mass-goers. The group who have fallen off are a combination of people who no longer identify in any way as Catholic and those who are cultural Catholics. A cultural Catholic is defined as identifying with Catholicism as part of one's culture rather than as a faith. A question that has to be asked (Rafferty 2015) is to what extent the Irish in the twentieth century had embedded their faith into the hearts and minds or were many simply cultural Catholics but too conventional to declare it. The cultural Catholic engages in some of the rituals of the Church, such as baptisms and funerals, but does not participate in it as a driving force directing a particular world view. According to the US-based Pew Research Centre (2015), cultural Catholics still adhere to some beliefs such as the importance of having a relationship with Jesus, praying and giving to charity. They are not hostile to the Church, and almost half report that they see themselves as potentially returning to it at some time in the future.

Cultural Catholicism is similar to what Alport and Ross (1967) described as an extrinsic religious orientation, to be distinguished from an intrinsic orientation in which the person integrated the codes of their faith into their personal conduct in so far as was possible. The latter are often identified with religious practices that are inaccurately viewed as dry and arid, based on convention and habit rather than on any deeper perspective. This will be discussed further below.

While it is clear that the number of Catholics who practise their faith has declined in Ireland, a further observation outlined above is that few of those who do practise speak out to challenge myths or to advocate for their faith. Apart from lack of knowledge, why the silence? In 1974, political scientist Elisabeth Noelle-Neumann wrote a paper entitled 'The Spiral of Silence: A Theory of Public Opinion', followed by a book of broadly the same title in 1993. This theory has become a classic in explaining the role of the mass media in directing public debate. This is relevant to the discussion about Catholicism in Ireland and to its role in the marketplace. According to this theory, people have a quasi-statistical sense that deters them from voicing an opinion if they perceive themselves to be in the minority because they fear being isolated. Their perspective on what is the majority opinion that comes through the lens of the mass media and may be inaccurate. In the view of Noelle-Neumann, the spiral is only broken and the silence terminated when a highly educated, affluent or cavalier minority who disregard media and social opprobrium, speak out. Thus, the spiral is time-limited. Only time will tell if the spiral has yet been broken in Ireland, but the omens are not positive at this point, as the Catholic Church hierarchy are in hiding from the media and there is an absence of Catholic intellectual thought and discourse. However, a number of new, articulate bishops have recently been appointed, and a new archbishop and papal nuncio have emerged from the fog. They and some new lay spokespersons for organisations such as Catholic Comments are coming to the fore. Other non-denominational organisations, like the Iona Institute (of which I am a patron), have also stepped into the breach, speaking on issues such as the right to conscientious objection, the benefits of denominational education and traditional marriage.

In summary, weekly mass attendance has declined, and cultural Catholicism is on the rise, as is atheism (but to a much lesser than is assumed). The church-going public has not been educated on matters of faith, and there is a spiral of silence among those committed to their religion. Some of the understandable hostility to Catholicism because of child abuse by clerics is fanned by myths about religion in general and about Catholicism in particular, which reinforce the negative stereo-type of this faith. These will be considered below.

Celibacy makes priests paedophiles

With the seemingly high prevalence of child abusers in the ranks of the Catholic Church, many came to accept the truism that this would not have occurred if priests had been allowed to marry. The idea of celibacy, inimical to modern society, is seen as outdated and even dangerous. The Catholic Church, being the only Christian Church to mandate clerical celibacy, is increasingly seen as having no currency in guiding the lives of ordinary people. Public commentators frequently argue that these abuses would not have happened if priests were allowed to marry. The question is do Roman Catholic priests sexually abuse children with greater frequency than clerics from other churches, which do not demand celibacy, or in comparison to other non-religious occupations? Insurance companies that cover all denominations, such as Guide One Centre for Risk Management, which has more than 40,000 church clients, does not charge higher premiums for the Catholic Church, which suggests that from a financial risk perspective claims against the Church are not uniquely high.

The best international evidence on the incidence of clerical abuse comes from research commissioned to investigate sexual abuse by Catholic priests in the USA. The John Jay College of Criminal Investigation showed that between 1950 and 2002, more than 10,000 individuals had come forward to report clergy perpetrated child sexual abuse (John Jay College 2004). The estimated prevalence of child sexual abuse by diocesan priests according to the allegations against them was 4.3 per cent, and among priests from religious orders 2.7 per cent . These figures compare with national US data from the general population that suggests between 5 and 10 per cent of men are sexual abusers (Wingert 2010). Turning to the victims, a study from the Netherlands (Langeland et al. 2015) on the prevalence of non-familial sexual abuse in almost 2,500 subjects over the age of forty, identified non-familial abuse overall in 14 per cent of the population and abuse by Catholic clerics overall was in 1.7 per cent of subjects.

However, the public overestimates the proportion of clerics who sexually abuse minors and underestimates the proportion who have been convicted (Goode et al. 2003). This was confirmed in a poll in 2011 conducted by Amárach for the Iona Institute which found that 42 per cent of respondents believed that over 21 per cent of priests were guilty of sexual abuse while 72 per cent overestimated the actual proportion abusing compared with the 4 per cent figure provide by John Jay University.

Catholic guilt

The belief in Catholic guilt is common in popular culture, and the term itself suggests that there is something particular about it that separates it from other types of guilt or from similar feelings in other faiths. The belief is that the Church engenders guilt, especially about matters of sexual morality and to a lesser extent about other matters, which were repressive and unnatural. Yet it is often forgotten that prior to the sexual revolution most societies had views on sexual morality that frowned on pre-marital sex and single parenthood, and this was not unique to Catholic countries. For example, in countries such as Britain, sexual acts were linked to medical and psychological problems such as masturbatory insanity (Stengers and van Neck 2001), for which restraining devices were developed, are on display at the Science Museum in London.

The Catholic Church has always recognised that some people are overly scrupulous seeing minor peccadillos as major transgressions about which they are especially preoccupied. This leads to frequent confessions of the same wrongdoing. Its attitude, far from encouraging such guilt, has been to discourage the repetitious behaviours around confession and to encourage the individual to accept forgiveness. These were referred to as scruples and in some cases were linked to a psychiatric disorder called obsessive–compulsive disorder (OCD), in which the person repeatedly ruminates on the same theme, to the extent that their day-to-day functioning is impaired. The historical link between scruples and OCD comes from the knowledge that St Thérèse of Lisieux, known as the Little Flower, experienced anguished preoccupations in her teenage years. Her autobiography *Story of a Soul* details these.

There is another condition in which false beliefs about imagined wrongdoings also occurs, and that is in the most severe form of depression, known as psychotic depression. In this illness, the person believes that they have committed a heinous crime and sometimes will give themselves up to police as murderers or as guilty of other crimes. There is no causal link between OCD, or psychotic depression, and Catholicism, as research now shows.

A small Italian study of fifty-four individuals concluded that religious groups scored higher than individuals with a low degree of religiosity on obsessional features such as the over-importance of thoughts, perfectionism and responsibility, from whence the conclusion that religion might play a role in some of the features of OCD (Sica et al. 2002). A study from Boston University found that among thirty-three subjects with OCD and twenty-four with anxiety, no particular religion was more common than any other in OCD patients, and they were no more religious than those with anxiety (Steketee et al. 1991). In the largest study of its kind, the US Universities of California and of Notre Dame examined the concept of Catholic guilt among US teenagers. The authors found no evidence that Catholic teenagers experienced more guilt than non-Catholic teenagers, nor was there any evidence that more observant Catholics had more guilt than those who were less observant (Vaisey and Smith 2008).

Popular culture regards guilt as something negative that should be eschewed. Yet guilt is not necessarily negative. It can be constructive when it recognises one's failings and weaknesses and acknowledges any hurt caused to others. Guilt of this type is beneficial to the individual and to society, reducing harmful actions. Researchers with an interest in guilt describe constructive and non-constructive guilt (Walinga et al. 2005). Non-constructive guilt, on the other hand, festers and is an unrelenting burden on the individual. In contrast, the absence of guilt is the hallmark of a psychopath and is a state that is detrimental to the well-being of others. It eschews right and wrong and does not learn from previous mistakes. Walinga et al. (2005) confirmed that when compared to a control group orthodox Catholics and Protestants experienced more guilt overall but it was constructive in nature and was highest among Catholics.

Shame and guilt are often erroneously seen as similar. Shame is defined as the person's response to how others might view him whereas guilt is the person's own reaction to the transgression. Secularists claim that going to confession engenders shame repentance and that this in essence gives the individual permission to continue as before rather than engendering true remorse and ultimately bringing about behavioural change. However, two recent studies rebut this presumption. The preventive value of guilt and shame was examined in a study by from George Mason University (Tangney et al. 2014). The subjects were 476 prison inmates who were interviewed shortly after release and one year later. Guilt, shame and blaming others were examined. Guilt reduced reoffending while shame did not. The analysis showed that shame predicted an increase in recidivism through its connection to externalising blame, but when blame was not directed to others shame had the same effect as guilt in reducing repeat offending. On a related theme, McCay et al. (2013) found that those who recalled the religious rituals of absolution and atonement donated much more money to charity than those who recalled the transgression without being absolved of it. The authors suggested that the findings 'complement a cultural evolutionary approach to religious pro-sociality, whereby religious practices evolve to the extent that they contribute to high levels of co-operation' among those in the group (McCay et al. 2013: 206).

In summary, the limited research that is available on 'Catholic guilt' suggests that, contrary to public perceptions, guilt among Catholics is neither negative nor specifically associated with mental-health pathology. Instead, it is positive and leads to pro-social behavioural change. Yet the myth is uncontested.

God is dead, thank God

It is common currency that institutional religion is dying in Ireland, as it is worldwide. Its death has been forecast since the Enlightenment, which pitted science against religion, one believed to be the truth, the other superstition. The French Revolution had as one of its objectives the destruction of religious practice and of the Catholic faith itself. Not only were bishops and priests massacred and churches destroyed but the word 'Sunday' was abolished and street names with any religious connotation were replaced (Tallet and Aiken 1991: 1–28).

Then Nietzsche proclaimed that 'God is dead' in his work *The Gay Science* (1882), in which he gave an account of God's murder. In *Thus Spoke Zarathustra*, a popular text in the 1960s, his antagonism towards the Judaeo-Christian world view is apparent, as instead of God he evokes images of fire, animals, earth, plants and other primal elements in his portrayal of the solitary, sage-like Zarathustra who seeks to live in a higher realm of existence called the *ubermenschlich* (superhuman).

Freud regarded religion as an activity of the 'neurotic' and as a means of avoiding the inevitability of death. During the 1960s, *Time* magazine ran a cover on Good Friday claiming that Americans were jettisoning religion with the question,

'Is God Dead?'. The lead story (Elson 1966) argued that anything which could not be demonstrated by scientific method was 'uninteresting or unreal'. Yet, some forty-eight years later, in 2014, a national Gallup poll found that 56 per cent of Americans felt that religion was very important in their lives.[1] And fifty-nine years after the *Time* magazine predictions that God was dead, *National Geographic* magazine, in its December 2015 issue, ran a front-page story entitled, 'Mary: The Most Powerful Woman in the World'.

Meanwhile, a number of new atheist philosophers, and four in particular, have become known as the Four Horsemen of the Non-Apocalypse, and their prominence has been obvious since the turn of the millennium. These are Richard Dawkins, Daniel Dennett, Sam Harris and Christopher Hitchens. Many of today's atheists do not accept that religion should be tolerated but argue that it should be countered and expunged from the public square.

Religion is delusional

In the book *The God Delusion*, Dawkins articulated a strident view in claiming that to believe in God was irrational and amounted to a 'delusion'. Since a delusion is a psychiatric symptom, defined as a false, unshakeable belief that is out of context with the social and cultural norms (Casey and Kelly 2009), the use of this term in respect of belief in God suggests that those holding such beliefs are psychiatrically ill. This dogmatic view is common among aggressive secularists, much as the Communist Party in Russia regarded those who voiced opinions opposed to it were regarded as ill and committed to psychiatric institutions with a diagnosis of 'sluggish schizophrenia'.

Who better to challenge the view that religious beliefs are delusions than an eminent psychiatrist? Professor Andrew Sims, a former president of the Royal College of Psychiatrists, and Emeritus Professor of Psychiatry at Leeds University, addressed this head on in his book *Is Faith Delusion? Why Religion Is Good for Your Health* (2009). With forensic detail, he examines the meaning of the word 'delusion' and considers its manifestations in clinical practice. He says, 'Delusion has become a psychiatric word: it belongs to psychiatry and it is the task of the psychiatrist to decide what is, and is not delusion' (Sims 2009 221). He points out that delusions are held by very few members in society and that their subject matter is time-specific. In other words, a person with delusions will be uncommon in his social group, and the content will be recognised as out of the ordinary within that group. The content will relate to what is current at the time, so during the Cold War delusions were often concerned with spies and the KGB. Those with religious delusions will actively 'spread the word' even in situations where it is inappropriate, whereas the traditionally religious person does not stand out from their peers in any way and will only discuss their beliefs in specific settings. Delusions are associated with mental illness and ultimately self-neglect and neglect of others with whom the person has a relationship. By contrast, the person with strong religious beliefs is able to work and lead a successful, fulfilling professional and private life. Thus, the ordinarily religious person is not marked out in any way except by their beliefs, while the individual with religious delusions is less well able to function in society and may be seriously impaired in day-to-day living. Sims powerfully points out, 'Faith is not delusion. Believers – members of the Church – would not be able to maintain their organisation if they knew that their tenets were false. It is not a shared pretence imposed by a super-class upon inferiors' (Sims 2009: 223).

Spirituality, religion: good guy, bad guy

Ask any person in Europe if they are religious, and they are more likely than not to describe themselves as spiritual but not religious. In the past, religion and spirituality were seen as being hand in glove, with one reflecting practice, the other the personal experience of God. With the growth of the New Age movement, the two have become unbuckled, and spirituality is now not even focused on a personal God but on broad feelings of the transcendent. According to Zinnbauer et al. (1997), the public also sees them differently also (see Table 11.1). In general, religion is viewed negatively while spirituality is seen positively, linked as it is to autonomy and individualised beliefs. Thus, religiousness is pitted against spirituality.

So the modern construct called spirituality is heterogeneous and means different things to different people. Hill et al. (2000) point out that currently there are many definitions of spirituality, some of which are linked to God, others of which are simply lifestyles, such as vegetarianism. While previously spirituality and religious activities, such as prayer, fasting and meditating were inextricably linked, the new understanding views spirituality as something that everybody possesses and that is uncoupled from a religious core (Koenig 2008). According to Koenig, there are now four categories that define peoples' religious involvement:

1. Spiritual and religious: This classification represent the traditional view of the relationship of one to the other.
2. Spiritual but not religious: This is the newest group.
3. Neither religious nor spiritual: This is the secular group.
4. Religious but not spiritual: This group has received little scientific attention.

These groups are exemplified by a study (King et al. 2006) that carried out face-to-face interviews with over 4,200 adults in England. They found that 17.7 per cent identified themselves as neither religious nor spiritual, 13.1 per cent described themselves as spiritual but not religious, while 69.2 per cent described themselves as religious and spiritual. Interestingly, nobody described themselves as religious but not spiritual. In their analysis, they found that

Table 11.1 Public perception of religion and spirituality.

Religion	Spirituality
Authoritarian	From within
Denominational	Personal
Linked to community	Autonomous
Ritualistic	Not hide-bound
Stipulates behaviours and rituals	Morality individualised
Personal god or supernatural	Supernatural unnecessary
Beliefs	Experiential

common mental disorders were no more prevalent among the non-religious group in comparison to the religious group but were most common in the group self-identifying as spiritual. The group that are spiritual and religious conform to the traditional view of the relationship between these attributes. The person engages in religious practices and adheres to beliefs and rituals associated with the specific tradition as well as engaging in activities such as meditating, fasting and reading illuminating texts. The group described as spiritual but not religious tend to view religiousness in a negative light, as shown in Table 11.1 above, to be more independent of others, to hold 'New Age' beliefs and to have mystical experiences (Zinnbauer et al. 1997). They view spirituality and religion as non-overlapping constructs.

The third group in the list above, those who are neither religious nor spiritual, are regarded as secular and are not much studied, and many of the New Atheists, wishing to avoid the word 'spiritual', belong in this group, partly because they do not ascribe to the idea of 'transcendence', which they see as a relic of religiousness.

The fourth group, religious but not spiritual, have not received any attention, nor are they mentioned in the scientific literature specifically although they are similar to the group who, in the past, attended church because they had to or because of social expectations rather than from a true faith (Allport and Ross 1967) and showing an extrinsic religious orientation.

These groups are of more than anthropological interest given the findings of the King study (2006). Similarly, a Canadian study (Baetz et al. 2004) examined over 70,000 adults as part of a longitudinal study. After controlling for confounders, those who attended church more frequently had significantly fewer depressive symptoms, while those who stated that spiritual or religious values were important to them or perceived themselves to be spiritual or religious, but who were not involved in religious institutions, had higher levels of depressive symptoms. Another study on suicidal behaviour (Rasic et al. 2009) found that self-harm behaviour such as overdosing and cutting was lower in a group who self-identified as religious in comparison to those who identified as spiritual. While not proving that religions causes fewer symptoms, these studies clearly point to an association between religiousness and good mental health and challenge the simple dichotomy between religion as bad and spirituality as good.

As well as being of interest to psychiatrists, the grouping and understanding of these attributes are relevant to evangelisers lest they assume that those who say they are spiritual are automatically focused on a monotheistic deity. Many, if not most, may not have any interest in a sacred religious core and may instead have appropriated a privatised vision.

Where are we now and where do we go from here?

The public at large continue to engage in varying degrees in activities related to our faith that include children receiving the sacraments, generativity, a desire to have our children educated in religious schools and around a 33 per cent weekly attendance at mass. Many might say our faith resilience has been very impressive given the scandals that the Church in Ireland has brought upon itself.

It is also easy to be dispirited by the state of Catholicism in Ireland from the clergy to the people in the pews. Yet it is important to turn to other countries and continents to witness the changes in religious attitudes and practices there. Examining how parishes have been rebuilt in the USA, after sexual abuse scandals similar to ours, would be instructive. Signs of religious sprouting in France in the past year or two are most encouraging, as is the growth of religion in China.

When one objectively examines religion, away from Western Europe, where it is certainly in decline, the omens are very different from those suggested by militant atheists. As Micklethwait and Wooldridge (2010) point out, there has been a rise in faith across the globe from South America to China to Nigeria. This too is the opinion of one of the foremost figures in the field of the sociology of religion, Rodney Stark. He and Roger Finke focus on the USA in their 2005 book. They use an economics analogy to make the case that churches which are in a free market economy for religion fare best as they will be in competition with others for souls while they languish when they have a monopoly or when their 'product' is insufficiently differentiated from their competitors. That is to say, adapting teachings to suit popular culture will make those denominations less, rather than more, appealing. Moreover, they also argue that even in Roman Catholicism, notwithstanding its international base and hierarchical structure, success comes from 'intense faith with a vivid sense of other worldliness' (Finke and Stark 2005: 143). In the context of Ireland, this finding must give cause for concern, especially if the findings in the Dolan review are correct and if the allegations concerning the attitudes among trainers to traditionalist seminarians are substantiated.

The momentous scandals in which the Irish Church has been embroiled have, not surprisingly, made many hostile to it. Church attendance rates have plummeted but are still above the averages in most European countries. Catholic Christians in Ireland now have little knowledge of what their religion stands for.

These are most likely unconnected to the sexual abuse scandals since they happened before many of our young people were born. This deficiency is probably better explained by their poor education in the fundamentals of the faith. This neglect has culminated in fear of engaging in religious debate, even by those committed to their faith, lest they are pilloried by the seemingly powerful ascendancy of a hostile media and joked about at the dinner parties of the libertarian 'intelligentsia'. It is reassuring that the feature which holds sustains religion, according to Finke and Stark's thesis, is the very one that its opponents of religion want changed, that is, doctrinal fidelity.

The new media have facilitated the spread of diverse philosophies worldwide. Because of their reach, no country is immune from their influence. Withstanding the challenge from various ideologies requires knowledge of one's faith and the personal conviction to state it. The New Testament used parables to speak directly to the people. This made the Word of God experiential. It surely demands that we make full utilisation of all media forms to tell the stories that have formed our faith. As well as tweeting, Facebooking, YouTubing and so on, there is an imperative to engage with other faiths, Christian and non-Christian, since they too are likely to be under pressure from secularising forces. Nevertheless, these interventions require us to be educated about our faith and to have the courage and language to speak to a secular audience, and these initiatives must come from lay people now that the days of clericalism are over. It is easy to become despondent but perhaps, just as we were urged to pray for the conversion of Communist Russia when we were children, the time has come for us to invite the children of a Christianising Russia to pray for us.

Note

1 Gallup Historical Trends (2014) available www.gallup.com/home.aspx (accessed 3 January 2016).

Works cited

Allport, G. W and J. M. Ross (1967) 'Personal Religious Orientation and Prejudice', *Journal of Personality and Social Psychology*, 5:4, 432–43.

Baetz, M, R. Griffin, R. Bowen, H. Koenig and E. Marcoux (2004) 'The Association between Spiritual and Religious Involvement and Depressive Symptoms in a Canadian Population', *Journal of Nervous and Mental Disease*, 192:12, 818–82.

Barry, Cathal and Greg Daly (2015) 'Bishops Rebel over Maynooth Seminary "Heave"', *Irish Catholic*, 2 July, available at http://irishcatholic.ie/article/bishops-rebel-over-maynooth-seminary-%E2%80%98heave%E2%80%99 (accessed 6 September 2016).

Casey, Patricia and Brendan Kelly (2009) *Fish's Clinical Psychopathology*, 3rd edn, London: RCPsych Press.

Dawkins, R. (2006) *The God Delusion*, London: Bantam Press.

Dooley, Mark (2011) *Why Be a Catholic?* London: Burns & Oates.

Elson, John T. (1966) 'Toward a Hidden God', *Time*, 8 April.

Finke, R. and R. Stark (2005) *The Churching of America, 1776–2005: Winners and Losers in Our Religious Economy*, New Brunswick, NJ: Rutgers University Press.

Goode, H., H. McGee and C. O'Boyle (2003) *Time to Listen: Confronting Child Sexual Abuse by Catholic Clergy in Ireland*, Dublin: Liffey.

Hill, P. C., K. I. Pargament, R. W. Hood, M. E. McCullough, J. P. Swyers, D. B. Larson and B. J. Zinnbauer (2000) 'Conceptualising Religion and Spirituality: Points of Commonality Points of Departure', *Journal for the Theory of Social Behaviour*, 30:1, 51–77.

John Jay College of Criminal Justice (2004) *The Nature and Scope of Sexual Abuse of Minors by Catholic Priests and Deacons in the United States, 1950–2002*, United States Conference of Catholic Bishops, available at http://www.usccb.org/issues-and-action/child-and-youth-protection/upload/The-Nature-and-Scope-of-Sexual-Abuse-of-Minors-by-Catholic-Priests-and-Deacons-in-the-United-States-1950–2002.pdf (accessed 6 September 2016).

King, M., S. Weich, J. Nazroo and B. Blizard (2006) 'Religion, Mental Health and Ethnicity, EMPIRIC: A National Survey of England', *Journal of Mental Health*, 51:2, 153–62.

Kline, P. M., R. McMackin and E. Lezotte (2008) 'The Impact of the Clergy Abuse Scandal on Parish Communities', *Journal of Child Sex Abuse*, 17:3–4, 290–300.

Koenig, H. G. (2008) 'Concerns About Measuring "Spirituality" in Research', *Journal of Nervous Mental Disease*, 196, 349–55.

Langeland, W., A. W. Hoogendoorn, D. Mager, J. H. Smit and N. Draijer (2015) 'Childhood Sexual Abuse by Representatives of the Roman Catholic Church: A Prevalence Estimate among the Dutch Population', *Child Abuse and Neglect*, 46, 67–77.

Maschi, David (2015) 'Who are "Cultural Catholics"?' Pew Research Centre, available at http://www.pewresearch.org/fact-tank/2015/09/03/who-are-cultural-catholics (accessed 6 September 2016).

McCay, R., J. Herold and H. Whitehoude (2013) 'Catholic Guilt? Recall of Confession Promotes Prosocial Behaviour', *Religion, Brain and Behavior*, 3:3, 201–9.

Micklethwait, J. and A. Wooldridge (2010) *God Is Back: How the Global Rise of Faith Is Changing the World*, New York: Penguin.

Neolle-Neumann, Elisabeth (1993) *The Spiral of Silence: Public Opinion, Our Social Skin*, Chicago, Ill.: University of Chicago Press.

Nietzsche, Friedrich (1999) *Thus Spake Zarathustra*, trans. Thomas Common, Philadelphia, Pa.: Pennsylvania State University.

—— (2001) *The Gay Science*, trans. and ed. Bernard Williams, Josefine Nauckhoff and Adrian Del Caro, Cambridge: Cambridge University Press.

Rafferty, Oliver P. (2015) 'The Catholic Church in Ireland and Vatican II in Historical Perspective', in Niall Coll (ed.), *Ireland and Vatican II*, Dublin: Columba, pp. 13–32.

Rasic, D. T., S. L. Belik, B. Elias, L. Y. Katz, M. Enns and J. Sareen (2009) 'Spirituality, Religion and Suicidal Behaviour in a Nationally Representative Sample', *Journal of Affective Disorders*, 114:1–3, 32–40.

Roof, W. C. (2001) *Spiritual Marketplace: Baby Boomers and the Remaking of American Religion*, Princeton, NJ: Princeton University Press.

Rosetti, S. (1995) 'The Impact of Child Sexual Abuse on Attitudes toward God and the Catholic Church', *Child Abuse and Neglect*, 19:12, 1469–81.

Sica, C., C. Novara and E. Sanavio (2002) 'Religiousness and Obsessive–Compulsive Cognitions and Symptoms in an Italian Population', *Behaviour Research and Therapy*, 40:7, 813–23.

Sims, A. (2009) *Is Faith Delusion? Why Religion Is Good for Your Health*, London: Bloomsbury Academic.

Steketee, G., S. Quay and K. White (1991) 'Religion and Guilt in OCD Patients', *Journal of Anxiety Disorders*, 5:4, 359–67.

Stengers, Jean and Anne van Neck (2001) *Masturbation: The History of a Great Terror*, Basingstoke: Palgrave Macmillan.

Tallet, F. and N. Aitken (1991) 'Dechristianising France: The Year II and the Revolutionary Experience', in Frank Tallett and Nicholas Atkin (eds.), *Religion, Society and Politics in France since 1789*, New York: Hambledon Press, pp. 1–28.

Tangney, J. P., J. Stuewig and A. G. Martinez (2014) 'Two Faces of Shame. The Roles of Shame and Guilt in Predicting Recidivism', *Psychological Science*, 25:3, 799–805.

Vaisey, S. and C. Smith (2008) 'Catholic Guilt among US Teenagers: A Research Note', *Review of Religious Research*, 49:4, 415–26.

Walinga, P. J., J. Corveleyn and J. van Saane (2005) 'Guilt and Religion: The Influence of Orthodox Protestants and Orthodox Catholic Conceptions of Guilt or Guilt-Experience', *Archives of the Psychology of Religion*, 27, 113–36.

Wingert, Pat (2010) 'Priests Commit No More Abuse than Other Males', *Newsweek*, 4 July.

Zinnbauer, B. J., K. L. Pargament, B. C. Cole, M. S. Rye, E. M. Butter and T. G. Belavich (1997) 'Religion and Spirituality: Unfuzzying the Fuzzy', *Journal for the Scientific Study of Religion*, 36, 549–64.

12

Irreconcilable differences? The fraught relationship between women and the Catholic Church in Ireland

Sharon Tighe-Mooney

Introduction

In the introduction to *From Prosperity to Austerity*, Eamon Maher and Eugene O'Brien write, in the context of attempts to voice caution during the Irish boom, that the consensus between government, the media and business interests held 'that anyone who opposed the current ideology was against progress, was rooted in the past, or was incapable of seeing the benefits to all of our exceptional prosperity' (2014: 5). The Catholic Church was in no position to voice its concern about these developments at the time, in the wake of the child-abuse and Magdalene laundry revelations. Moreover, the response in the public forum to the litany of Church-related offences has been to reject the institutional Church and, consequently, impede the creation of a space for the evaluation of the cultural legacy of Irish Catholicism. As a result, attempting to explore aspects of the Catholic Church without falling into outright condemnation of the entire institution and of its members is deemed insular, 'against progress' and 'rooted in the past'. It can be argued that the public rejection of Catholic Church teaching is an attempt at individual reassertion and autonomy in the wake of discovering that the institution in which we placed our faith and trust has been found undeserving of that faith and trust. Yet to ignore the legacy of the Catholic Church in Ireland is to deny the most enduring and forceful facet in the shaping of Irish society.

In an interview in 2002, the well-known writer John McGahern (1934–2006) remarked, 'Ireland is a peculiar society in the sense that it was a nineteenth century society up to about 1970 and then it almost bypassed the twentieth century' (*The Guardian*, 6 January 2002). That 'peculiarity' is most evident when it comes to the rapid nature of change in family life. Ireland has changed from a largely homogenous society, loyal to the tenets of Catholicism, to a multicultural society with access to contraception and divorce, in a remarkably short space of time. Indeed, the role of women at the heart of that change, given the strong relationship between women and the Catholic Church in the past, has yet to be fully appreciated. Additionally, while there have been important cultural advances for women in terms of their role in society, the one institution that has not altered its perception of women to any great degree is the Roman Catholic Church. Moreover, scripture is used by the teaching authority of the Church to uphold women's secondary status and exclusion from ministry in the Catholic Church.

This chapter will examine the main events of the past thirty-five years in the context of the weakening hegemony of the Catholic Church in juxtaposition with the growing awareness by Catholic women that they had framed their lives by edicts promulgated by a celibate male-dominated institution that had supported double standards in an area in which it was most vocal. The consequences of this ethos have been traumatic, with generations of Irish women in particular having paid a heavy price in terms of the approximately thirty childbearing years of their lives that were framed by a strict regime of enforced selflessness and a system of severe penury for those who did not conform. I will begin with a brief overview of the historical context of the relationship between women, priests and religious and then examine how evolving mores were framed by an issue about which the Church was particularly vocal, namely contraception, which reflects the conflict between the Church and women for control of the female body. Major events, such as the death of Ann Lovett and the Kerry Babies controversy, as well as the accounts of moving or weeping statues of Our Lady, will be contextualised in an attempt to give readers a feel for the *Zeitgeist* of the time. Then I will turn my attention to the ordination of women, the interdiction of which, in my view, seeks to exclude women from leadership roles in the institution and, furthermore, is a stance that is at odds with contemporary society. The reiteration of the Church's position on this teaching in 2010 will be considered in the wake of the contemporaneous revelations of wrongdoing by some church personnel: Bishop Eamon Casey, Fr Michael Cleary and the child-abuse scandals. Finally, a survey conducted by sociologist Betty Hilliard that frames this thirty-year period, will be utilised to discuss how the lives of Irish women were particularly affected by Church teaching and how attitudes changed, especially in relation to the unquestioning obedience to Church teaching.

The historical context

It is an historical fact, Mary Kenny writes, that 'no one has forged, sustained, or upheld the faith of Catholic Ireland more purposefully than the women of Ireland' (2000: 11). The relationship between church personnel and women developed from the middle of the nineteenth century onwards. Priests and nuns took an interest in what women were doing, and the Church, Tony Fahey argues, promoted 'a familial piety which reflected the increasing nuclearisation of the family and the growing importance of women as the moral centres of family life' (1992: 263). The family was important, therefore, because it provided the space for the socialisation of the future members of society. In that capacity, the Irish mother played a crucial role in the development of modern Irish society, a development that was heavily influenced by the Church. The Catholic Church world view held that in the home, woman exercised the 'natural' vocation for which nature had intended her. Moreover, she imitated the toil and self-denial of priests and nuns, thereby fostering vocations among her children or resigning them to the limitations of life in Ireland at that time. In the Catholic Church ethos, therefore, women had a defined role; that of mother, nurturer and carer of the family. It was, in short, a vocation. In this way, Irish mothers became the propagators of the faith both in the home and in the community. In *Moral Monopoly*, Tom Inglis describes how this role was central to both the continuation of the Catholic ethos and the acceptance of the limited roles offered by society in the early twentieth century (1998: 178–200).

The Irish State, underpinned by the 1937 Constitution that embraced Catholic social teaching in terms of the family and women's place in the family as mother, was slow to embrace any semblance of autonomy for Irish women. This included the right to regulate fertility. With the assertion of 'natural law' (or 'God's law') promulgated by the Church, and upheld by the ban on contraception enacted by the Fianna Fáil government in 1935, no forum for discussion about contraception was possible in Ireland. A study conducted by Betty Hilliard, in the 1970s and again in 2000 in Cork City as part of a project on family research, interviewed women who had become mothers in the 1950s and 1960s. What is striking about the study is that the questions posed were not specifically on the topic of sexuality. Rather, as Hilliard wrote, 'most of the following material emerged in response to a very general question about life when these women were rearing young children' (2004: 139). A significant theme among the participants was motherhood as the central role of women's lives, as well as the experience of high birth rates. Hilliard remarked, 'In talking about their experiences of sexuality, motherhood and the Church, the respondents painted a picture of domination, ignorance and fear' (2004: 139). A notable finding that emerged from the study was a very poor understanding of the actual process of childbirth as, Hilliard was told, it was a topic that was not discussed. This created a culture of fear about childbirth, about pregnancy itself and of the risks of continuous childbearing. For these women, therefore, the reproductive aspect dominated sexual activity, and intercourse was beset with fear.

Hilliard's study reflects the long-lasting and deep-rooted sway that the Church had exercised over the institution of motherhood. The physical consequences of sex were entirely women's responsibility. As women's value in the Catholic Church world view is intrinsically linked to motherhood, the physical demands of repeated pregnancies on women were of little concern to the male hierarchy.[1] Prioritising motherhood over other concerns such as the health of both mother and child, or whether there were adequate material provisions available, led to much suffering and hardship for generations of Irish women who were deprived of access to artificial forms of contraception. This edict was ruthlessly enforced as can be gauged by the comments of many respondents in Hilliard's study who reported being refused absolution in confession for voicing concerns about risking another pregnancy due to poverty or ill health. The Irish State upheld Catholic Church teachings by banning the use of contraceptives, as well as written material giving information about or alluding to contraception. Consequently, securing legal autonomy in this regard was not an easy matter. Hilliard noted, 'Although there were some references to political figures, power and control were almost universally associated with religion by respondents' (2004: 155). This reflects the power of the Church in affecting state regulations in this regard.

On the matter of contraception, there was great expectation of a change of heart from the Vatican in the 1960s. However, expectations were not fulfilled. In his encyclical, *Humanae vitae* (1968), Pope Paul VI (1963–78) reaffirmed traditional Church teaching and stated that preventing pregnancy by abstinence was the only acceptable means of contraception, because in abstinence, 'the married couple rightly use a faculty provided them by nature' (Section 16). In this way, the merits of celibacy predominate the issues of childbearing and human sexuality. In addition, although women are mentioned in the body of the encyclical, they are not specifically greeted, blessed nor addressed directly in their emotional and physical role as bearers of children. The Vatican would seem to have made its judgement without actually 'seeing' the women at whom the issue was targeted. The response from the 'faithful' was disbelief and disappointment. At the same time, Kenny writes that even in the aftermath of the first wave of the feminist movement in the 1960s, 'the Catholic view that God and nature intended sexual intercourse to be fruitful was quite widely held as a correct principle, even if it was not always practiced or observed' (2000: 127). While on the one hand faith in the sustenance of the Catholic Church ideology of welcoming all new life was the ideal; on the other hand, much human suffering was involved, especially for females. As well as the physical and emotional demands on mothers, decades of poverty and sustained emigration had shown that God did not always provide. The dichotomous situation was arguably best summed up by the writer Kate O'Brien. In *Pray for the Wanderer*, Nell Mahoney ponders 'the binding vows and obligations of marriage', a rite that has the procreation of children as its primary aim. Her thoughts reflect the dilemma of the Catholic believer, as she 'could not admit, any more by her fastidious nerves than by her religious training, the pitiful exigencies or crude materialistic ethic of birth control – though baffled indeed, too, by the appalling problems and horrors of unchecked fecundity' (1951: 109). Ultimately, as Chrystel Hug remarks, 'in this domain, Catholic morality was particularly cut off from the reality of contraceptive practice, which accounts for its demise' (1999: 9). The topic of contraception, therefore, put into doubt, for the first time, the validity of Church teaching.

While a robust Catholic society was still evident when John Paul II (1978–2005) visited Ireland in 1979, gradual changes in state law had begun. Jenny Beale notes, 'Issues relating to the changing status of women have acted as focal points for controversy over the wider changes in values and attitudes in Irish society' (1986: viii). In early 1971, Mary Robinson, then a senator, attempted to introduce a Bill proposing to liberalise the law on contraception. The Bill was not allowed a reading in the Seanad, and so it could not be discussed. In fact, she had to make seven attempts in total before being successful (Hug 1999: 94). In May 1971, a group of Irish feminists caused quite a stir when they travelled to Belfast by train and returned to Dublin with contraceptive devices in order to demonstrate the illogical nature of the law. In 1973, the Supreme Court agreed that while there was a constitutional right to marital privacy that allowed for the use of contraceptives, the Act forbidding their import or sale was, nevertheless, not repugnant to the Constitution. In other words, contraceptives could be used legally but not obtained legally. As a result of this anomaly, a series of Bills was proposed, but the enthusiasm to see them through appeared to be lacking in the Irish government. Eventually, in 1978, and largely due to the consistent work for women's reproductive rights by Mary Robinson, Charles Haughey introduced the Health (Family Planning) Bill. In this Bill, which became an Act in 1979, contraceptives could be prescribed by doctors on medical grounds and obtained in selected pharmacies. It was, therefore, extremely restrictive, but at least it was now under the remit of the Department of Health rather than the Department of Justice, which removed any former criminal associations from the issue of contraception.

The movement of discussion about these matters from the private to the public sphere was facilitated by a new afternoon radio programme, *Women Today*, first broadcast on 31 May 1979. This show, which allowed women to speak about issues of concern in their lives, together with the iconic broadcaster Gay Byrne's vital role in facilitating public discussion of formerly taboo topics, meant that for the first time people started hearing about the lives of ordinary people. Additionally, journalists such as Nell McCafferty and Gene Kerrigan, who have been writing political commentaries since the 1970s, continued to highlight issues of concern, such as the Kerry Babies case.[2] In this way, personal stories that had been formerly masked by collective ideology began to emerge. The effects on women of state legislation and church edicts were verbalised, and the predominant mood was that women had had enough. However, when John Paul II visited Ireland, the year after his appointment to the papacy, the idea that motherhood should be a woman's only role in life was still to the fore. In his address at Shannon Airport on the day of his departure, the Pope said, 'May Irish mothers, young women and girls not listen to those who tell them that working at a secular job, succeeding in a secular profession, is more important than the vocation of giving life and caring for this life as a mother' (John Paul II 1979: 80–1). This continues to be the Vatican position. Many women, however, were no longer willing to be defined merely by this one aspect of their lives.

While great enthusiasm was displayed for the papal visit, it was arguably more about seeing and hearing a world-famous figure than acting as a marker for the renewal of Catholic devotion. James S. Donnelly remarks, 'Indeed, the openly acknowledged purpose of the Irish hierarchy in inviting John Paul to Ireland was largely that of halting or at least slowing the damaging inroads of materialism and secularism on the attachment of Catholics to their ancient faith' (2002: 271). Additionally, in his memoir *Staring at Lakes*, Michael Harding writes:

> In some ways, the papal visit was the funeral of Catholicism in Ireland. After the cheers of the assembled millions had died away … Irish society found that it couldn't really stomach the harsh tone of Rome's teachings and bit by bit went off to gorge and be lost in a frenzy of secular self-improvement. (2013: 97–8)

The signs of decline had been there from the 1960s, as noted by the writer Desmond Fennell, who argues that there was no reason why decline in belief, as had happened in Europe, would not be mirrored in Ireland. As literacy, education and advances in science and technology facilitated an increase in living standards, Christianity had been abandoned. Fennell's thesis is that the Church had failed to understand the new developments and, moreover, had failed to frame the changing society in a Christian context. His reasoning, it can be argued, was borne out by the subsequent issuing of *Humanae vitae*, which was another example of, as Fennell puts it, a 'failure to know the times' (1962). The Church also failed to appreciate the changing role of women in society. Additionally, another aspect of the feminist movement that had an impact on the relationship between women and the Church was access to education. Women began to read scripture for themselves; they could now study theology and could communicate with women around the world. The Catholic Church's ambivalent attitude towards women could now be seen in the interpretations of scripture written by men over the centuries on the subject of women. This knowledge and awareness, combined with the sexual revolution, in the view of Mary T. Malone, 'often stretched the relationships between women and their churches to breaking point' (2000: 22). In addition, as women became involved in all aspects of public life, their almost total exclusion from the organisational arm of the Catholic Church began to rankle.

The signs of the alienation of women from the Catholic Church from the time of the Pope's visit onwards can be suggested by their engagement in areas that were intrinsic to Church teaching. In 1979, the Family Planning (Health) Act to legalise contraception, albeit in very limited terms, was enacted and came into law the following year. Also in 1979, the Censorship Board's authority to ban books about or referring to contraception was withdrawn. The relationship between women and the Catholic Church at this point was succinctly described thus by Tom Inglis:

> In terms of maintaining its power, the problem for the Catholic Church was that once women began to gain control of their bodies … the bonds that tied them to the home and rearing children gradually loosened. As that happened, the consolation and compensatory power which the Church in Ireland provided for women over the last hundred years was no longer as necessary because they were able to gain entry to the positions, resources and prestige to which they have previously been denied access. (1998: 63)

There is little doubt that many of the changes in Irish society were driven by women. Moreover, it can be argued that the issue of contraception best reflects the initial gap between lived experience and ideology and, in the aftermath of *Humanae vitae*, doubt as to the credibility of Church teaching began to feature in the Irish cultural psyche.

In the 1980s, a series of events exposed the cultural hegemonic Catholic landscape to the rigours of a conflict between physical reality and spiritual ideology, particularly in relation to the policing of female sexuality.

Church, State, women and the 1980s

By 1980, limited contraception was available. In 1982, the first minister of state for women's affairs and family law was appointed. Nuala Fennell (1935–2009) had worked as a freelance journalist and was a staunch advocate of women's rights.[3] In 1983, an amendment to the Constitution was passed by referendum seeking to prevent any possible legalisation of abortion and instating equal status in law to a mother and her foetus. The bitterness of the campaign was a reaction to the perception of a growing loosening of the bond between church and people. One of the most damaging consequences for women was the new discourse that positioned them as a potential threat to the unborn child; in other words, as potential killers of innocent babies.[4] This was the context that preceded the death of Ann Lovett and the Kerry Babies fiasco, both of which occurred in 1984.

In February 2014, Maynooth University held an event to mark the thirty-year anniversary of the death of Ann Lovett in Granard, Co. Longford, on 31 January 1984. Christy Moore performed 'The Middle of the Island', a song he had recorded with Sinéad O'Connor and which evolved from lyrics sent to him by Nigel Rolfe under the title, 'The Ostrich'. The opening line, which is repeated in the song, captures the cultural focus on sexuality, in terms of the policing of female sexuality, and, at the same time, the silence surrounding the topic: 'Everybody knew, nobody said.' Moore writes that the song is not only a memorial to Ann Lovett, who is not named, but a reminder of 'young girls left to die in cold stone grottos while a country kneels at the altar, like an ostrich' (2000: 28). Ann Lovett died after giving birth to her son in a grotto dedicated to the Virgin Mary. In the absence of being able to seek or accept help, she had turned to a statue that symbolises the ultimate loving mother, albeit one that is wholly unconnected with sex or sexuality.

Given that this was not an immaculate conception, the father of Ann's baby escaped national notoriety. There was little impetus to force men to confront the consequences of pre-marital sex in either practicable or public terms. It was women and their children who were incarcerated as well as vilified by church and society. 'Purity', as the most important attribute of the Catholic woman, in imitation of the mother of Jesus, has a long history in the Church. Moreover, the control of sexual behaviour was a feature of Irish nationalism from the nineteenth century onwards and was accentuated after Independence in the drive for the moral and cultural uniqueness of the newly independent Irish people. Thus, church, state and society, all of the opinion that the threat to sexual morality resided in the bodies of women, ensured that females who did not conform to the ideal Irish woman were rendered invisible. As Marjorie Howes notes, 'Irish culture has long had, for better or worse, a keen sense of the public determinants and consequences of the apparently private realm of sexuality' (2002: 923). The organs of 'public consequences' were particularly oppressive for Irish women.

Ann Lovett's death marked a shift in mood. People asked themselves what kind of society would allow a young girl and her baby to suffer such a fate. The answer was a Catholic-dominated one, in which, as Inglis argues, status was tied up with the public participation in Catholic ritual and the need to be deemed respectable (1998: 11). In response to the deaths of Ann and her son, hundreds of letters were sent to the *Gay Byrne Show* on RTÉ radio. Women wrote about their experiences and described previously untold stories of pregnancy outside marriage. As a result of the volume of letters received, Byrne dedicated an entire show to the reading of women's experiences. Indeed, the facilitation of the stories on the national airwaves ensured that not only were these topics no longer taboo but that the human cost to maintaining the façade of Catholic respectability was articulated.

In April that same year, the Joanne Hayes story, involving the death of two babies, broke. At the end of the year, in December 1984, the Kerry Babies Tribunal was set up, with, it should be noted, all-male investigating, legal and expert teams.[5] Similarly, as with the case of Ann Lovett, the proceedings emphasised how much the focus was on women in these situations. In other words, although the responsibility for sexual morality was largely vested in women, it was enforced by men, in both Church and State. The remit was to investigate why Ms Hayes had confessed to giving birth to a second child found near Cahirciveen, almost fifty miles away from her home. Instead, the Tribunal turned into an investigation and demonisation of Joanne Hayes. The vitriol and hostility expressed towards certain women anxious to assert their rights in relation to birth control and the equal right to life of the mother and child, during the 1983 constitutional referendum on abortion, now had a visible target. Worryingly, however, the death of two babies, both of whom were assumed to be Joanne's, appeared to be of far less interest than the extra-marital affair from which they allegedly arose.

Wider access to contraception, in that contraceptive devices were made legally available to all, including unmarried persons, was legalised in 1985, the year after these events. The final vote had taken place in the Dáil at the end of February. How much Ann Lovett's death and the vilification of Joanne Hayes influenced this outcome is open to speculation as it had taken over fifteen years to achieve. While on the one hand the loosening of the bonds between Catholic Church teaching and Irish society appeared inevitable in the wake of accounts of the deaths of young girls and newborn babies, as well as the legalisation of contraception, on the other hand, a curious phenomenon took place that suggests that the break from long-held belief in and obedience to Catholic teaching was problematic.

The moving statues phenomenon reinforces the opposing factions of an evolving liberal and secular society marked by uncertainty and a strongly held belief system that dealt in absolutes, framed by a strong unquestioning adherence to Catholic teaching. As Margaret MacCurtain notes, 'a familiar system of Catholic representation, the Marian wayside shrine, became the vehicle for interpreting the moral anxiety that engulfed Catholic believers in the aftermath of the angry exchanges that accompanied the 1983 Eighth Amendment to the Constitution' (2008: 161). From February to September 1985, there were over thirty accounts of moving or weeping statues of Our Lady. The most famous one is the moving statue of Ballinspittle, Co. Cork, which is near Kinsale, but the first alleged event took place in Asdee, Co. Kerry, just two months after the Kerry Babies Tribunal had been set up. As the most popular figure in folk religion, a renewed devotion to Mary, the perfect female icon and loving chaste mother, was particularly relevant in the context of abortion and the portrayal of Joanne Hayes, who, as Tom Inglis notes, 'was made into a kind of exotic, sexual predator, who was not just very different from other Irish women, but represented a threat to them and to every decent Irish man' (2003: 222).

With the Church being particularly vocal on the issues of sex and the control of women's bodies, the institutional Church was failing to meet the religious needs of the people as provider of access to the transcendent. In some ways, the apparitions were a response to this gap in a folk-religious sort of way.[6] There were claims of healings by people who visited the sites. Many saw the face of Our Lady of Ballinspittle change to that of either Jesus or Padre Pio. Others saw the 5 foot 8 inch concrete statue rock from side to side. By early August, some 100,000 people had visited the grotto in Co. Cork.[7] While this suggests a show of religious piety, Eamon McCann found that the mood at the grotto in Ballinspittle was matter-of-fact and, furthermore, that nobody expressed a view of the events as transformative. Rather, the experience appeared to suggest a deep yearning for reassurance that faith in God was justified (McCann 1985: 33–7). The fact that so many people, and women in particular, collectively imagined or felt that they had experienced something mystical at various grottoes around the country, suggests a subconscious plea for reassurance about the 'rightness' of adhering to the rigid regulation of the body in light of the public discourse, discussion and bitter exchanges around what Nell McCafferty termed, 'the war of the wombs' (1985a: 58). The phenomenon of the moving statues in one way served to reassert the comfort and security of long-held beliefs. Then again, the effects, if any, were brief, and, as McCann found, not 'transformative'.

In 1984 and 1985, therefore, the clash between cultural and religious ideology and the move towards an individual interpretation of religious ethics and morals was played out to an unprecedented degree in the public forum. There is little doubt that these events had focused, to a degree hitherto unseen and unheard in public, on individual personal consequences in terms of the Church's theology of sexuality. In the context of Catholic teaching, females such as Joanne Hayes and Ann Lovett had transgressed the very essence of the perfect Irish Catholic woman, modelled on the Virgin Mary: self-sacrificing, subservient and all-loving, and largely disinterested in sex. At the same time, they also embodied the dichotomous dilemma of the Irish Catholic female, esteemed as a married mother, shamed and vilified as an unmarried one and otherwise of no great import. The Catholic Church's implicit attitude was, and still is, that women are valued for their contribution to the perpetuation of the faith, for their role as mothers (married only) and as carers of others. In her self-sacrificing, vocational role as mother, the Catholic woman has neither the right nor the expectation of any other means of fulfilment. Up to the 1980s, wider society perpetuated this world view. However, the events outlined above provoked questions about aspects of Church teaching in the context of Irish societal values. In the decade to follow, the recounting of the physical, mental and sexual abuse visited upon women and children by church personnel in industrial schools and Magdalene laundries would serve to loosen the bond between the Church and the women of Ireland even further.

Church, State, women and the 1990s

The right to autonomy, begun by Irish women in the 1970s and persisted with throughout the 1980s, began to come to fruition in the 1990s. This also signalled the growing chasm between women and the Church as the series of referendums that took place in Ireland directly contravened Church teaching. At the same time, the pull between tradition and change featured strongly. In 1990, Mary Robinson, a known proponent of women's rights, was elected as president of Ireland. In May 1992, it was revealed that the revered Bishop Eamon Casey had fathered a son. This was a pivotal moment in the perception of the Church as moral authority. In November 1992, a referendum was held in the wake of the 'X Case' on three abortion-related issues. The right to travel and the right to information were upheld. The following year, the fathering of two children by the well-known 'singing priest' Fr Michael Cleary was reported, just after his death. In 1995, the referendum legalising access to divorce was carried. In October 1997, Mary Robinson was succeeded by Mary McAleese as president of Ireland.

Legally, women now had the ability to make decisions about their bodies, their marriages and their lives both outside of and within the context of family matters, about which Pope John Paul II had spoken so passionately during his 1979 visit. Moreover, the gradual shift in cultural views about women meant that participating in all aspects of life was no longer taboo. Motherhood was no longer the only defining factor of a woman's life. She could now also be considered as a person in her own right. In the church context, the remaining years of this decade were framed by a series of revelations of physical and sexual abuse by clerics and religious. By the end of the 1990s, the most influential and important institution in Ireland, the Catholic Church, had been shown to be seriously deficient in human kindness and to be incapable of or indeed unwilling to police its own ethos of sexual morality, as well as showing itself to be largely indifferent to the people its personnel had abused. Moreover, there was little expression of sincere remorse for the shortcomings that had been exposed. Rather, the Church was eventually compelled to address the situation by outside forces. The most important aspect of a relationship, trust, had been broken.

Since Vatican II, the dignity of the human person and the equality of all the faithful are stated core principles of the Catholic Church, 'no inequality on the basis of race or nationality, social condition or sex' (Vatican II 1965: 13). However, rather than concerning themselves with the series of unfolding scandals across the world, as well as in Ireland, or indeed attempting to explain to Catholics why such penury had been visited on those who were regarded as having transgressed by a church founded on the principles of love and forgiveness, John Paul II decided to act on the issue of women and ministry in the Catholic Church. The Pope reiterated the thoughts of Paul VI who had addressed the question in 1976, on foot of the Vatican's Pontifical Biblical Commission being unable, after examining scripture, to answer the question one way or another.[8] In the apostolic letter, *Ordinatio sacerdotalis* (On Reserving Priestly Ordination to Men Alone), John Paul II employed his full authority to put an end to the discussion: 'I declare that the Church has no authority whatsoever to confer priestly ordination on women and that this judgment is to be definitively held by all the Church's faithful.' Just a few months after the publication of *Ordinatio sacerdotalis*, the record of offences committed by Fr Brendan Smyth across Ireland, the UK and the USA, stretching back to the 1950s, was revealed. Smyth was a prolific paedophile who used his position of trust to rape and sexually assault dozens of young children over a forty-year period.

Three years later, John Paul II took further action on the questioning of Church teaching by issuing an apostolic letter *Ad tuendam fidem* (To

Defend the Faith), which is a document issued on the Pope's own initiative (*motu proprio*) and personally signed by him. The document authorised key additions to the code of Canon Law, and a number of changes were implemented. Changes to canon law are quite rare, and in past centuries there have been only a few such alterations. In any case, John Paul II opened the letter by stating that the changes were needed to 'protect the faith of the Catholic Church against errors arising from certain members of the Christian faithful'. This was in response to the many Roman Catholic theologians and religious personnel who had questioned Church teachings on topics such as female ordination, priestly celibacy, artificial methods of birth control and homosexuality. In this way, discussion and debate about how to confront the changing mores were firmly suppressed. This left little room for Catholics, either lay, professed or ordained, to discuss and debate openly the role of Catholicism in a changing world. Fennell's thesis about the Church's failings in this regard, made almost thirty years earlier, seemed prescient. A year later, in 1999, RTÉ broadcast a three-part documentary, *States of Fear*, made by Mary Raftery. The series detailed the sustained abuse suffered by children in Church-run industrial and reformatory schools in Ireland between the 1930s and the 1970s. By the end of the decade, therefore, rather than offering a model for the Christian message of love and forgiveness, the absolute moral authority had been found to be highly immoral at times.

Church, State, women and the 2000s

As the new millennium dawned, Ireland was a very different society from the one that Pope John Paul II had encountered in 1979. Women had achieved legal rights, more personal autonomy and the right to participate in the public sphere. In 2004, Mary McAleese was re-elected president of Ireland. In the context of the Catholic Church, the issue of abuse continued to dominate the public forum. Indeed, these scandals proved to be a major turning point for the participants in Hilliard's study of family and motherhood undertaken in the 1970s, and again in 2000. Hilliard concluded her study by noting that among the respondents there had been 'changes in thinking and practice' in the intervening twenty-five years. She remarked that by the time of the second interview: 'a new degree of reflexivity and awareness appears to have developed; in particular an awareness of having been dominated by forces outside themselves which had far-reaching effects on some of the most intimate aspects of their lives, including fertility, sexual relations and religious practice' (Hilliard 2004: 154). In other words, revelations of sexual abuse, impropriety and immorality had further fractured the relationship between women and the institutional Church. These accounts, as well as the experience of incidents of humiliation, embarrassment and censure in the confession box in the context of their sexuality, Hilliard wrote, 'significantly coloured and in cases changed respondents' relationships with the Church' (2004: 149).

In 2010, Benedict XVI (2005–13) updated *Normae de gravioribus delictis*, a document originally composed by Pope John Paul II in 2001 that contains a series of regulations or 'norms' and lists the most serious 'crimes' identified by the Church. In the introduction to the modifications, Cardinal William Levada listed the new additions, which include the following: 'The attempted ordination of a woman has also been introduced as a delict in the new text, as established by the decree of the Congregation for the Doctrine of the Faith on 19 December 2007.' A delict is a crime or violation of canon law. As Fiona Govan explains in *The Telegraph*, 'Women attempting to be priests, and those who try to ordain them, already faced automatic excommunication but the new decree enshrines the action as "a crime against sacraments"' (*The Telegraph*, 15 July 2010). The same body charged with investigating child-abuse cases was now in charge of investigating the 'crime against sacraments' that included any actions in terms of women and the priesthood. The Church, therefore, was focused on the shoring up of tradition rather than on introspection or a questioning of its practices. Given the zealousness with which the suppression of debate about women and the priesthood, among other topics, was dealt with by the Church, in contrast to the lacklustre approach to child-abuse investigations, Catholic women could not fail to see the extent of their exclusion. Additionally, on top of the penury visited upon 'erring' women and children and the often-harsh face of the Church with regard to people's intimate lives in the past, continuing to attend church services constitutes a moral dilemma for many women who feel a loyalty to their faith but not to the institutional Church.[9]

Hilliard noted the following transition in loyalty to Church teaching in the years that separated the questioning of her participants: 'A clear shift took place in the basis of morality; this was a movement away from a pre-existing moral order propounded by the Church, towards a more individualistic morality based on a greater confidence in the legitimacy of one's own experience' (2004: 159). In the findings of a 2012 *Amárach* survey, commissioned by the Association of Catholic Priests in Ireland, the growing distance between Church teaching and societal practice is also recorded: '3 in 4 find the Church's teaching on sexuality irrelevant to them and/or their family. [...] The younger age cohorts are the least likely to find the teachings pertinent to them' (*Amárach* 2012: 34). Additionally, at a recent presentation, Mary T. Malone recounted that young women see the Church as at best irrelevant and at worst evil. She also related that repeated studies have shown that in the main, religious faith and creeds are passed on by mothers and grandmothers (Malone 2015). While an older female cohort remains loyal to the Catholic faith, and I would argue that this is often in spite of the institutional Church, their daughters are not taking up the baton of propagating the faith. There is little doubt that unless the Vatican engages with female Catholics, both religious and lay, the propagation of the faith cannot be assured.

Conclusion

In this chapter, I have attempted to trace the trajectory of the decline of the relationship between the Catholic Church and the women of Ireland. The 1980s were tumultuous in this regard as the changing status of women both fuelled and served as a site for cultural change in Irish society. Moreover, the tug of war between the Church and women centred on the issue of bodily autonomy, with *Humane vitae* serving as the watershed document that provoked debate about birth control around the world. The response in Ireland to the encyclical was more muted, but it marked the beginning of the separation between Church teaching and private practice. Moreover, the public discussions in the 1980s about Ann Lovett and Joanne Hayes, and the many other women who told similar stories of being pregnant outside of marriage, moved the debate from the realm of Catholic ideology to lived reality. For many women and their children, the 'dignity of the person' proved an empty principle.

In the 1990s, the trust bestowed on the Church and its personnel as moral guardians was seriously fractured when it was found to have gravely erred in the area in which it had been most vocal. In addition, rather than show mercy to those whom the Church deemed to be sinners in the sexual realm, it had punished women and their children to an extraordinary degree. In addition, the reputation of church personnel who continue to work for the good of others has been tainted by association. Rather than proactive engagement, explanation or research on these matters, the Church has been concerned with issues such as upgrading the 'sin' of ordaining women, amending canon law, silencing those who try to discuss aspects of Church teaching on gender and sexuality, as well as demanding that all Catholics assent to such dictates without question. The reiteration by Pope Francis that the topic of women in ministry is not up for discussion has reinforced the institutional rejection of the voices, bodies, experiences and contributions of women.[10]

The former status accorded to the Catholic Church has been eroded as a result of the Church's own resistance to confronting and acknowledging its flaws. While many welcome the decline of Catholic Church hegemony and its absolutist ideology, which was supported and upheld by the Irish State, it can also be argued that in its wake there is an absence in the cultural fabric that has yet to be filled. While the 'unbinding' between church and society has taken place in the public forum, the private forum is to a large extent undocumented and unknown. As the Catholic Church has not undertaken, despite everything that has happened in the past thirty-five years, any real examination of itself, its ethos, its structures, and its theology of sexuality in particular, the trajectory of decline is set to continue. Moreover, the failure of the Vatican to recognise that engagement with women is central to the continuation of the faith suggests that the legacy of Irish Catholicism will not be bequeathed to the next generation. It cannot, therefore, be assumed that the 'faith of Catholic Ireland' will be 'forged, sustained, or upheld' into the future by 'the women of Ireland'.

Notes

1 The long-standing belief, derived from Ancient Greek medical conviction, and as understood by two of the most influential church fathers, Augustine and Aquinas, that the uterus was merely a vessel for the man's seed and did not play an active part in the reproduction process, underlies the reasoning behind the disregard for women's physical and mental health in their capacity as bearers of children (Uta Ranke-Heinemann's *Eunuchs For Heaven: The Catholic Church and Sexuality* (1990): 222–3).

2 See, for instance, Nell McCafferty's *A Woman to Blame: The Kerry Babies Case* (1985b), Gene Kerrigan 'The Kerry Babies Case' (1985a), 'The Kerry Babies Case: An Analysis of Mr Justice Lynch's Report' (1985b) and 'We Led the Fight for Family Values' (2015).

3 Nuala Fennell was co-founder of AIM (1972), a family-law reform lobby and of ADAPT (1973), a support group for deserted wives. She also founded Women's Aid (1975), a refuge for battered wives, and was a member of the Council for the Status of Women.

4 For an account of the history of the struggle 'against the suppression of fertility control' in Ireland, see Pauline Conroy's 'Maternity Confined in the Struggle for Fertility Control' (2004).

5 One female guard was involved in the original investigation.

6 The Bishop of Cork, Dr Michael Murphy, and his fellow bishops heartily disapproved, and priests were discouraged from commenting on or engaging with the events, although the extra stimulus for prayer was welcomed. The hallmark of an apparition is a direct personal experience of the divine. Such experiences occur outside of the institutional Church framework and are, therefore, not under the management of church personnel. However, as the role of the Church is as facilitator or conduit for a relationship with the divine, such occurrences can undermine its authority. As a result, the Church eventually appropriates enduring 'holy' sites, such as Lourdes and Knock. See Lawrence J. Taylor's *Occasions of Faith: An Anthropology of Irish Catholics* (1995).

7 Other sightings of unusual occurrences were recorded at Ballydesmond and Courtmacsherry in Co. Cork; Mount Melleray in Co. Waterford; Camolin, Glenbrien, and just outside Wexford town, on the Rosslare road, in Co. Wexford; and in Co. Sligo, where four young girls saw an image of Our Lady and what looked like St Bernadette in the sky over a remote field.

8 The commission's report was never made public. Moreover, it is not listed on the Vatican website. It is known about only because it was leaked to the press. See Angela Hanley's *Whose la Carte Menu? Exploring Catholic Themes in Context* (2014).

9 This is a view I heard expressed by female audience members at a number of presentations on the topic of reform in the Catholic Church in 2014 and 2015.

10 At the impromptu press conference held aboard the papal plane in July 2013, Patsy McGarry reports: 'Pope Francis said, 'on the ordination of women, the Church has spoken and said no. Pope John Paul II, in a definitive formulation, said that door is closed' (2013).

Works cited

Amárach (2012) 'Contemporary Catholic Perspectives', Draft 2, available at www.amarach. com/assets/files/ConsumerForesightArchive/ACP%20Survey%20Findings%20 April%202012.pdf (accessed 1 November 2014).

Beale, Jenny (1986) *Women in Ireland: Voices of Change*, Dublin: Gill & Macmillan.

Conroy, Pauline (2004) 'Maternity Confined in the Struggle for Fertility Control', in Patricia Kennedy (ed.), *Motherhood in Ireland: Creation and Context*, Cork: Mercier, pp. 127–38.

Donnelly, James S. (2002) 'The Troubled Contemporary Irish Catholic Church', in Brendan Bradshaw and Daire Keogh (eds.), *Christianity in Ireland: Revisiting the Story*, Dublin: Columba, pp. 271–86.

Fahey, Tony (1992) 'Catholicism and Industrial Society in Ireland', in J. H. Goldthorpe and C. T. Whelan (eds.), *The Development of Industrial Society in Ireland*, Oxford: Oxford University Press, pp. 241–63.

Fennell, Desmond (1962) 'Will the Irish Stay Christian?', *Doctrine & Life*, 12:5, 246–65.

Govan, Fiona (2010) 'Vatican Says Women Priests a "Crime against Faith"', *The Telegraph*, 15 July, available at www.telegraph.co.uk/news/worldnews/europe/vaticancityand holysee/7892666/Vatican-says-women-priests-a-crime-against-faith.html (accessed 15 April 2015).

Hanley, Angela (2014) *Whose à la Carte Menu? Exploring Catholic Themes in Context*, Dublin: Columba, pp. 154–6.

Harding, Michael (2013) *Staring at Lakes*, Dublin: Hachette Books.

Hilliard, Betty (2004) 'Motherhood, Sexuality and the Catholic Church', in Patricia Kennedy (ed.), *Motherhood in Ireland: Creation and Context*, Cork: Mercier, pp. 139–59.

Howes, Marjorie (2002) 'Introduction: Public Discourse, Private Reflection, 1916–70', in Angela Bourke, Máirín Ní Dhonnchadha, Margaret MacCurtain, Siobhán Kilfeather, Maria Luddy, Mary O'Dowd, Gerardine Meaney and Clair Wills (eds.), *Field Day Anthology of Irish Writing*, vol. IV: *Irish Women's Writing and Traditions*, Cork: Cork University Press, pp. 923–30.

Hug, Chrystel (1999) *The Politics of Sexual Morality in Ireland*, London: Palgrave.

Inglis, Tom (1998) *Moral Monopoly: The Rise and Fall of the Catholic Church in Modern Ireland*, 2nd edn, Dublin: Gill & Macmillan.

—— (2003) *Truth, Power and Lies: Irish Society and the Case of the Kerry Babies*, Dublin: University College Dublin Press.

John Paul II (1979) *The Pope in Ireland: Addresses and Homilies*, Dublin: Veritas.

—— (1994) *Ordinatio sacerdotalis*, 22 May, available at http://w2.vatican.va/content/ john-paul-ii/en/apost_letters/1994   /documents/hf_jp-ii_apl_22051994_ordinatio- sacerdotalis.html (accessed 28 April 2015).

—— (1998) *Ad tuendam fidem*, 18 May, available at http://w2.vatican.va/content/ john-paul-ii/en/motu_proprio/documents/hf_jp-ii_motu-proprio_30061998_ad- tuendam-fidem.html (accessed 28 April 2015).

Kenny, Mary (2000) *Goodbye to Catholic Ireland*, rev. edn, Dublin: New Island.

Kerrigan, Gene (1985a) 'The Kerry Babies Case', *Magill*, 30 May, pp. 16–51.

—— (1985b) 'The Kerry Babies Case: An Analysis of Mr Justice Lynch's Report', *Magill*, 1 November, pp. 4–34.

—— (2015) 'We Led the Fight for Family Values', *Sunday Independent*, 8 March, p. 36.

Levada, William (2010) 'A Brief Introduction to the Modifications Made in the *Normae de gravioribus delictis*', available at www.vatican.va/resources/resourc es_rel-modifiche_ en.html (accessed 29 April 2015).

MacCurtain, Margaret (2008) 'Introduction to "Moving Statues and Irishwomen"', in *Ariadne's Thread: Writing Women into Irish History*, Galway: Arlen House, pp. 161–74.

Maher, Eamon and Eugene O'Brien (eds.) (2014) *From Prosperity to Austerity: A Socio- cultural Critique of the Celtic Tiger and Its Aftermath*, Manchester: Manchester University Press.

Malone, Mary T. (2000) *Women and Christianity: The First Thousand Years*, Dublin: Columba.

—— (2015) 'Women in the Church: Is This the Elephant in the Room?' Presentation delivered at All Hallows College, Dublin, 11 March.

McCafferty, Nell (1985a) 'Virgin on the Rocks', in Colm Tóibín (ed.) *Seeing Is Believing: Moving Statues in Ireland*, Mountrath: Pilgrim Press, pp. 53–8.

—— (1985b) *A Woman to Blame: The Kerry Babies Case*, Dublin: Attic Press.

McCann, Eamon (1985) 'A Most Impressive Sight to Behold', in Colm Tóibín (ed.), *Seeing Is Believing: Moving Statues in Ireland*, Mountrath: Pilgrim Press, pp. 33–7.

McGahern, John (2002) 'The Whole World in a Community', *The Guardian* [online], 6 January, available at www.theguardian.com/books/2002/jan/06/fiction.features (accessed 29 April 2015).

McGarry, Patsy (2013) 'Australian Priest First to Be Excommunicated by Pope Francis', *Irish Times*, 26 September, available at http://www.irishtimes.com/news/social-affairs/religion-and-beliefs/australian-priest-first-to-be-excommunicated-by-pope-francis-1.1541165 (accessed 26 September 2016).

Moore, Christy (2000) *One Voice: My Life in Song*, London: Hodder & Stoughton.

O'Brien, Kate (1951) *Pray for the Wanderer*, London: Penguin Books.

Paul VI (1968) *Humanae vitae*, 25 July, available at http://w2.vatican.va/content/paul-vi/en/encyclicals/documents/hf_p-vi_enc_2507196 8_humanae-vitae.html (accessed 29 April 2015).

Ranke-Heinemann, Uta (1990) *Eunuchs for Heaven: The Catholic Church and Sexuality*, trans. John Brownjohn, London: André Deutsch, pp. 222–3.

Taylor, Lawrence J. (1995) *Occasions of Faith: An Anthropology of Irish Catholics*, Dublin: Lilliput.

Vatican II (1965) '*Lumen gentium*', *Acta Apostolicae Sedis*, 57, 5–75.

13

The Catholic twilight

Joe Cleary

All we have gained then by our unbelief
Is a life of doubt diversified by faith,
For one of faith diversified by doubt:
We called the chess-board white – we call it black.
Robert Browning, 'Bishop Blougram's
Apology' (1885)

Introduction

It has been obvious for decades that Catholicism in Ireland is undergoing a crisis of historic proportions. That crisis is commonly defined in terms of a litany of clerical and religious-run institution abuse scandals, an ageing clergy, a loss of institutional authority and increasing levels of indifference to religion generally. Catholic influence in the areas of education, health, political policy and legal practice has been rolled back. The changes also extend into the realms of the sacred, and the liturgical: Catholic churches are frequently packed to or beyond capacity at Christmas or for Easter Week services, communions and confirmations remain important rites of passage for most families, and Irish Catholic funeral rituals retain their importance. But Sunday masses, holy days and confessional obligations no longer regulate ordinary time for most of the population as they once did. Activities outside of the church such as pilgrimages and cemetery Sundays are still popular, but other aspects of quotidian devotion have retracted. Fewer houses display religious icons or statuary; home-based devotions are rare; religious medals and rosary beads are becoming outmoded. All in all, this long crisis has brought about transformations not only in religious practice but also in the entire lifeworld of modern Ireland.

Though the changes under way are profound, the difficulty is to know how best to interpret them. Many scholarly works invoke a sense of total collapse or even terminal crisis – like bell peals, the funereal book titles toll a passing: *Irish Catholicism since 1950: The Undoing of a Culture* (Fuller 2002); *Is Irish Catholicism Dying? Liberating an Imprisoned Church* (Kirby 1984); *The End of Irish Catholicism?* (Twomey 2003); *Change or Decay: Irish Catholicism in Crisis* (Hoban 2000). Still, while such titles draw legitimate attention to a contemporary sense of an ending, a focus on 'the death of Irish Catholicism' may obscure more than it reveals. Do changes of the kind described above actually represent the death of Catholicism in Ireland or rather the unravelling of the Devotional Revolution Catholicism constructed after the Great Famine (1845–50)? And if that Devotional Revolution Catholicism is now in free fall, might some different version of Catholicism emerge in its place? After all, the Catholicisms of the pre-modern era, the Counter-Reformation, the Penal Law and pre-Famine era, and of the Devotional Revolution period were of quite different character, and some post-Devotional Revolution Catholicism now emerging might also differ significantly to these earlier manifestations. Or are the kinds of changes now under way involved best captured by the term 'secularisation', and, if so, does this mean that Ireland is now belatedly undergoing processes largely in step with those that have taken place earlier in the UK and Western Europe? Or is it more accurate to say that Ireland is not so much being 'secularised' as undergoing a longer-term transition from Christianity towards some new, more indeterminate but socially consequent 'spirituality'? Questions of this sort can be suppressed by a consistent stress in the media and much of the academic literature on the absolute decline and fall of Irish Catholicism. On the one side, some secular commentators seem almost vengefully eager to announce the death of Irish Catholicism; on the other side, low-bar optimists search for signs of continuing religious vitality or imminent recovery with a desperation that recalls Theodor Adorno's acerbic riposte: 'they have gradually come to intone their *Te Deum* whenever God is denied because at least his name in mentioned' (Adorno 1990: 372).

This chapter will examine, in necessarily exploratory mode, three hypotheses. First, it will consider the notion that the collapse of Devotional Revolution Catholicism is leading not to the demise of Catholicism in Ireland as such but rather bringing Irish conditions into closer line with those of Catholicism globally. This way of seeing matters implies that Ireland in the century between the Famine and the 1950s was more of an aberration in Catholic terms transnationally than it is now; in other words, the challenges which the Catholic Church currently faces in Ireland are closer to those it confronts in other continents than was the case some generations ago. If this is correct, Irish Catholicism is not so much in total free fall as 'regressing' from an exceptional intensity to something like a more general Catholic mean. Second, the essay will discuss the secularisation thesis and consider what this analytical model highlights or occludes. Though many who accept the secularisation thesis view with equanimity what Catholic catastrophists view with dread, the two approaches have more than may appear in common. Finally, contemporary changes will be analysed not in terms of a transition from religion to secularism but conversion to a new 'spirituality' on the rise globally.

It is always difficult to grasp the direction of seismic historical changes of the kind at issue here; therefore, the object of this essay is simply to open lines of analysis that may stretch the scope of contemporary debate a little. Its intention is not to provide answers but to display some of the analytical complexities of the situation brought about by the decline of Catholicism in contemporary Ireland. Ours may be an era of 'dead certainties', but when assurances wane, intelligent questions ought at least to take their place.

The Devotional Revolution and its legacies

The term the 'Devotional Revolution', coined by church historian Emmet Larkin, refers to the accelerated development of the Catholic Church in Ireland in the wake of the Famine. Before the Great Famine, Larkin maintained, that church which had been institutionally weakened by the Penal Laws and had confronted a demographic surge in the early nineteenth century, lacked the human and material resources to address the spiritual needs of the often only nominally Catholic population. Low ratios of clergy to laity in this pre-Famine period were aggravated by lapses of clerical discipline in some dioceses, and, in many regions, levels of lay compliance with canonical obligations such as mass attendance or receiving the sacraments were poor. (David Miller later corroborated this picture by demonstrating that nearly universal weekly mass attendance was largely confined before the Famine to the relatively affluent south-eastern countryside and a few towns [Miller 1975]). However, other such historians, notably Kevin Whelan, have suggested that while the Catholic Church may have been institutionally weakened during the Penal Laws, religious conviction remained strong, but the character and practice of this pre-Devotional Revolution 'vernacular Catholicism' was quite different to the more pietistic version instituted after the Famine (cited in Cleary and Connolly 2005: 138–9). Led by Paul Cullen, archbishop of Armagh (1850–52) and of Dublin (1852–78), the Devotional Revolution describes a concerted phase of church-building and parish reorganisation that strengthened the Catholic Church's institutional infrastructure across most of the island. In the same era, the Church also extended its influence into the areas of education and health as many new Catholic religious organisations such as the Presentation Sisters (founded in Cork in 1775) or Christian Brothers (founded in Waterford in 1802), fired by a sense of zeal, expanded clerical-run educational and other services, especially after Catholic emancipation in 1829.

Furthermore, the Devotional Revolution imposed a greater degree of doctrinal and devotional regulation as Cullen, an ultramontanist, used his influence in Rome to appoint reform-minded bishops, promote parish missions and introduce a variety of new devotional practices from Europe. Concomitantly, pre-Famine 'vernacular Catholic' practices were replaced by more church-centred modes of worship and unorthodox 'traditional' folk-practices, including raucous wakes and keenings, belief in the *sidhe*, and the celebration of pagan fertility rites or feast days, were vigorously suppressed. The upshot, Larkin argued, was that by the end of the nineteenth century a much higher percentage of the Catholic population in Ireland complied with the canonical requirements for religious practice than in any other part of Europe (with the possible exception of Poland) and continued to do so until the late twentieth century. Nevertheless, despite the widespread success of the Devotional Revolution, the idea of a single, uniform Catholicism is best avoided. Some forms of pre-Famine Catholicism and of folk religion remained popular, their strength and endurance varying regionally and in class terms, even after the Devotional Revolution had been consolidated.

By the time the Irish Free State was established in 1921, Catholicism's close association with nationalism and its strong institutional infrastructure were such that it was able to command support across a wide variety of social fields and classes. In Northern Ireland, Catholicism became a major support system for a beleaguered Catholic nationalist minority abandoned to a 'Protestant state for a Protestant people'. Bolstered in the south by the self-assertiveness of an emerging Catholic middle class assuming state power but retaining in Northern Ireland something of its historical role as the religio-cultural patron of an oppressed community, the Catholic Church was able to command high levels of allegiance from nearly all social classes in Ireland itself and also to service the Irish diaspora in the UK, Australia and the USA, and even to promote an array of missionary activities in Africa, Asia and South America. Hence, 'Irish Catholicism' in the period from the Famine to roughly Vatican II may be said to refer not just to Catholicism on the island of Ireland but to the elaboration of a Catholicism intertwined with Irishness that was expanding across the anglophone world and into several parts of the British Empire and beyond. For many of those who identified with this version of Catholicism, Ireland represented the epicentre of a spiritual empire it nurtured with vocations and missionary and administrative zeal.

Though the idea of the Devotional Revolution is widely accepted, its larger historical implications have arguably been under-explored. To begin with, if that revolution led to an unusually tight affiliation (though sometimes fractious) between Catholicism and nationalism in the nineteenth century and to an even tighter one between Catholicism and the new Irish State in the twentieth, then this surely suggests that what is anomalous about the Irish situation is its timing rather than its intensity. After all, a mutually validating link between church and an emerging nation-state had been common all across early modern Europe: Catholicism was crucial to the consolidation of the absolutist states in Spain, France and Austria, just as Protestantism was to the English or Swedish absolutist states or to the Dutch Republic. What was unusual about Ireland in European terms, then, was that the bonding between the dominant religion, nation and state was, because of several centuries of English colonial rule, 'delayed' until well into the twentieth century. Moreover, because the Devotional Revolution took place in the nineteenth century, and preceded the early twentieth-century political revolution that led to the formation of the state in 1921, the Catholic Church had a considerable 'headstart' on the Free State; it already had an island-wide institutional network and could command a level of popular support from the people that the post-Partition, post-Civil War state had still to earn. Furthermore, one of the things that made that church–state bond seem even more anomalous by European standards was that it was tightened, after Independence in 1921, in an epoch when such bonds were slowly, though very unevenly, being loosened in many other parts of Europe.

Even so, the degree to which Ireland was out of step with other societies or its next-door neighbour ought not to be exaggerated. The 31st International Eucharistic Congress, held in Dublin in 1932, is widely taken to represent an acme of Catholic religious fervour and Irish nationalist triumphalism: some quarter of the total population of the Free State attended the final papal mass in the Phoenix Park in June of that year, and the celebration of the struggle to preserve the Catholic faith over millennia and to free the Irish nation after centuries of British rule was intricately linked in the symbolism of the occasion. However, in her study of religion in Britain after 1945, Grace Davie describes the coronation of Queen Elizabeth II in June 1953, nearly a quarter of a century after the Dublin Eucharistic Congress, in terms of an even more spectacular identification of religion, state and nation. Davie notes that the occasion 'undoubtedly brought together the Church of England, the monarchy and the nation in an act of sacralisation, witnessed for the first time by a television audience numbered in millions' (Davie 1994: 31). For Davie, the coronation was less an expression of a pre-existing English consensus than a deliberately crafted effort to construct a consensus, and the same might surely be said of the Dublin Eucharistic Congress of 1932, coming as it did in the immediate wake of intensely divisive Treaty debates, Partition and the Civil War. While some have described the post-Independence Irish State as a 'theocracy', assuming it an aberration to the more secular Western European norms of the twentieth century, it may be the case that what was 'exceptional' about the bond between religion, nation and state in Ireland was actually its relative brevity.

An institutionally maintained link between dominant religion, nation and the state endured for several centuries in England, Spain, Sweden and Holland (to cite just a few examples). But in the Republic of Ireland's case, that linkage was for a variety of reasons – these ranging from the challenges of the women's movement to the need, against the backdrop of the Troubles, to create a stronger case for a non-denominational state more hospitable to Protestants and unionists, to European Economic Community membership – already being severely contested by the 1980s, just seven decades after the foundation of the State. Because it had been consolidated so late and was, as a result, historically out of step with developments elsewhere in Europe, particularly after the 1960s, the drive to loosen or dissolve the state–nation–religion nexus in southern Ireland came much sooner after the creation of the state than it had done in many other European societies. The bonds between religion and state tightly knotted and then gradually loosened over centuries in states such as the UK, Holland, Austria or Spain were tightened and relaxed in Ireland in less than one century.

What might this mean for any understanding of the situation of Irish Catholicism today? For one thing, it means that contemporary Ireland is not leaving behind, as Catholic mythologists sometimes imply, 'an age of faith' that abided over centuries, for a new atheism, but, rather, that the country is, after a relatively brief period of unusually high levels of religious practice and orthodoxy, and particularly close levels of church–state affiliation, 'reverting' to more unexceptional conditions of practice and power. As the once remarkably robust institutional infrastructure of the Devotional Revolution – with its well-staffed and well-run parishes, young and highly motivated religious and lay organisations and evangelical ambitions at home and overseas – begins to downsize, and as the Catholic Church's influence over the educational system slowly contracts, the high levels of doctrinal instruction and practice that could once be maintained inevitably diminish. This in turn leads to a looser, less doctrinally informed and less well-regulated versions of Catholic practice, and to a more amorphous sense of Catholic identity and community. There is nothing aberrant about this either in Euro-American or even global terms. Nearly everywhere in the 'First World' the Catholic Church has to contend with fewer vocations, bigger staffing and organisational challenges and communities whose sense of Catholic doctrine or commitment to Catholic practice is generally lax. And, in the 'Third World', huge population increases, mass poverty and the overlay of Catholicism on non-Catholic religious cultures create heterogeneous situations that broadly recall those that obtained in pre-Famine Ireland; such situations create their own forms of doctrinal irregularity and uneven practice. Conceived in this light, it might be more useful to think of religious change in contemporary Ireland not so much in terms of 'the death of Irish Catholicism' as in its refashioning. A once exceptionally dynamic and charismatic Irish Catholicism, combining evangelical charisma with extraordinary institutional–bureaucratic ability, has 'cooled' to become a little more like many other Catholicisms elsewhere.

A 'melancholy, long withdrawing roar'? Secularism, religion and Irish modernity

The model of religious change sketched above disputes some of the more apocalyptic versions of Catholic collapse. It also interrogates the diagnostic usefulness of the parallel between the fates of the Irish language and that of Catholicism uncritically alluded to in much of the contemporary literature on the subject. That parallel, itself tending towards a catastrophic conception of matters, is usually attributed to Fr Peter Connolly, who apparently predicted that 'When Irish

Catholicism goes, it will go so fast that no-one will know what is happening' (cited in Kiberd 2005: 283). One year after Pope John Paul II's visit to Ireland in 1979, Connolly speculated that Catholicism would one day be discarded by the Irish people with the same unsentimental pragmatism and speed that they had in an earlier era abandoned the Irish language to accommodate anglophone modernity. Connolly's analogy, recycled in recent times by Declan Kiberd, Brendan Hoban and others, captures the swiftness of language change in the late nineteenth century and religious change in the late twentieth. Nevertheless, the analogy suffers obvious limitations. The Irish language was more or less peculiar to Ireland and therefore remarkably vulnerable in a vastly wider and continuously expanding anglophone world (and in any event to speak of its abandonment without reference to the convulsion of the Famine and the institutional power of the national school system is to overstate some supposedly innate sense of Irish pragmatism); Catholicism, in contrast to the Irish language, is a world religion, and religions generally have displayed remarkable endurance across dramatically different geo-historical circumstances.

On the other hand, the Irish State was able to provide a lifeline through the education system (however belatedly, half-heartedly or ineptly this support came) to sustain the Irish language or stave off its terminal decline at least; though the Catholic Church has probably received even more indirect state support than the Irish language has done, the ongoing separation of church and state in the present moment means that Catholicism will, unlike the Irish language, almost certainly have to depend less on the State in the future. One cannot imagine the State sponsoring the equivalent of Raidió na Gaeltachta or TG4 to shore up a declining Catholicism, for example. The decline of Irish, and more recently of Catholicism, has inevitably brought Ireland culturally closer to the rest of the Anglo-American world, itself historically Protestant, and this is where Connolly's parallel is perhaps most suggestive. But even if it is now culturally closest to Anglo-America than anywhere else, Ireland has also been more deeply politically integrated into the European Union in recent decades, and thus now straddles these two wider social universes. Religious change in those European and Anglo-American contexts is variable and complex, and it is consequently difficult to predict how changes in these wider zones will impact on Ireland in the future.

Nevertheless, while the hypothesis that Catholicism in Ireland is not so much dying as undergoing a sea change to some still-emerging, laxer post-Devotional Revolution version, offers one way to think about ongoing developments, this model possibly exchanges a too-catastrophic with a too-moderate conception of religious change. Whereas the first model considered implies that one variant of Catholicism will eventually be replaced by another, the secularisation model implies that the decline of religious practice in the advanced capitalist world is inexorable. In that latter model, religious decline follows a steady downward line, even if subject to minor periodic 'religious revivals', as the slow, unswerving processes of industrialisation (or post-industrialisation) and urbanisation (which ultimately brings even the most rural regions into its ambit), and of the division of labour and the diminution of the public sphere, take their toll. Secularisation, in this understanding, means that religion suffers an irreversible loss of social significance and becomes increasingly a largely privatised minority practice with few social consequences. No longer able to mould the collective intellectual apprehension of society or guide its effective organisation, religious institutions may survive in secular societies but do so in a world dominated by capitalist and technocratic rationality where large metaphysical questions are accorded little validity. For those who view religion sympathetically, secularisation represents the dissolution of moral community and coherence, a disenchantment of the sacred and a slippage of any higher sense of existential purpose. For those who view secularisation sympathetically, it is regarded as a gain for personal freedom and conscience and an advance of rational over magical or delusional thinking.

These irreconcilable religious and secular conceptions of the world have agitated Irish society for nearly half a century or more at this stage. A whole series of national referendums on matters such as divorce, abortion and gay marriage have never simply been about the subjects immediately before the electorate; in a deeper sense, they have also been contests between religious and secular world views. In this respect, devout Catholics have mostly opposed what secularists construe as rational and overdue positive change; for the opponents of such change, the struggles in question are construed as attempts to stave off the largely amoral instrumental logic and selfish individualism of a secular society. But while constitutional and legislative struggles over such matters have sharply divided Irish society in voting terms, most individuals are probably, to greater or lesser degrees, internally divided and navigating their lives with value systems partly religious, partly secular, neither terribly conceptually coherent. Thus, the lines taken from Robert Browning cited at the head of this essay may quite accurately describe a general structure of feeling in Ireland since the late 1960s: many in Ireland have exchanged a life of faith diversified by doubt for one of doubt diversified by faith. On the whole, though, the secular forces have been slowly but surely becoming ascendant, and after initially adopting an intransigently hostile stance to change, the political, business, educational and media intelligentsias now increasingly endorse that secular advance as 'progressive'. The religious opposition, once powerful and still organisationally able to mobilise strong showings on single-issue campaigns, appears increasingly demoralised, resigned to rearguard actions to stem the tide of faith's 'melancholy, long, withdrawing roar' but utterly unable to mount any campaign for national reconversion to counter the secular de-conversion.

While events on the ground certainly seem to support the secularisation model of change, some sociologists have pointed out that model's conceptual limitations. Though approaching things from opposite ends of the faith–rationality value divide, the catastrophist model and the secularisation model share the assumption that modern history is undergoing a long, painful transition from 'an age of faith' to 'an age of reason'. In the European context, this assumes that medieval Europe was dominated by a shared or largely homogenous religious world view and that the emergence of capitalist modernity inaugurated a long process of attrition whereby, from an earlier position of uncontested dominance, the Christian religion initially underwent a violent scission into Catholic and Protestant denominations and all of these then gradually began, especially after the Enlightenment, to wither. For secularisation-model attritionists, the social functions once exercised by the Church are taken over by modern state institutions and re-functionalised on the basis of instrumental reason and humanistic goals. However, those who dispute this secular attritionist model argue that it presupposes, just as do the most nostalgic Christians, what Bryan Turner calls 'a backward-looking utopian view of medieval Christianity in which people were "really" religious' (1983: 144). This 'age of faith' is then taken as the baseline from which later modern societies represent, depending on one's view of religion, a decline or an advance.

But some sociologists of religion have argued that Christianity in medieval Europe may have been much weaker than commonly assumed. In pre-modern Europe, David Martin suggests, the mass of the rural population lived outside of the religious influence of the Church and was largely engaged in survival struggles (2014). To the extent that there was an 'age of faith' at all, religious instruction and practice was largely the preserve of a small Latinate elite (whose contribution to modern European culture was nostalgically charted by Ernst Robert Curtius in his *European Literature and the Latin Middle Ages* [Curtius 2013]), but the lower social orders had comparatively little or only patchy knowledge of religious doctrine. Moreover, Martin contends, if the strength of religion in the medieval period has been overestimated by both nostalgic Christians and progressive secularists, the secularisation of modern consciousness has been equally so. In fact, despite the putative rise of technocratic reason, all sorts of superstitions and irrationality persist in the modern world, and religion can still display remarkable strength in situations where subaltern groups can convert religious difference into collective social or political effort. The 'rise' of religious fundamentalism in some of the more underprivileged sectors of US society or of political Islam in the Middle East, Asia and in diasporic ghettoes in Europe evidences as much. Those who dispute attritionist secularist theories as excessively linear, totalising and teleological contend that modern history does not trace one long receding tide of faith but has undergone more jagged and dialectical processes of religious ebbs and revivals.

Whatever view one ultimately takes, the debate opens up interesting considerations for the contemporary Irish situation. If one accepts the view, associated with David Martin and others, that religious cultivation and commitment has generally been strongest among the more elite classes and that the lowest social classes tend to be less systemically religious or altogether indifferent, then it might be argued that the most significant religious change in modern Ireland has occurred among the middle or professional classes rather than evenly across society in general. After all, the improving middle classes had, historians agree, provided the backbone of the Devotional Revolution, and it was to such classes that the country's elite Catholic secondary schools, modelled on Victorian English Protestant counterparts, had catered. The 'social professions' of medicine, law, teaching, nursing and local government were once highly regulated by both the Catholic and Protestant churches, and, in recent decades, these professions have regularly become sites for clashes between religious and secular value systems. Today, however, the same professions are often to the fore in state-led secularisation drives. In other words, the Irish middle classes, once the most doctrinally informed, socially influential and observant bearers of Catholicism, have, in the professional-collective sense at least, now exchanged or relaxed their faith and adopted a more secular–capitalist value-system.

This obviously does not mean that the Irish lower classes are currently more religious than the dominant classes. Even if the Irish lower classes were unusually well integrated into the Catholic Church thanks its exceptional dynamism during the Devotional Revolution, they were probably still more unevenly under its control than were their middle-class counterparts. Or, to put it another way, whereas the middle classes were better socialised into Devotional Revolution Catholicism, the lower orders were more likely to be dependent on the welfarist services of the Church or to experience the brunt of its coercive power. Less protected by social status, leaving school earlier, emigrating more frequently and in higher numbers proportionally, less able to enter the higher professions, including the clergy, the working classes generally experienced shorter and less rigorous religious training than the dominant classes. But where the most misfortunate – the indigent, orphans, unmarried mothers, illegitimate children, the disabled – came under Church authority, they were subjected to the full coercive force of its carceral institutions in ways that the better-off classes were largely spared. The combined results of more uneven religious education and greater social distance from a fundamentally middle-class church created a working class that was never strongly anti-Catholic in the manner of the more ideologically committed republican, anarchist, socialist or communist working classes in certain regions of twentieth-century Europe. But the Irish working class was also never (except perhaps in Northern Ireland) as politically Catholic in any organised sense as were its counterparts in those areas of Europe or the USA where Catholic and working-class social mobility were more affiliated.

If the Irish middle classes, especially in the higher professions, are now becoming increasingly secular, and if neo-liberalism is also (as is widely agreed) aggravating already significant class cleavages, will religion and class conflict become more closely imbricated in the twenty-first century? Certainly, something of this sort seems to have occurred in the USA where beleaguered sections of the lower orders in run-down rural regions or post-industrial cities have embraced modes of Evangelical Protestant fundamentalism. No major Irish political movement or political party that is at once economically neo-liberal and socially neo-conservative has emerged to date in the Irish Republic, so for the moment this kind of American-style fundamentalist Christian mobilisation seems unlikely outside of the Northern Irish 'Bible Belt'. On the other hand, economic egalitarianism and Catholic teaching are not inevitably at odds, and the Catholic working classes of Irish origin very strongly inclined towards Labour politics in twentieth-century England, Wales and Scotland just as some of the more working-class Catholic regions of Europe gravitated towards Christian or secular socialism.

The contemporary Irish left's commitment to secular liberalism and its (moderate) anti-clericalism means that any alliance between a more socially minded Catholicism, were it to gather force, and the radical left seems unlikely in early twenty-first-century Ireland. That allowed, Grace Davie has noted that even as its authority waned in Britain, the Anglican Church, once intimately affiliated with the Conservative Party, became embroiled in several political controversies during the Thatcher years and moved moderately leftwards as the British political elites moved rightwards by embracing a callous neo-liberalism. It is not unlikely that the Irish Catholic Church will, despite its antipathy to sexual and gender policies embraced by the left, also find itself impelled to move in liberal-left directions as the once socially conservative and overtly Catholic parties, Fianna Fáil and Fine Gael, become more openly neo-liberal and secular and espouse an aggressive neo-liberal capitalism. Declining authority and less cosy church–state relations are wholly compatible with increased Catholic critical activity in the public sphere.

If the secularisation model of change is taken, in its most extreme version, to mean that religion in advanced capitalist societies diminishes to virtual social nullity, then Ireland, north or south, cannot yet be said to be a secular society. However, if that model is taken, more modestly, to imply that religion generally is receding in importance and seems likely to continue as such, then the empirical evidence to confirm this is weighty. Nevertheless, this still does not say much about the likely social consequence of such change. Contrary to assumptions, a decline in popular religious belief does not lead inevitably or directly to positive gains for rational or humanist thinking: modern popular culture can support the most preposterous farragoes of superstition, conspiracy theory, brutality and vulgarity. By the same token, a decline of religion does not necessarily prepare the way for more rational or progressive forms of politics. If ours is, to recall a phrase used earlier, an age of 'dead certainties', then it is also the case that the decline of once-dominant religions and the decline of socialism have been largely concurrent in contemporary Europe, both waning rapidly, if regionally unevenly, since the 1960s. Indeed, as church congregations have diminished in Ireland, so too have other forms of social collectivity such as trade-union membership, political-party membership and so on. The decline of Catholicism, then, may well have created the clearing space and potential for new forms of collectivities to emerge: the women's movement and the gay and lesbian movements may be evidence of these new collectivities, but the largely fatalistic reaction of the contemporary generation of Irish people to the massive global and local crisis of neo-liberalism after 2008 would seem to attest, rather, to a rather alarming sense of social atomisation and apathy. If twentieth-century Catholicism offered a weak and broadly 'anti-modernisation' critique of capitalism and socialism a strong and 'ultra-modernisation' critique, the retreat of both since the 1960s means that capitalist rationality now goes less challenged by broad-based popular movements than ever, this even though the long-term social and environmental consequences of late capitalism are dire.

Catholicism and New Age spirituality

Secularisation theories propose that in modern societies religion generally declines and that it wanes also in its various manifestations: its charismatic, sacralising and ritual functions diminish; its institutional strength and clerical command decrease; intellectual authority subsides. However, critics of secularisation theory contend that this model's conception of religion is too wedded categorically to monotheistic concepts of religion. The idea that all religions require well-regulated membership of organised institutions such as churches, mosques or synagogues is, they argue, to overlook the fact that many religions – Hellenistic, Native American, Australian Aboriginal, African animist – never assumed such form to begin with. Whereas secularisation theory presumes a general trajectory from religious belief to non-belief, counter-theories argue that when once-dominant religions decline much of the population may become indifferent or atheistic but substantial sections also convert to alternative or new religions. Thus, in many parts of Latin America, a once-dominant Catholicism is now challenged by varieties of Protestant evangelicalism; Islam is now the second largest religion in Italy and France, just as in England, for long monopolistically Protestant, successive migrations inwards from various parts of the Empire have created substantial Catholic, Islamic and Hindi religious communities.

On a macro-level, sociologists such as Colin Campbell and Steve Bruce have explored phenomena that might be described as the Westernisation of Asian religious practice and the Easternisation of Euro-American practice. That is to say, in the age of high imperialism, Catholic and Protestant missionary movements headquartered in Europe and America launched major evangelisation drives on all other continents, but, after the decline of formal empire, 'the West' has also been busily importing elements of religions from the regions it had earlier evangelised. This importation has been eclectic. Former Christians have rarely converted in large numbers to other monotheisms (Islam or Judaism) or to Eastern religions such as Buddhism or Shinto; instead, they have syncretically adapted elements of Buddhism, Zen, Sufism, animism and so forth, in various forms of New Age spiritual practice. For some theorists, this new spiritualism represents a contemporary counter-trend that challenges the secularisation model of change.

Because the crisis of Irish Catholicism is quite recent, the full significance of New Age spiritualism in Ireland is difficult to evaluate and the wider phenomenon hard to categorise in any case. For many, religious and secular alike, the new spiritualism will appear an absurdity because it claims neither the mythic nor doctrinal coherence and integration of Christianity nor the empirical scientific commitments of secular rationalism. New Age spiritualisms, moreover, take very different forms to either Catholicism or Protestantism because they usually do not require affiliation to churches or even sects, they are not regionally organised in the manner of parishes or dioceses, and they usually have few if any doctrinal creeds or formalised ethical or disciplinary requirements. Instead, they are more commonly associated with festivals, retreats, therapies and contemplative or mindfulness exercises. Campbell and Bruce observe that whereas Christianity, which is a religion of difference, posits a categorical distinction between a perfect deity and a postlapsarian imperfect humanity, which can only realise its own goodness by subjecting itself to God's will and obeying his laws, New Age spirituality repudiates any such distinction. Instead, it stresses an a-priori cosmological oneness between the individual and creation and assumes that the human self is fundamentally good (or holy) and that where badness exists it does so as a result of negative life experiences or environmental circumstances. In other words, childhood or relationship traumas, the standard workaday stresses of modernity and physical or mental illnesses can all damage the fundamentally healthy core self, and the purpose of New Age spiritualism is to restore damaged individuals to a condition of spiritual well-being, thereby freeing up their optimal potential. Thus, Bruce argues, 'In much New Age spirituality, therapy is the manifest, not the latent, function. Good health, self-confidence, prosperity and warm supportive relationships are no longer the accidental by-products of worshipping God; they are the [end] goals sought through the spiritual activity' (Bruce 2002: 85). Hence the high importance attached to meditation, relaxation exercises, alternative 'holistic' healing, oneness with nature and self-seeking techniques in such spiritualism. For most commentators, New Age spirituality is intimately connected to the highly individualistic character of late modernity and wedded to ideas of self-realisation. Whereas Christianity and other monotheisms require from the devout considerable elements of strict self-discipline, and many Eastern religions (and some forms of Christian mysticism) advocate goals of self-abnegation or self-emptying, for New Age spiritualism, salvation means the realisation of the optimal self.

By its nature, it is hard to calculate how significant New Age spiritualism is or may become because its adherents cannot be statistically counted in the way of church attendees can, its practices are extremely eclectic and its epistemology is highly relativist and non-integrated. In seeming paradox, new spirituality has a strong primitivist and anti-modern thrust – syncretism and holism are preferred to the compartmentalising logic of Enlightenment rationality, and ancient or non-European religions are preferred to those associated with Western modernity – but yet it seems largely compatible with late capitalist subjectivism, consumerism and multiculturalism. Given the new spiritualism's capacity to mix primitivist anti-modern impulses with postmodern syncretism and relativism, Ireland may well offer a hospitable habitus for New Ageist growth. Because it is one of Europe's remoter peripheries and possesses only a weak legacy of industrial capitalism but a strong indigenous legacy of 'Celticism' and romanticism, the country's association with the non-modern offers much to appeal to New Age sensibilities. Furthermore, the very intensity of Devotional Revolution Catholicism, and the strong sense of ignominy attached to Catholicism's current decline, may well have provoked a real zealous backlash, something that may benefit New Age spiritualism, which is generally much more liberal than Catholicism in terms of sexual and gender politics and much more at ease with multiculturalism. And now that it is a neo-liberal hub of post-industrial software, pharmaceutical and digital enterprise, Ireland also has a late capitalist economy that generates the needs and neuroses that New Ageism strives to satisfy. The Irish Revival, a phenomenon commonly linked to a crisis of southern Protestantism, displayed, even in the heyday of the Devotional Revolution, many features that resemble contemporary New Ageism: a preference for primitive paganism or pre-modern 'Celtic Christianity' to post-Reformation Catholicism or Protestantism and a syncretic mixing of occultism, Oriental theosophy, mysticism and folk religion. Now, when Devotional Revolution Catholicism is now longer nearly the power it was in the Revival period, and when many Catholics are arguably experiencing a historic religious crisis roughly equivalent to that experienced by Protestants in the late nineteenth century, New Age spiritualism may well have found optimal conditions in which to flourish in contemporary post-Celtic Tiger Ireland.

Some commentators argue that the new spiritualism represents, in the words of Paul Heelas and Linda Woodhead, 'a tectonic shift in the sacred landscape that will prove even more significant than the Protestant Reformation of the sixteenth century' (2005: 16). In recent decades, the capitalist 'West' has seen off its arch-rival, communism, and triumphed globally, but Christianity, its once-dominant religion, is, they argue, mutating into a new amorphous 'spirituality'. Sceptics such as Bruce dispute this, claiming that contemporary New Age spirituality is a weak minority enthusiasm that cannot even match the social effects of nineteenth-century Dissenting Protestantism. For Bruce, the new spiritualism, coming after the bureaucratisation of Catholicism and the liberal-rationalisation of Protestantism, constitutes a final historical stage in the secularisation of Christianity. As such, New Age spiritualism is, in his view, only a diffuse consumerist dabbling, the last weak vestige of the sacred in 'the West', not a resurgence but a final petering out of religion in a feeble hipster whimper.

There would be every reason to support Bruce's thesis were one to focus only on New Age festivals, retreats and therapy clinics. However, given its amorphous nature, it may be the case that the new spiritualism has to be more broadly conceived as something with the capacity to inhabit well-established religious and secular institutions that are not at all consciously New Age. After all, as the stricter orthodox versions of Catholicism and Protestantism wane, many of the more liberal versions of Christianity increasingly display things in common with New Ageism – folk masses, outdoors sunrise services at Easter, walks on sacred ways, revivals of 'Celtic Christianity' and so forth – and even traditional religion itself sometimes reinvents itself for consumption in therapeutic terms. Moreover, as Catholic and Protestant control of mass education contracts, educational philosophy is arguably becoming both weakly religious and weakly secular, and is often philosophically New Ageist now at all levels from kindergarten to university. Therapeutic conceptions of learning and loudly professed commitments to the optimisation of individual potential are fundamental to the credos of many forms of education, especially in the humanities and social sciences, and this new spiritual entrepreneurialism goes hand in hand with the commercial entrepreneurialism also increasingly prominent in educational mission statements. Viewed in this context, New Age spirituality is not merely a minor fringe religion or trendy secular counterculture but is infiltrating and rewiring the self-understanding of the postmodern institutions of church and state apparatuses alike. And, like earlier forms of Christianity, which at once offered 'weak' critiques of capitalist exploitation, acquisitiveness and materialism but nevertheless legitimated capitalism for fear of more atheistic secular systems such as republicanism, socialism or communism, New Ageism offers to meliorate the worst effects of capitalist alienation without at all proposing systemic anti-capitalist alternatives.

Conclusion

Do these rival models of religious change support any strong conclusions about our present moment? Few enough. The first model suggests that Irish Catholicism is not so much dying as subsiding after an unusual period of dynamism and rigour to broadly level off at some wider international Catholic mean; the second that it is in terminal decline but still at some distance from that endpoint; the third that religion in post-Catholic Irish society is slowly but ineffably mutating into a diffuse spirituality. For the time being, the situation is decidedly mixed and better described in terms of an interregnum rather than in those of decisive endings or new departures. In the short term, it is hard to tell for whom the bell tolls – for a dying Christianity or for the more left-leaning secularists who, blindsided by one of history's many ruses, might have been more careful about what they wished for. Much will depend in the several decades ahead on how cannily religious, political and social movements make sense of the volatile present conjuncture and on how intelligently or ineptly they respond to it. For the moment, the Catholic Church is certainly in disarrayed retreat, socialism and social republicanism still struggling, with no guarantee of success, to create a new vision of society with genuine mass appeal, and neo-liberal capitalism is still ascendant, though riven by contradiction nationally and globally. To imagine that contemporary Ireland is now finally catching up on and fighting out some belated version of the religious vs. secular wars fought earlier in nineteenth- or twentieth-century Europe is to mistake the current conjuncture quite seriously; the wider international terrain in our time has changed dramatically from that of earlier centuries, and it is on this latter terrain that Irish religious struggles will be played out in the next few decades. In other words, it is more useful to recognise that both religious and secular forces today are historically highly mutable, and so too, consequently, are the lines and terms of conflict between them. To be attentive to such change is the only way to avoid rehashing the tired old battles of the past, which are typically fought in the name of the future they simultaneously sabotage.

Works cited

Adorno, Theodor (1990) *Negative Dialectics*, trans. E. B. Ashton, London and New York: Routledge & Kegan Paul.

Bruce, Steve (2002) *God Is Dead: Secularization in the West*, Oxford: Wiley/Blackwell.

Campbell, Colin (1999) 'The Easternisation of the West', in Bryan Wilson and Jamie Cresswell (eds.), *New Religious Movements: Challenges and Responses*, London and New York: Routledge.

Cleary, Joe and Claire Connolly (eds.) (2005) *The Cambridge Companion to Modern Irish Culture*, Cambridge: Cambridge University Press.

Cresskey, James G. (2014) *Harnessing Chaos: The Bible in English Religious Discourse since 1968*, London: Bloomsbury Academic.

Curtius, Ernst Robert (2013) *European Literature and the Latin Middle Ages*, trans. Willard R. Trask, Princeton, NJ: Princeton University Press.

Davie, Grace (1994) *Religion in Britain since 1945*, Oxford: Blackwell.

Fuller, Louise (2002) *Irish Catholicism since 1950: The Undoing of a Culture*, Dublin: Gill & Macmillan.

Garelli, Franco (2014) *Religion Italian Style: Continuities and Changes in a Catholic Country*, Farnham: Ashgate.

Green, S. J. D. (2011) *The Passing of Protestant England: Secularisation and Social Change, c. 1920–1960*, Cambridge: Cambridge University Press.

Heelas, Paul and Linda Woodhead (2005) *The Spiritual Revolution: Why Religion Is Giving Way to Spirituality*, Oxford: Blackwell.

Hoban, Brendan (2000) *Irish Catholicism in Crisis*, Sligo: Banley House.

—— (2012) *Where Do We Go from Here? The Crisis in Irish Catholicism*, Dublin: Banley House.

Kiberd, Declan (2005) *The Irish Writer and the World*, Cambridge: Cambridge University Press.

Kirby, Peadar (1984) *Is Irish Catholicism Dying? Liberating an Imprisoned Church*, Cork: Mercier.

Konieczny, Mary (2013) *The Spirit's Tether: Family, Work, and Religion among American Catholics*, Oxford: Oxford University Press.

Larkin, Emmet (1976) *The Historical Dimensions of Irish Catholicism*, New York: Arno Press.

Martin, David (1969) *The Religious and the Secular*, London: Routledge & Kegan Paul.

—— (2014) *Religion and Power: No Logos Without Mythos*, Farnham: Ashgate.

Miller, David W. (1975) 'Irish Catholicism and the Great Famine', *Journal of Social History*, 9 (autumn), 84–7.

—— (2005) 'Landscape and Religious Practice: A Study of Mass-Attendance in Pre-Famine Ireland', *Éire-Ireland*, 40:1–2, 90–106.

Turner, Bryan (1983) *Religion and Social Theory*, London: Heinemann Educational Books.

Twomey, Vincent (2003) *The End of Irish Catholicism?* Dublin: Veritas.

Wesses, Anton (1984) *Europe: Was It Ever Really Secular?* London: SMC Press.

Whelan, Kevin (2005) 'The Cultural Effects of the Famine', in Joe Cleary and Claire Connolly (eds.), *The Cambridge Companion to Modern Irish Culture*, Cambridge: Cambridge University Press.

Wilson, Bryan and Jamie Cresswell (eds.) (1999) *New Religious Movements: Challenges and Responses*, London and New York: Routledge.

Index